Inspired by her travelling  and storytelling parents, Honor Auchinleck has led a peripatetic life. With her husband, Mark, who served in the British Army, she has moved home nineteen times, living, working and travelling in five different countries on three continents.

Born in Melbourne in 1953, educated by correspondence schooling, as a boarder at Toorak College and at the Australian National University, Honor has always had strong ties to Australia. In the thirty-four years she lived overseas, she never lost touch with her roots, returning frequently to the old family home, Towong Hill.

Honor has taught English as a second language, worked as a freelance features writer and photographer on expatriate newspapers and for two years was a judge for the Commonwealth Essay competition in London. She has also worked in archaeology.

She has two grown-up children, and she and Mark now live in Melbourne and on their property, formerly part of Towong Hill, where they raise Aberdeen Angus cattle.

Elyne Mitchell

A DAUGHTER REMEMBERS

HONOR AUCHINLECK

CENTENARY OF THE CREATOR
OF THE BESTSELLING *SILVER BRUMBY* SERIES

HarperCollins*Publishers*

HarperCollins*Publishers*

First published in Australia in 2012
by HarperCollins*Publishers* Australia Pty Limited
ABN 36 009 913 517
harpercollins.com.au

Copyright © Honor Auchinleck 2012

The right of Honor Auchinleck to be identified as the author of
this work has been asserted by her under the *Copyright Amendment
(Moral Rights) Act 2000*.

This work is copyright. Apart from any use as permitted under the
Copyright Act 1968, no part may be reproduced, copied, scanned, stored
in a retrieval system, recorded, or transmitted, in any form or by any
means, without the prior written permission of the publisher.

HarperCollins*Publishers*
Level 13, 201 Elizabeth Street, Sydney NSW 2000, Australia
31 View Road, Glenfield, Auckland 0627, New Zealand
A 53, Sector 57, Noida, UP, India
77–85 Fulham Palace Road, London W6 8JB, United Kingdom
2 Bloor Street East, 20th floor, Toronto, Ontario M4W 1A8, Canada
10 East 53rd Street, New York NY 10022, USA

National Library of Australia Cataloguing-in-Publication data:

Auchinleck, Honor.
  Elyne Mitchell: a daughter remembers / Honor Auchinleck.
  978 0 7322 9349 9 (pbk.)
  Includes bibliographical references.
  Auchinleck, Honor – Childhood and youth.
  Mitchell, Elyne, 1913-2002.
  Mothers – Biography.
  306.8743092

Cover design by Natalie Winter
Typeset in 11.5/15.5pt Adobe Caslon by Kirby Jones
Printed and bound in Australia by Griffin Press
The papers used by HarperCollins in the manufacture of this book are a natural, recyclable
product made from wood grown in sustainable plantation forests. The fibre source and
manufacturing processes meet recognised international environmental standards, and carry
certification.

5 4 3 2 1   12 13 14 15

To Mark, Sarah and James with love and gratitude

*When you set out on your journey to Ithaca,
pray that the road is long,
full of adventure, full of knowledge.*

Constantine P. Cavafy, 'Ithaca'

Contents

Author's Note		xi
Prologue		1
1	For Fear of a Nightmare	5
2	A Name Like Honor	11
3	Cranky Ghosts	21
4	Working in a Wild Museum	29
5	Shards of Memory	40
6	Each Item Had a Story	49
7	Brilliant Times and Places	57
8	'Like a Wave Lifting Everything'	62
9	Where There Are Roses There Are Usually Thorns	67
10	A Naughty Blue Leopard with a Great Big Smile	73
11	The Bittersweet Schoolroom	78
12	So Many Stories	92
13	The Coming of the Brumbies	105
14	Out of Eden	115
15	Paradise for her Daughter	121
16	Crucifix in the Pudding	124
17	Pushing the Boundaries	128
18	Undercurrents	133
19	Beyond the Family	142
20	War Secrets	146
21	War Friends and Waterskiing	158

22	Another World	163
23	Visitors to Our World	166
24	Typical Upper Murray Fun	172
25	Early Skiing	186
26	Skiing Is Serious	195
27	The Magic of Summer Skiing	202
28	Adventures on the Alpine Way	210
29	Skiing the World	218
30	Accident and Intrigue	228
31	Moths in the Lamplight	234
32	Toorak College	239
33	A Bid for Freedom	254
34	A Love of Freedom	258
35	The Time Warp	266
36	'A Man Who Would Have Sons'	284
37	Wings to Find My Life	299
	Notes	309
	Bibliography	315
	Acknowledgements	319

Author's Note

My parents, Tom and Elyne, left rich manuscript and correspondence archives, from which I have done my research. Both Tom and Elyne wrote about similar subjects. In the early years after they were married they wrote together articles for *The Australian and New Zealand Ski Year Book*. After the Second World War their interests diverged, although Elyne continued to draw inspiration from some of Tom's family stories and sources.

In writing *Elyne Mitchell: A Daughter Remembers*, I have also drawn extensively on Elyne's travel journals and my own diaries and memory. Throughout the text I have reproduced conversations I recall having with various family members and friends. In particular, my father, Tom, was a wonderful raconteur who often repeated his stories, so that I remember them almost word for word.

I accept full responsibility for any factual errors.

Prologue

My mother, Elyne Mitchell, was already an established writer before I was born. By then she'd had six books published and a number of articles, but her big break hadn't yet come. When it did, in 1958, Mum had been writing for more than twenty years and had given birth to four children: Indi, Harry, me and John. Her success was unexpected and quite thrilling.

In November 1956 Mum had written to her friend and fellow writer Henrietta Drake-Brockman explaining her new direction: 'I should have been writing another novel [for adults] but instead of that I am writing a book for Indi.' Less than a year later, on 28 September 1957, Mr Voss Smith, the Australasian manager of the English publishing house Hutchinson, wrote one of the most encouraging letters Elyne could ever have hoped to receive:

> *I am sorry for the slight delay concerning 'The Silver Brumby' but can now advise that I have read it, so has our Sales Manager and also our outside reader. We all agree it is excellent, and the Reader comments –*
>
> *'I think I can say it is one of the finest juvenile horse stories I have ever read.'*

> *For your information, although we don't usually pass this information on to the author at this stage, the Reader comments inter alia –*
>
> *'The author writes with beautiful simplicity, her sense of the dramatic allows drama to arise from the action of the story and is never marred by a cascade of adjectives. There is a nobility and dignity about these wonderful animals – her painting of the Australian scene is marvellous, matching in the beauty and dignity, the horses who live there.'*

Only eleven months later, on 6 August 1958, Mr Voss Smith was again writing enthusiastically to my mother, this time about *Silver Brumby's Daughter*. He explained that he had not been in a hurry to get this manuscript to the London office as 'I want their full concentration on "The Silver Brumby" and didn't want anything else to be considered until this was published as a certainty in time for Christmas here.' On 23 December Mr Voss Smith once again wrote, wishing Mum a happy Christmas and also telling her that he estimated world sales of *The Silver Brumby* would be in the region of 13,000 by the end of that year. It was a wonderful achievement, and the reviews were ecstatic. Mum marked in red her journalist friend Pamela Ruskin's remarks:

> *An Australian classic, and one of the most beautifully written children's books of the last decade, is Elyne Mitchell's story of the wonderful Silver Brumby. Thowra roams the Australian Alps and valleys, wild and free and ever in danger from his enemy, Man.*[1]

Mum's real talent lay in creating the characters of her animals – such as Thowra, the magnificent and illusive Silver Brumby, and Beni, the friendly, wise kangaroo – rather than people in her marvellously evocative descriptions of the bush. As a

Prologue

young girl I read *The Silver Brumby* and fell in love with the horses, the indigenous animals, the mountains and the bush. Mum gave her imagination a much freer hand with animals than she did with the two-legged characters in her earlier novels and short stories.

Weaving tales about the world of wild fauna and flora offered Mum a pleasurable escape into an imaginative world. It was a form of release that she could not find in her immediate domestic environment. By the time Mum started writing *Silver Brumby's Daughter* she was highly attuned to observing and understanding fauna and flora – a result of her many prewar and wartime expeditions into the mountains on horseback, skis, foot and later via car. With the success of the first two Silver Brumby books, her interest and delight in every conceivable aspect of the bush began to soar. Through her stories she breathed thrilling magic into the Australian bush, not just for herself and my sister, Indi, and me, but also for generations of children across the world.

The success of *The Silver Brumby* rewarded the hard work that went into it. With four young children and John just a baby, born in November 1955, throughout 1955 and early 1956 Mum wrote and typed only a few pages a day. She said that she wrote *The Silver Brumby* 'between [her children's] correspondence school courses and lifting the baby out of the biggest puddle'.[2] In the 1950s Mum usually had domestic help – a cook, a cleaner and a gardener (who also milked the five Jersey cows) – but she had to oversee, sometimes assist the staff, and cope with any problems that cropped up. It is hard to imagine how she managed to write successfully, bring up a family and run a house. Many people said she was remarkable, which indeed she was. Some people realised it must have been difficult too.

I felt that many aspects of my formal primary education were sacrificed for her later success while she wrote *Kingfisher Feather* and *Winged Skis* and was trying to write another adult novel. While Mum's books added fabulous degrees of magic to my childhood, I do have some regrets about my schooling. Her attention often seemed to be elsewhere when I was struggling with my correspondence lessons.

As I grew up I realised that *The Silver Brumby* was a very useful key to understanding Mum; it could help me in that long and interesting journey. I can still hear her voice and her perceptive wisdom in these words:

> *Kunama reminded [Thowra] of Bel Bel, with her inborn wisdom. Perhaps, like Bel Bel, she would be given an even greater wisdom than the wisdom of mares, because she, too, being cream, would lead a hunted life, and must be wise in order to survive. Mares, Thowra knew, with foals to look after as well as themselves, often had a special understanding of the bush and weather. If like Bel Bel and Mirri, they were 'lone wolves', their wisdom, knowledge and cunning could be very great – that was why Bel Bel had been almost as much leader of the herd as Yarraman; that was why he, Thowra, having learned from Bel Bel, seemed magic to the other horses and to the men. Anyway, he knew – as soon as he saw Kunama prick her small ears, then shiver, as seven black cockatoos passed overhead, flying, crying, that she would need everything he could teach her and all her own inborn wisdom, too, if she were to remain free and wild, and live her life in the mountains.*[3]

Mum often wrote that black cockatoos foretold bad weather or even danger. She also knew that danger was the downside to Paradise, and that nothing in life can be taken for granted: you have to be wise to survive, wild horses and people alike.

Twenty years after writing *The Silver Brumby*, black cockatoos came into our own lives.

1

For Fear of a Nightmare

Not long after Mum died, I was back in our old family home at Towong Hill, near Corryong in north-eastern Victoria. I dreamed about trying to open the door of the wardrobe in my bedroom. The full-length mirror in the door had been loose for as long as I could remember. It rattled and scraped whenever I opened and closed it. The wardrobe was half of a pair; it stood at one end of a much larger piece of furniture on the dark side of the room, furthest from the windows. A shorter shelved cupboard above three deep drawers separated the two long cupboards. It was a late Victorian prefabricated item of furniture dating from the turn of the twentieth century when the house was built. A hundred years later, in the early years of the twenty-first century, the piece had some curiosity value.

In my dream, instead of opening my wardrobe to the usual clothes jumbled on hangers and a disorderly collection of shoes, to my horror I saw hastily but firmly nailed graffiti-covered sheets of compressed pine wood, the kind used to board up disused buildings in the down-at-heel suburbs of big cities. That filthy wall was severing me not just from the little that remained of my clothing but from my childhood memories, as if I had never belonged at Towong Hill. I woke and sat bolt upright, turning on the light and leaping from bed. I *had* belonged, and I didn't want to lose any more connection with my past. I'd lost too much already with Mum's death. I opened my desk drawers and pulled out the scrappy bits of paper, letters and notebooks that I had kept down the years and thrust them into my overnight bag. It was through Mum that I would start remembering because she had been right at the centre of my life until well into adulthood.

Shortly after Mum's funeral in Corryong in March 2002 I returned to Towong Hill before my husband, Mark, and I were due to go to Ankara for Mark to take up his appointment of defence attaché at the British Embassy. I knew Mum's work reasonably well and I was interested in her writing, so I hoped to collect and assemble her archive. My cousin Richard Chauvel had travelled up from Melbourne with me and stayed and helped for a weekend. It was an awkward job because Mum never really filed anything systematically. Particularly in her latter years, she didn't spend much time on maintaining an orderly environment in which to work – of much greater importance to her was putting time and effort into thinking, research and creative writing. Dusty manuscripts bulged from collapsing manila folders, correspondence burst from envelopes, elastic bands, ribbons and pieces of string. Papers spilled out everywhere from overfilled cardboard boxes and had become scattered. The carers who assisted in Mum's later years clearly didn't understand what the manila folders and bundles of papers were about, nor did they have the time to find out.

Initially I took on the job of unofficial executor, but it soon became official. This was both extraordinarily illuminating and at times deeply distressing, the papers and photographs evoking all kinds of memories and emotions: laughter, gratitude, deep regret and the knowledge that her death ensured that some misunderstandings and mysteries would linger on, with little or no possibility of further explanation unless I happened upon clues as I gathered, sorted and explored.

I began by dividing the material into broad categories and removing private correspondence so the archive could be professionally assessed. As I worked, I searched the dusty desks, bookcases, walls, and other nooks and crannies of Towong Hill, remembering the companionship of my brother Harry fixing his radio set, and stimulating conversations with Mum about anything from David Campbell's poetry to where kingfishers nested. Often Dad could be persuaded to tell stories from the old days when his grandfather, old Thomas Mitchell, first came to the Upper Murray. Now silence filled those familiar spaces.

But my work with the archive gave me the chance to preserve my memories, to try to understand Mum better and make up for some of the opportunities I hadn't taken when she was alive. Mum died on 4 March 2002; Dad had died eighteen years earlier on 4 February 1984. It was as if Mum's sixty-year writing life, which I was trying to pack up, might disintegrate before my eyes if I was not careful, taking with it many of my remaining connections with my childhood. I worked carefully and quickly, wanting to get as much done as possible before returning to my own life on the other side of the world. The dream exposed my fear that, with my departure early the next day, I would lose some of the most treasured memories of my mother and of my childhood.

The following morning I began my travels south to Melbourne International Airport and from there back to England, where I had to pack up and move from our army quarters, see our daughter, Sarah, who was studying in London, and then, with my husband, Mark, and son, James, drive across Europe to Ankara.

I was daunted by both the work required for Mum's archive and the preparations for attaché life, as well as all the travel before me. If

I focused on what I had to do for the archive stage by stage, it would be just manageable. Yet Mark's role in Ankara would require more of me. Never had I felt so torn between two threads: the past and the immediate future at opposite ends of the earth, pulling strongly against one another. Nevertheless I felt certain that I had to know where I'd come from to form some idea of where I was going.

For as long as I could keep my eyes open on that flight and at every other opportunity during the journey from Melbourne to London, I thought about my parents, and Mum in particular. I needed to remember and record my childhood to ensure I would be firmly rooted in my identity and not lose my past. My parents' stories were inextricably interrelated with my own.

Some of Mum's last words were still ringing in my ears: 'There is so much to talk about – but I can't talk here,' she said, indicating that the local hospital was not the appropriate environment for the things she wanted to say. She wanted to go home but never had another chance to, and she hardly uttered another word. There was so much I wanted to know. I wanted to find the mother I had known in my childhood before I began to lose her. Death and illness in the family as well as physical distance had separated us many years before she died. As a child I was thrilled by the stories she wrote and told and now, in my grief, I wanted to go back to the late 1950s and early 1960s, particularly those happy times when I was learning to read and Mum was writing the first four books in the Silver Brumby series.

Mum would read the first few paragraphs of *The Silver Brumby* with me, making sure I identified each word as she said it. Sometimes she had to read the same chapter over and over again and answer masses of my questions. I wanted to know whether the Ramshead Range really looked like a ram's head, with curly horns like a merino ram. Once I asked her if she would take us to see the place where Thowra was born. She seemed both vague and worldly wise when she replied, 'You will know it when you find it yourself one day.' Now I think of her remark whenever I climb the Ramshead.

I wanted to find the woman behind the tall, lean, fit figure, once effortlessly beautiful and later with a weathered, tanned face, crisscrossed with lines of happiness, endeavour and sorrow. In her later years she was often difficult, prickly, highly critical and thoughtlessly determined to get her own way, but she was also exceptional, both as a person and as a mother. She was charismatic and compelling, and I wanted to accept and understand her the way she was, warts and all.

Writing down my memories would help me to separate memory from dream, and good dream from bad. At that stage I didn't plan to write a memoir. I had often kept a journal, particularly when I travelled, and I had written travel features for newspapers. Recording my memories meant that I had to put into words what the significant characters in my family looked like, what they did, and the events and family occasions in which they took part. As I wrote, I discovered that I knew a lot about Mum, but I couldn't write about her without writing about Dad too.

I had my own notes about my memories of my parents and the ambience of the house and garden at Towong Hill, and the materials I had been seeking out and assembling for the archive also acted as *aides-memoire*. All I had to do was write it all down.

Before the plane had even taxied down the runway at Tullamarine on that trip back to Europe, the gum trees in the surrounding countryside flashing past, memories were tumbling like Mum's photographs and letters spilling from a box, landing in no particular order.

The first scene that sprang to mind was more about my eldest brother, Harry, than Mum. One brilliant winter morning Harry lobbed a small stone on the ice on the trough at the end of the backyard outhouse. It skated over the swirly ice patterns that distorted the reflections of both the sky and our faces as we leaned over it, our breath forming misty clouds before our eyes. Then he chucked a bigger stone that broke the glittering surface into sharp angular fragments. We scooped some out of the freezing water, dumping the ice shards on the ground and sorting out shapes – swords, scimitars, diamonds and triangles sparkling in the early morning sunrays. It was the first time I remember really enjoying Harry's company.

Mum and Dad were standing deep in conversation and came over to see what we were doing – things of natural beauty were their passion. They remarked how thick the ice was, much thicker that year than the last as it was even colder. Dad asked us not to throw stones in the trough, saying we'd need to get them out. Mum mentioned one chilly winter in England during the First World War when ducks had their feet frozen to the ice on a pond. (Mum was born in Melbourne just eight months before the First World War, but lived with her family in England while her father, Harry Chauvel – later to become a general and be knighted – served in Egypt, Gallipoli and Palestine.) Mum could always tell a story. Dad could too, but he often concentrated on factual and practical matters.

Soon the shapes began to melt and the sky clouded over; the magical memory fades. Later Harry thoughtfully dragged me backwards against a fence to scrape manure from the backside of my corduroy trousers. He'd been trying to keep me out of trouble and we'd been running around, testing cowpats to see if ice formed on them, until I'd slipped. Fleeting though those moments were in my mind, the visions that imprinted themselves on my memory began to gather brilliance with passing years.

Meanwhile, in my handbag, a small newspaper clipping seemed to weigh more than it should. Deciding that it belonged to me, I'd put it with my passport and ticket in my hand luggage. The cutting seemed to rob some of the magic of memory: I wished I hadn't found it, but I had, and it was both illuminating and cathartic.

2
A Name Like Honor

Naturally I have no memory of it, but I was told soon enough that my birth had provoked discord and a family rift that echoed throughout my childhood. It was all to do with the spelling of my name, though there was more to it as neither of my parents ever mentioned to me that I was nameless for my first couple of days of life – this I discovered from the crumpled, yellowing newspaper clipping from 1953 that I'd found after Mum died, stuffed in the back of a drawer in her upstairs bedroom at Towong Hill. Mum hadn't kept up photograph albums and scrapbooks since the beginning of the Second World War, so I shouldn't have expected it to have been preserved in any organised way, though I'd often wished she would treasure and care for family memorabilia more. Headed 'Daughter', the clipping reads:

> *A name has not yet been decided on for the daughter born to Mrs T.W. Mitchell, wife of Mr Mitchell MLA, at St Andrew's Hospital on Sunday. They already have a girl called Indi, and a boy, Walter Harry. He was named after his grandfathers, the late Mr Walter Mitchell and the late General Sir Harry Chauvel.*

Elyne Mitchell: A Daughter Remembers

> *Mrs Mitchell has written several books. Her first novel, 'Flow River, Blow Wind', was published recently.*[1]

I stared at the crumpled cutting on first finding it. What did Mum call me when I was nameless? Was I just 'baby'? Or perhaps she didn't call me anything at all. There was little point asking such questions when Mum was no longer alive to answer them, but I still wanted to know. Indi, who may have remembered the story, was not with us when Mum died and had not stayed after the funeral. Being the youngest of the family, John would only have heard the story second-hand, if indeed he knew anything at all, but he didn't seem to share my interest in archives and family history anyway.

At birth I'd landed with a bump on a busy stage in the midst of a powerful play in which all the actors seemed to know their parts well, while my name and role were yet to be defined. To end my namelessness Mum called me Honor after Dad's beloved sister and her own close wartime friend. Aunt Honnor Lodge was known to the family as simply Aunt Hon, but she spelled her name with a double 'n'. Mum, who was frequently firm about her opinions, was adamant that I only needed one 'n', though I suspect life would have been easier if I had been given two to keep Dad's family happy.

'Mummy insisted,' Dad explained rather uncharacteristically and plaintively years later when I asked about the spelling of my name. He called Elyne Mummy – spelling it Mummie in letters – just to get under her skin. My siblings and I called her Mum or Mother and tried not to take much notice of Dad's irritating tease. 'I am not your "Mummy",' Mum's exasperated reply would echo through the dark downstairs corridor at Towong Hill, and she'd shake her head of short, wavy, almost black hair with frustration as she strode purposefully back to her desk in the front hall. Four children were enough without a tease of a husband looking for a mother figure.

'I fought tooth and nail about the spelling of your name,' Mum told me. 'Having just one "n" is to help you make it your own name.' Had I listened to Mum, and if I'd felt right about it, my name could have been an inspiration.

Mum signed my birth certificate on 15 July, five weeks after my birth. Perhaps Dad had been too busy and Mum too taken up with two children and a newborn to complete the formalities. All the same I wondered if they delayed the registration of my birth simply because they couldn't agree about the spelling of my name.

Before my arrival, Mum wrote about me being a baby 'who will probably choose Coronation day to be born, when no one is interested in anything but the wireless. I'm afraid this infant has succeeded in holding up work on the next novel.'[2] Mum said she was disappointed because my imminent arrival had meant she was unable to attend any of the commemorations for the coronation of Queen Elizabeth II on 2 June. Dad had been the local member of parliament for six years by then and consequently went to some of them.

Mum was thirty-nine and Dad was forty-six when I was born. Perhaps because she was an older mother by the standards of the time, Mum had gone to Melbourne to stay with Granny in good time before the birth of each of us. Indi, the eldest, was six and Harry was just three, while John, of course, was still to come. Dr Rome, who was sure I was going to be a girl, was supposed to deliver me, but, after lingering, I finally arrived in a hurry in the early hours of 7 June 1953 before he could reach St Andrew's, the tall red-brick hospital overlooking Treasury Gardens in East Melbourne.

My birth was an easy one, which pleased Mum as she felt that giving birth was one of the most creative things a woman could do and it was immensely important to her. On 10 June she wrote to Granny M, Dad's mother, saying, 'The baby looks wonderful & I feel wonderful and [it] is such a marvellous thing to be able to prop yourself up & look at the babe having the cord tied and to have known all about it all the time.' Later in the letter she added, 'It would be lovely if we could manage another little boy soon.'

'On the morning of your arrival, I left home for Melbourne early,' Dad explained when I'd once asked what he was doing when he heard about my birth. 'There was a thick, clammy fog and I had a slow journey.' Towong Hill is just under five hundred kilometres north-east of Melbourne, the first third of which to Albury and Wodonga was mostly a dirt road in the early 1950s. So the entire journey probably took him most of the day. Perhaps my godmother Pat, daughter of Allan Knight, our manager, went with Dad, because years later when she visited me in England she proudly told me, 'I drove you home for the first time!'

At the time of Dad's telling of the story, it had been enough for me to know that he had come to the hospital in Melbourne to meet me. Now I would like to know what he thought about having another daughter, when it was that he and Mum decided to call me Honor, and how long he stayed. I knew he was there long enough to go to the Melbourne Club at the top of Collins Street, and he probably put the birth announcement in the paper. He might also have gone to see Indi and Harry, who were staying with Mum's mother, Granny Chauvel, nearby in Murphy Street, South Yarra

Granny M lived in Sydney and wrote to me only once, on the day after I was born. She died in early August that year and her warm, welcoming card was the first letter I ever received. She addressed me as 'Miss Honnor L. Mitchell', perhaps to reinforce her opinion that my parents should spell my name with a double 'n'. Later, Aunt Hon put in her tuppence worth, saying that the spelling of her name had done her well and she couldn't understand why it shouldn't suit the baby too.

Before I was born Mum had asked Aunt Hon, who was a talented artist, to draw a design that Mum, who embroidered beautifully, could use on my christening robe. Aunt Hon filled her drawing with musical instruments and notes. Although the drawings annoyed Mum, she kept them – or perhaps she just never got around to throwing them out. 'Your father and his sister are tone deaf,' she said once when Aunt Hon's name was mentioned. 'She can't even recognise the national anthem. Someone else always has to tell her to stand up!'

The drawings would have been done well before my arrival to allow time for Mum to complete the embroidery for the christening. But in the photographs it doesn't look as if I am wearing a christening robe embroidered with musical instruments. Granny M and Mum's maternal grandmother were both very musical, but perhaps Mum thought that to have musical instruments embroidered on my christening robe was like giving a baby a wish that was unlikely to come true. Or perhaps she was just too busy to do it. I have the drawing, and it doesn't look as if a tracing was ever taken from it. Mum often left stories frustratingly incomplete, leaving me wondering and often never finding out what really happened.

Dad usually sided with Aunt Hon as far as he could without straining his relationship with Mum to breaking point. He retaliated on the double 'n' by insisting my second name should be Lenore, after the wife of a family friend whom he knew better than Mum did. While the good Lenore could not have known it, Dad talked about her at Towong Hill as if she was a domestic goddess. If Mum was not sure how to do something, he would advise: 'Phone Lenore, she will know.' Mum hardly ever phoned her, and I don't think ever to ask her advice, though the two women got on well whenever they met.

My names could have been worse. Shortly after my birth, in one of the distinguished, high-ceilinged rooms at the Melbourne Club, a mischievous member suggested that my parents might name me Regina in honour of the Queen, whose coronation had taken place a few days earlier. Another ventured Corona

Elizabeth. I was spared that as Mum explained that 'the only Corona I've ever known was a very unpleasant girl at school'! Another worthy member suggested my parents might consider calling me Hilary after Sir Edmund Hillary, who made the first ascent of Mount Everest on 29 May, just over a week before my arrival. If they had taken up the suggestion Mum and Dad might well have argued about whether the name should be spelled with one 'l' or two! Later, when I went straight from correspondence schooling to boarding school at Toorak College, I could have done with all Sir Edmund's grit, courage and fortitude.

From my first awareness that there was controversy about my name, Honor with one 'n' was good enough for me. Learning to write it meant there was one less letter to print neatly and I had no intention of changing it just to keep others happy. I avoided using Lenore whenever possible, and as soon as I was able, I changed it. The double 'n' disagreement resurfaced within the family every now and then, sometimes in my hearing and sometimes not; it was as if my name was their concern and they didn't expect me to have an opinion about it. Once Dad realised I was sensitive about my second name he teased me pointedly, using both names instead of just Honor. Sometimes, but not always affectionately, he called me Blacksmith on account of my dark hair and complexion, and I began to loathe it just as much as Lenore. Smacky Blither, a derivative of Blacksmith, was more embarrassing still when he used it in front of visitors.

If I objected to nicknames, Dad's fast-spoken words would avalanche down on me; when he was angry it was like windblown hailstones stinging on bare skin. I knew it was better to stay quiet, watch, listen and bide my time. Training for the bar in London and being a member of parliament had taught him to argue cogently, to bluff and to speak loudly and with immense authority, even if on occasions he didn't really know what he was talking about.

Except for Aunt Hon, none of the immediate family was entirely exempt from extra names. Behind her back Dad sometimes referred to Granny as Lady Mum. Of course Granny somehow found out and didn't seem to mind, but Mum hated it. If Indi slept in Dad referred to her as Dormouse. Long before Barry Humphries used the term, he loved calling his kids Possums; and Mum and Dad called each other Possie before the war – Mum was Dad's Mrs Possie. Possums were Dad's favourite bush creatures; he'd dreamed about them while he was in Changi. If he had only called us Possum girls and boys and nothing else, I wouldn't have minded.

Even Dad's pale, smokey-green panel van, Gorgeous Gussy, did marginally better than we did as it only ever had one name; there was another mustard-coloured Fargo truck called the Yellow Peril, which was used for political duties. (Dad was a terror on the roads; no wonder he needed my godmother Pat to drive him.)

Dad mightn't have realised or even cared that his names and remarks got under people's skins; he had endured so much worse in captivity as a prisoner of war. He didn't necessarily mean to be hurtful or derogatory; he might have thought that a bit of teasing toughens kids up. That was true to a point, but sometimes he went too far.

'We also called you Blacksmith because you always bolted or ran for open doors,' Dad explained when I was older. It was a play on words – at one time blacksmiths made bolts. The moment he said this that I had a fleeting vision of myself as a toddler running out of the dining room door in bare feet, feeling the splinters in the verandah before the wooden boards were replaced with practical but characterless concrete. 'You never seemed to hear when we tried to stop you and we thought you were incapable of learning anything anyway,' Dad said. I have always been a little hard of hearing. Perhaps he was trying to shock me out of my dream world.

It was cruel stuff by today's standards and even when I was quite little I smouldered with indignation, but Mum and Dad didn't understand the connection between their remarks and my hurt and anger. Unusually, Mum agreed with Dad so I had no ally. I avoided further hurt by trying to keep quiet and not to cry or, more strategically, to be seen crying. I never knew if they misunderstood my silence as indifference, which might have encouraged them to express their feelings with even more emphasis. I was in a lose–lose trap that I desperately wanted to escape and so I became even deafer to such jibes.

If Mum had spelled my name with a double 'n', it would have been even more of a Mitchell family name, as Granny M's sister Jessie had married Timothy Honnor, who lived far away in England – they were the parents of Dad's twin cousins Pat and Patricia Honnor. The sisters were close and Granny M missed Jessie. Naming her daughter Honnor after Jessie's husband's family was a compliment to Jessie and her husband, and reminded Granny M of the happy times they had spent together in Sydney, London and Paris.

In our family, unusual names were not without precedent. Indi's name came from the Indi River, one of the tributaries of the Murray, and apparently in an indigenous dialect it means a water plant. It is a pretty name so I never thought about it as being particularly unusual. Harry was named Walter Harry Thomas after our grandfathers: Dad's father, Walter Mitchell, and Mum's father, Harry Chauvel. Mum and Dad had chosen Harry's name in autumn 1941, nine years before he was born, when they'd hoped to conceive before Dad went to the war in Malaya. I started calling my older brother just Harry, apparently because I couldn't manage saying Walter and Harry together. John inherited his three names from Dad's much-revered Uncle Jack (really John), Chauvel from Grandfather Chauvel, and Huon from ancestors on the Mitchell side of the family.

Strangely, I had never thought to ask Mum about the story behind her name while she was alive. Later, in a long telephone call to Mum's sister, Eve, in Harare, she explained that her parents had found the name Elyne (it is pronounced Ell-een) among family papers and that it is supposed to be Scottish for Ellen. 'It was,' Eve said, 'a difficult name with which to saddle a child!' As it turned out, it was an unusual name for an unusual person; Ellen would never have suited Mum.

Perhaps it would have been politic for me to quietly start spelling my name with a double 'n' and defuse the squabbling. But I didn't want to appease anyone and at twenty-three and young for my age – stubborn and sulky and perhaps more like a teenager than an adult – I took matters into my own hands. I would have quite happily ditched my entire name, but Honor was already part of my identity. Instead, I targeted my middle name. Rather than choosing another name from my extended paternal family, in 1976 I decided on a second name from Mum's side of the family. I didn't like my Granny Chauvel's name, Sibyl, but I thought Chauvel would do fine as a middle name. Dad continued to call me Honor Lenore if he felt like it; the fact that I refused to answer had no effect on him.

Grandfather Chauvel's first name was Henry, but he was always called Harry. Towards the end of the First World War he asked if he could be knighted as Sir Harry rather than Sir Henry Chauvel. He had set a precedent and I saw no reason why I shouldn't follow suit, although changing a name by deed poll signed in a Melbourne solicitor's office was far less romantic than using a knighthood won on the battlefield to make the change.

Mum never commented to me about my name change. It might have been polite to ask her if I could use her family name, but I didn't think she would like it. With my jet-black hair, olive skin and shortish, sturdy legs, like Dad's, I looked more like a Mitchell than a Chauvel. I wished my legs would grow and stretch out into elegant, athletic-looking legs like Mum's – she had a fabulous figure.

Granny Chauvel's last gift and message to me before she died in 1979 was a copy of Alex Hill's biography of my grandfather, Sir Harry Chauvel. In spidery writing, she inscribed it inside the front cover: 'To Honor Chauvel Auchinleck with her grandmother's love.' My choice of middle name and the fact that I had married an army chap must have been okay with Granny, but I never saw her again to thank her properly. The memories of her wise guidance, support and encouragement when they were really needed stood out like beacons, just like the memory of Harry breaking the ice on the trough and scraping the cowpat off my trousers on a winter's morning long ago.

3
Cranky Ghosts

Initially I found it hard to reconcile the discord surrounding my name with the beautiful home in which I grew up. Naively, I thought beautiful places were supposed to be happy, or at least that people who lived in beautiful places had happy lives in the end, just like in fairytales. When people remarked how lucky I was to grow up in such a wonderful home – or told me I had a beautiful name – I usually agreed. But it wasn't entirely like that.

I began to realise that very little about our house fitted together logically. It was an anomaly – a large, urban-looking, two-storey house built of homemade bricks at the turn of the twentieth century, and tucked away on the edge of the bush and the High Country far from Sydney and Melbourne. Naturally, there was a story behind it.

Dad's father, Walter Edward Mitchell, or Granddaddy M, as even Dad respectfully called him, was one of eight children and of three surviving sons, the others being Peter Stuckey, who lived at Bringenbrong, and John Francis Huon (Jack) who lived at Khancoban House. Granddaddy M had two older sisters: Elizabeth, born in 1853, and Mary Annie, born in 1862. There were two younger sisters: Emma Isabella, known as 'Pinkie', born in 1867 and Henrietta Eveline, or Eva, who was the afterthought, born in 1873. Dad hardly spoke about Elizabeth and Mary Annie, but he said his Aunt Eva was wild. She put someone's good English hunting saddle on a steer and when she tried to mount, the steer bucked her off and vanished into the bush. The hunting saddle was never seen again.

In accord with the times, it was only Granddaddy M and his two brothers who inherited land from my Great Grandfather Mitchell. Except for tales of Aunt Eva's daredevil doings and some fond stories of Granddaddy M's favourite sister, Pinkie, it seemed that once the girls married, they faded from the immediate family story.

Dad said that Granddaddy M had the house designed and built by his sister Eva's husband, Soley Peck. Granddaddy M wanted a family house in which Granny M, the Paris-trained violinist from a distinguished banking family in Sydney, might be happy.

I know some of the story of Winifred Dibbs' and Walter Edward Mitchell's unlikely courtship. Granny M was twenty-seven when she met Granddaddy M in 1902. Granddaddy M's sister Pinkie, who was married to Dr Willie Chisholm, introduced them at her house in Macquarie Street in Sydney. It seems Pinkie thought it was time to find a suitable bride for her brother. Perhaps Granny M was attracted to the sensitive, thirty-seven-year-old bushman with a singing voice 'of some range'.[1] They were married on 28 April 1904. Granny M's matchmaker sister- and brother-in-law became lifelong friends, and friendship has flourished between subsequent generations of Chisholms and Mitchells.

In the early years of the last century there was a strong umbilical cord linking Towong Hill to Sydney. Just like Granny M's family home, Graythwaite in North Sydney, the front of the house and one side elevation at Towong Hill are surrounded by verandahs and balconies, and almost all the main reception rooms and bedrooms have fireplaces with wooden surrounds of shelves, cupboards and mirrors. Granny M had tried to create her own oasis on the edge of the bush. Her home became a house of contrasts between the realities of country life and the dreams and desires of a woman who had lived in a city mansion overlooking Sydney Harbour, studied in Paris and travelled widely.

The house Granddaddy M built was an uneasy one. It was the second house on the site, the first one having been a prefabricated structure erected by a previous owner, James Findlay, over about four years from 1868. It was in fact two smallish houses with verandahs that stood roughly on the site of the present house and garden. Dad said that Mr Findlay lived in one house while Mrs Findlay lived in the other, thus unwittingly setting a precedent. By the time Dad told me the story, Mum and Dad were living at different ends of the house. There were also reports that mighty battles used to take place between the Mum Findlay faction and the Dad Findlay faction in the open space between the houses. The differences of opinion between Mr and Mrs James Findlay continued after they both died, because they don't lie side by side in the old Corryong Cemetery. Ultimately even more distance separates my parents' final resting places, with Mum buried in the Lawn Cemetery in Corryong and Dad's grave on the ridge overlooking the homestead at Towong Hill.

The second house at Towong Hill – our home – was one of the first two-storey houses in the district to have a staircase with carved railings and posts. There was a septic tank for sewage and acetylene gas lighting. Ornate chimney pots and carved finials rather ostentatiously topped the gabled galvanised-iron roof. The house alone set the family apart as being different. Beyond the garden were spectacular views of the Dargals Range and the western face of Australia's highest peaks on the Main Range.

When I saw Granny M's violin in a junk cupboard in the linen room, Mum told me that after her marriage Granny M's hands had become rough from domestic chores and gardening, and she never played her violin again. It might have been her way of coping with regressing ability, but I wonder whether she regretted sacrificing one of her greatest sources of pleasure and interest. Instead she turned her attention to running the house with what Mum saw as absolute and terrifying perfection; fifty years later her beautifully handwritten inventories of bed and table linen and the tasks for household staff were still pinned inside the doors of the linen room cupboards.

While there were few neighbours with whom to socialise, Granny M had a busy household with extended family and friends coming to stay and travellers needing beds and meals. Just like her mother and her sisters in Sydney, Granny M was immersed in running the house and bringing up her children, but she also had an excellent business brain. She was not only a wise adviser and staunch source of support for the cattle station and thoroughbred horse stud Granddaddy M had set up, she was also a dedicated nurse in times of illness. Mum often said that Granny M loved people to be ill so that she could look after them. Unfortunately her skills were called upon all too soon.

In 1913, immediately prior to the First World War, Granny and Granddaddy M travelled with Dad and his sister, Honnor, to Klosters in Switzerland in search of a cure for Granddaddy M's ill health. He was suffering from terrible headaches accompanying Bright's disease, a degenerative kidney condition; he was also devastated at the way his brother and business partner Peter was treating him. Apparently Uncle Jack had warned Granddaddy M that Peter would let him down. Dad never told me exactly what happened, but the P. & W. Mitchell Partnership was dissolved in 1915–16, just a year before Granddaddy M's death. As a result, Peter Mitchell took the family homestead at Bringenbrong, across the state border from Towong Hill in New South Wales, while Walter Edward (Granddaddy M) took Towong Hill and a property called Indi near Biggara. Encouraged by the resolute Granny M, he arranged for someone else to bid for the well-known and jointly owned racehorse Trafalgar at public auction for 7500 guineas[2] so Peter would not know that his estranged brother was the buyer. The hurt from the falling out with Peter exacerbated Granddaddy M's headaches and on one occasion a doctor in Albury told Peter that his bad temper and harsh business practices were endangering his brother's health.

After the division of partnership assets, Granddaddy M had large weatherboard stables built for the thoroughbred stud at Towong Hill; though no longer used as stables, they still stand today. Over the main door he had the date '1916' painted – the date the two brothers completed their separation.

'Dad, did you ever meet Peter?' I asked him one time when I was in my late twenties and we were passing Bringenbrong homestead in his noisy truck.

'Only once,' Dad shouted. 'He was sitting on a shooting stick outside some stockyards. When I asked Granny M who that foxy-looking old man was, she replied, "He is your Uncle Peter and if he speaks to you, you must be very polite." He never spoke to me.'

'So why didn't Granddaddy M and Great-Uncle Peter get on?'

'The fundamental cause of the change in Peter's nature was a love affair,' Dad replied, apparently not wanting to go into too much detail. 'Peter fell in love with the daughter of one of the local landholders, a worthy kind of girl, reports said, but the stern old Thomas Mitchell, my grandfather, said she was not good enough for Peter and the marriage was called off. Granny, your Great-Granny Mitchell, ruled the family with a rod of iron right up until her death in 1897. Peter brooded and over the years became more and more egocentric, thoroughly eccentric and selfish. He was cranky, too. He could quote the Bible and Shakespeare and he liked fast women.' I was married when Dad told me this, otherwise he wouldn't have mentioned fast women.

'The Bible and Shakespeare couldn't have been that bad, and fast women were probably interesting and good fun,' I suggested, playing devil's advocate in my attempt to get to the bottom of this story.

'It wasn't like that with Peter – he was an unkind troublemaker,' Dad retorted. 'He spread rumours about people and wrote anonymous letters and then sat back to watch what happened.'

I went on to ask Dad how much he thought Peter might have felt upstaged by Granddaddy M's marriage in 1904 and the wonderful house he had built with the help of partnership money. Dad explained that Peter could have afforded to do what he wanted with the homestead at Bringenbrong, but he didn't do much. All the same, he didn't seem to want Granny and Granddaddy M to have a nice place either. Nothing that Dad told me really explained why Peter was able to pour so much acid on Granddaddy M. Perhaps Walter was simply too much the gentle, sensitive, hard-working bushman, though I did wonder if Granny M – the slim, talented, determined, well-educated and well-connected city girl – disliked her brother-in-law and whether the feeling was mutual.

Granny M stayed at Bringenbrong during her first visit to the Upper Murray before she was married and again while the house at Towong Hill was being built. Peter had ruled at Bringenbrong since his father died in 1887 and his mother ten years later, and maybe he didn't want competition from anyone, let alone his younger brother's competent, highly organised new wife. An album dating from Winifred's visit in 1903, about a year before she married Walter Edward, holds a sepia photograph of a beautifully dressed Granny M killing a snake in the Bringenbrong homestead garden. She doesn't look like a lady with whom to tangle.

Dad told me that for his Grandfather Thomas, my great-grandfather, Sunday was a day of rest and he wouldn't let the family play cards. Mrs Scammell, who cooked at Towong Hill, once told Mum that Thomas Mitchell was so religious that he wouldn't let his children do anything but read the Bible on Sundays and later, as a result, none of them would go to church but they could all spout the Bible backwards. Old Thomas Mitchell had moved the family to the Upper Murray from Tangambalanga in 1875 when he bought Bringenbrong from the Douglas family. Apparently he was a hard-working, rather cranky disciplinarian. No wonder Peter was cranky too. According to the not particularly objective John T. Francis, author of *Lives of Romance*, which was facetiously known by Mum and Dad as 'the Family Bible', Peter 'was short and stout, clean shaven, with bluish grey eyes and straw-coloured hair – not exactly an attractive personality to most women'.[3]

On 24 April 1908, four years after attending Granny and Granddaddy M's wedding, Peter was married in the City Hall in Manhattan to New Zealand-born Jeannie Watson Muir, or 'Tui' as she preferred to be called. Some said the unworldly Peter had thought he was courting a widow rather than a divorcee who was reputed to have been a barmaid. Whatever the truth, the marriage divided the two brothers more profoundly than the Murray River filled with snowy floodwaters could ever have done. So by the time I arrived in the world, discord was no newcomer to our family.

John T. Francis also had an opinion about Tui: 'From her youth, Jeannie was a born schemer and adventuress, whose sole aim was to get rich by entrapping some wealthy man as a husband, or as a protector.'[4] Francis's family history was paid for by Tui's sister's husband who coincidentally was called John Mitchell, but was no relation of our family. Louise, John's wife and Tui's sister, had run away and scandal ensued. Contemporary convention required Granny M to call on her new sister-in-law at Bringenbrong homestead. Granddaddy M was opposed, and in any case Granny M refused to call, thus deepening the rift still further. Whatever happened, Great-Uncle Peter and I share birthdays and I have more than a passing interest in him. I wonder what his side of the story was?

Granddaddy M died on 18 September 1917 when he was only fifty-two, a month short of his fifty-third birthday. Dad was eleven and Aunt Hon was nine. The cause given on his death certificate is chronic nephritis. He and Granny M had been married for only thirteen years. On hearing the news Uncle Peter is said to have remarked 'Poor Wally!', indicating he might have had some residual affection for his brother. I never thought to ask Dad if his uncle attended Granddaddy M's funeral or if he contacted Granny M. Granny M, together with Aunt Hon, soon moved to Sydney to be close to Dad (who was shortly to start at the newly opened Cranbrook School) and Granny M's family. Granny M owned a house in Wentworth Street, Point Piper, just a short distance from the school. During the summer holidays the house at Towong Hill was 'opened' and the family returned.

Stories about life at Bringenbrong and the house at Towong Hill were eccentric from the outset and I loved them. Dad colourfully recounted how both his parents were 'crack shots' and maintained the shape of the macrocarpa tree by sitting in chairs on the lawn and 'shooting off any protruding branches and twigs'. Aunt Hon was a good shot too, only she didn't stop at pruning the macrocarpa. She also trimmed some of the gargoyles and finials on the house.

4
Working in a Wild Museum

When Mum and Dad moved into Towong Hill in January 1936, after their wedding on 4 November 1935 and their honeymoon in New Zealand, the second house on the site had not really been a permanent family home for any length of time since 1917. Dad had had a long association with the house and surrounding property, and the family assumed that, as he had inherited it, he would ultimately make it his home. But it was his Uncle Jack's Khancoban Station, where he had spent a number of school holidays, that he knew best.

My great-grandfather Thomas Mitchell was so incensed when his son Jack married his cousin Fanny that, with exception of the acreage at Khancoban, he disinherited him. Khancoban had no house, no yards, no fencing or stock. As a result, Uncle Jack owed money to the bank for the rest of his life. He was a bucolic man who swore like a trooper and he became a surrogate father to Dad. In Dad's eyes he could do no wrong. Uncle Jack taught Dad all he knew about bushcraft, cattle, working in the forge, plaiting stockwhips, using a lathe to carve wood and loving the land in a way a city dweller never would have done.

I loved listening to Dad's stories about Uncle Jack and Aunt Fanny and their house at Khancoban and he loved telling them.

He had already written about them while he was in Changi, in his unpublished memoir 'Midway Peak'. He had such a good memory that once he had written something down, he knew it by heart. He told me the stories so often that I can easily draw on my memory of the conversations, and repeat them almost word for word.

'Khancoban House, as Uncle Jack called it, was the usual sort of bush homestead, with a verandah that ran round four rooms and a central passage down the middle,' Dad would say. 'The kitchen was a separate building at the back and connected to the main house by a small side verandah. The dining and sitting rooms were in the front on either side of the passage.'

'What was it like staying there?' I used to ask, not that Dad needed any prompting.

'The house was old. You only needed the slightest breeze to lift the roof iron off the white-ant-eaten rafters, and when the wind really blew there was a hell of a racket of loose iron rattling around. I reckoned Uncle was lucky not to lose some of that roof. It was a bit risky getting up there to hammer down nails and there wasn't enough money to do many repairs. When you came in from a long day's work on the place, you didn't want to lean against the back verandah posts as you took off your boots or you were apt to find yourself sprawling in the garden on a cloud of white-ant-eaten splinters and Uncle Jack's curses,' Dad would go on.

'And of course we had to help Aunt Fanny bring the roast from the kitchen, often in the pitch darkness of a wet winter's night – remember, there was no electric light in those days – and you had to negotiate a couple of steps, then dodge the wood box and any loose boards. At the door you had to balance the dishes on the corner of an old treadle sewing-machine table and with hand and knee manage to get both the wooden door and the wire door open long enough to dash through. If you were not quick, one or other slammed on you. If you were lucky someone heard you and opened the dining room door; if they did not you had to draw up one knee, balance the dish on it, and grope for the door handle as best you could. No wonder my cousin Colin Chisholm wanted to build a decent house after he inherited Khancoban Station.'

Dad always blamed himself for Uncle Jack's death. 'During the term before I was due to spend the spring holidays at Khancoban, he wrote to me at school saying he'd bought a mob of Queensland bullocks and wanted a hand with them,' Dad said. 'I reckoned we'd have trouble and I was a bit apprehensive. I could almost hear his curses as I read his letter. Aunt Fanny was a real dear, like Mother – she always told me that his bark was worse than his bite but I couldn't get used to it.'

'So what happened?' I asked, in case Dad started talking about Aunt Fanny instead of Uncle Jack.

'We had trouble all right. Those bullocks were pretty big and wild, I was bungling, Uncle was shouting his head off, and there were men and beasts galloping all over the place. I got the bulk of the curses but everyone got some. I did not get actually hit with the whip and nor did my pony, but he was heavily flushed with rage.

'That evening was killing night and I was still nervous: we had a cranky killer in the killing pen, and I took three shots to kill him. This was a most heinous offence and if he hadn't already cursed me enough, he cursed me one hell of a lot more and I felt dreadful. Over dinner he chatted away pleasantly about old times at Tangambalanga but during the night he had a heart attack and died. The doctor said it was due to overexcitement and exertion.' That was 30 August 1921.

Dad was educated at Cranbrook School in Sydney where in 1918 he was one of the foundation students. Afterwards he was accepted to Jesus College, Cambridge. He then went on to study law and for the bar in London. Strangely, for a man with such a good memory, he found academic work difficult, at least initially. He said he couldn't have succeeded without Granny M's encouragement and support. Judging from his diaries, I suspect travel, sport and a very active social life had something to do with any academic difficulties. Nonetheless, he graduated with his BA in 1929 and was admitted to the bar in London in April 1931. He returned to Australia and was also admitted to the bar in New South Wales. An accomplished skier, by the end of winter in 1932 he held Australian and Victorian ski titles. Instead of practising as a barrister, by November 1932 he and Honnor were boarding a ship to visit Germany, spend Christmas in Switzerland and then race in Davos and Innsbruck, Austria, during the European winter of 1932–33.

Mum and Dad first met in November 1933. At that stage, Dad was more of a city dweller and sportsman than a bushman, and almost more English than he was Australian. Theirs was a relationship forged on the whirlwind of a few social meetings in Sydney and Melbourne and, by today's standards, when they announced their engagement on 20 March 1935 they scarcely knew each other. Mum let on when I was an adult that she had some misgivings and broke off the engagement briefly. She said she had no idea what to expect and knew virtually nothing about sex.

In January 1936 Granny M welcomed the newly married couple to Towong Hill before she left to stay with Aunt Honnor and Uncle Moreton at Blowering, eventually returning to live in Sydney.

The ghosts of Dad's cranky uncles across the border in New South Wales haunted the newlyweds at Towong Hill. Neither Peter and Tui nor Jack and Fanny had any children, so there were never any Mitchell first cousins living close by to alter the family dynamics. The God-fearing Mitchell family thought that Jack and Fanny couldn't have children because it was a sin to marry a cousin. Aunt Pinkie and Uncle Willie Chisholm's son Malcolm spent school holidays with Fanny and Jack, his aunt and uncle;

he was Jack's heir and like an older brother to Dad. Much to everyone's sorrow, Malcolm was mortally wounded on 26 August 1914 and died a few days later – he was the first Australian to be killed in the First World War.

When Uncle Jack died in 1921, Malcolm's younger brother Colin inherited the Khancoban property and built a new house. Peter died the same year and in his will set up a couple of scholarships, one at Duntroon and the other at Sandhurst in England. He stipulated that candidates 'must possess a sound and appreciative knowledge of parts of the Protestant Bible'. The will also attempted to ensure that none of his relatives could be beneficiaries. Peter was determined to fight the family beyond the grave and down the generations. When I was offered a glass of wine by the wife of the winner of the scholarship at Sandhurst, I drank a silent toast to my viperous old great-uncle and to the fine tales I had heard about him. Apparently the scholarship cheque was only sufficient to pay for a very few to have a drink or two – nobody was going to hit the tiles at my great-uncle's expense – but he hadn't written his will carefully enough to prevent the winner of either scholarship spending it on alcohol. Nor had he been clever enough to prevent me being the ultimate beneficiary of Tui's watch, left to me by a distant relative.

Arriving on a large sheep and cattle station with a thoroughbred horse stud as a somewhat intimidated twenty-two-year-old bride, Mum must have wondered how she was going to make the grand house at Towong Hill, with its short and mostly sombre history, her home. She must have wondered, too, what sort of life she and her cosmopolitan wanderer of a husband would be able to create in the bush. She must have searched every facet of her new environment for inspiration and clues as to what might lie ahead in life. At first she hated the house and was intensely lonely; if life had not worked out in the way Granny M and Granddaddy M had hoped, it also didn't work out in the way Mum might have expected or wished. I have often wondered if she ever felt her parents-in-law's tragedy could turn out to be a bad omen.

Mum and Dad never packed up our grandparents' possessions; it was as if they were forever guests in someone else's house. It is a wonder that Mum didn't exorcise as much as possible from the house to discourage the ghosts haunting her. She simply pushed their works of Shakespeare, Charles Dickens, Sir Walter Scott and a wide range of Granny M's French literature to the back of bookcases and, over time, placed her own books and papers in front. She repeated the process with other objects in the cupboard under the stairs, the pantry, my upstairs bedroom and the linen room, creating a complex stratigraphy of literature and possessions for the historical archaeologist. When I sorted out Mum's papers and belongings, Granny M's neatly ordered French paperbacks were disintegrating behind a collection of Mum's first editions.

At the time of their marriage, the only room that seemed to have been exclusively Dad's was his small, musty, book-lined study at the back of the house. Appropriately, he called it the 'Weasel Hole', and it would have been ideal for one person, or two people working closely together. When they moved into Towong Hill after their honeymoon, Dad had a desk put in for Mum. It was no more than a polished wooden bench, a small concession to his shy but ambitious bride. A large crepe myrtle blocked the view from the only window; the Weasel Hole was a serious work room.

From the Weasel Hole Mum and Dad planned their first skiing and walking trips in the mountains. In 1936 they rode from Geehi to the snowline and then skied to the Chalet at Charlotte Pass. They explored the Alps from all points of the compass: the Dargals Range at the northern end to Mt Pinnibar in the south across the border in Victoria. It was remarkable that Mum was able to meet such tough challenges – Dad was exceptionally fit as well as being an accomplished skier, having already won Australian and New Zealand titles. They were united by a love of adventure. If not explorers themselves, they saw themselves following in the footsteps of the explorers and perhaps even gathering some of the knowledge that the explorers hadn't recorded. The Weasel Hole was the base where they kept their maps and wrote their lists of food and equipment. One such list included tins of sardines, salmon, camp pies, various tinned fruits, 'cakes of chocolate' and a mouth organ. Mum only ever brought her piano accordion along when they were taking a packhorse, or on shorter outings when they took a vehicle into the bush for a picnic.

But it wasn't long before the world was again plunged into war. Dad was commissioned into the 2/22 Battalion and was assigned to the headquarters of the 8th Division. Before Dad left for Malaya in autumn 1941, the serious-minded couple drew up a program of study they were going to undertake while the war kept them apart. Mum's program included literature, philosophy and history.

The Weasel Hole was where Mum worked from the time of her first arrival at Towong Hill until after the war ended. During the war and as she gradually began to feel at home, she added her mountaineering books to Dad's shelves and had a glass-fronted bookcase built to accommodate her growing collection of volumes on philosophy, poetry and the craft of writing. It was at her desk in the Weasel Hole that she wrote to Dad when he first went away on active service, to her own family in Melbourne and to the wider family scattered between Sydney, Melbourne and Queensland, and further afield across the world. Here too she typed her diary and compiled the scrapbook containing press cuttings collected from their visit to New Zealand for the Inter-Dominion Ski Championships in 1936 and their trips in 1937 to Hawaii and in 1938 to North America, notably to Sun Valley and Banff. In the southern hemisphere winter of 1938 Mum and Dad skied in Chile and Argentina before going on to ski in Austria.

Many of Mum's letters, diary entries and notes eventually became part of her inspiration for future articles and books.

Mum wrote a good deal of her first book, *Australia's Alps* (1942), from the detailed letters she wrote to Dad (some from the Chalet at Charlotte Pass) about her ski expeditions to the Cascades, the Western Face and to Mawson's Hut and Jagungal. She never went alone. George Day, Colin Wyatt, Toddy Allen, cross-country ski champion Ken Breakspear and Jill Macdonald were among her most frequent touring companions. If Dad was ever jealous, he never let on. The few letters he wrote in 1941 from Malaya that I have seen were always encouraging and full of admiration – she was carrying on the life that they had agreed she should lead while he was away.

With the assistance and encouragement of her distant relative and family friend Ethel Anderson, at the end of the ski season Mum completed the manuscript of *Australia's Alps* back at Towong Hill in the Weasel Hole. In *Chauvel Country* (1983), Mum explained:

> *I don't know whether [Ethel] suggested the article on the Snowy Mountains which* Walkabout *published and which became the first chapter of* Australia's Alps, *but she knew I intended to write* Australia's Alps *and to do all the exploration on skis which Tom and I had always intended to do together. I sent each chapter to her as it was written and typed while at the Chalet, and she took six of them to Mr Cousins at Angus and Robertson, and her interest and his interest gave me the encouragement to go on.*[1]

In the early mornings and evenings following the news of the fall of Singapore on 15 February 1942, after which Dad was listed as missing, Mum began to write the diary that she, again with Ethel Anderson's help, turned into the book *Speak to the Earth*

(1945). *Soil and Civilization* followed and was published in 1946. Not knowing whether Dad was alive and often fearing the worst, Mum didn't hear until January 1943, via the Red Cross, that Dad was in Changi.

Even so, she didn't know he had been injured or anything about his health or the way he and his fellow POWs were being treated. From their shared experience in the mountains, she would have known that he had good survival skills and that he would have kept himself as strong and fit as possible. She might have felt that his military training with the Melbourne University Rifles Regiment, then his training with the 2/22nd Battalion and his courses at the gas, bomb and camouflage schools in Singapore in 1941 had not prepared him for an overwhelming enemy such as the Japanese. Indeed she must have wondered if even the most professionally trained men would have felt capable of withstanding the onslaught. She must have endured many anxious months, wondering what her future held, if indeed there was a future.

She would not have known then that Dad was being looked after by Dr Ken Burnside, or that Peter Chitty and other men from the Upper Murray would look out for him during the dark months and years of their captivity. Mum never discussed with me how she felt during that time, but having spent twenty-seven years as an army wife, with Mark often away on operational tours, I can imagine, to some degree, what she must have experienced.

After he returned from the war, Dad helped Mum with photographs to illustrate *Images in Water*, which came out the following year. It seems strange to think that the smallest room in the house nurtured two fine but increasingly divergent careers.

By the time of my first memories, Mum had expanded her writing space and moved to another desk in the front hall where there was more room. Dad quickly filled the void in the Weasel

Hole with piles of parliamentary papers and other material relating to his diverse array of interests. Soon Mum started writing her way round her home, ultimately using almost every room in one way or another as part of her writing space. When an idea came she wrote it down in the shorthand notebook she carried in her pocket, or on the back of an envelope, or on any other scrap of paper to hand. Sometimes the ideas became stories, or parts of stories, articles or poems. Otherwise, they were simply left in a drawer in case they held some inspiration in future. The house at Towong Hill could easily absorb a trail of books, notebooks, biros, broken pencils, broken typewriters, cardboard boxes and envelopes filled with manuscripts, notes, photographs, correspondence, shopping lists and all the other paraphernalia of family life.

Cupboards all over the house were stuffed full. Mum's sister, Eve, tells a story of how she and her husband, Ted, opened a cupboard in the spare bedroom downstairs (usually called the Bachelor's Room) and a pile of rolled maps and papers cascaded down onto his head. Ted was a very precise retired army officer who must have found it strange to be accommodated in such a wild museum. Similarly, the cupboard in the sitting room was filled with a wonderful collection of brilliantly coloured embroidery threads. Again, they threatened to decorate the head of anyone who opened the cupboard. Beneath the chaos lay Granny M's well-ordered possessions.

When I was a child my writer mother's possessive love affair with what she often referred to as 'that resonant, dream-filled house' and its surrounding countryside developed into a burning obsession. It was the epicentre of her world and imagination. Somehow, just as Dad had done when he returned after the war and Indi and Harry had done before me and John would do afterwards, I had to find a way to fit within the spoken and unspoken but nonetheless firm boundaries of Mum's well-established and essentially self-absorbed lifestyle. When Dad was at home he had his own equally firm but sometimes different boundaries. For me it felt like trying to establish an identity alongside a couple of warring gods in a Greek play – a tragedy, ultimately – without getting any more than my tail feathers caught and a metaphorical and literal sore bottom from the crossfire.

5
Shards of Memory

My earliest memory dates from August 1954 when I was just one year old. I was sitting in a pool of sunlight on the floor in the drawing room of my Aunt Margaret and Uncle Edward's house, Danbury, in Sydney's Bellevue Hill. There was a grandfather clock and sea-green silky curtains, the folds of which looked like gleaming, sinuous waves. My Uncle Edward, Mum's brother, had not much hair, slightly baggy eyes and a kindly smile. Aunt Margaret's brilliant blue eyes seemed to twinkle and dance merrily as she laughed and poured tea from an ornate silver teapot. The white walls of the house held some beautiful paintings and the sun seemed to pour in from the windows. It was so much brighter and lighter and like a tinkling fairyland compared to the sombre Towong Hill. But I can't remember anyone talking, or, at least, talking to me, while we were in Sydney.

'I am sure someone told you about the grandfather clock and the colour of the curtains,' Mum remarked with disbelief when, aged about ten, I was talking about that trip to Sydney and mentioned my memories. 'If you remembered the trip from Albury to Sydney at all you would remember Harry falling from the bunk in the sleeper on the train, right on top of you in your basket. You were too young to remember anything.'

I longed to say something but I didn't have the vocabulary to convey my annoyance that Mum should question the memories that were as clear as sharp colour photographs in my mind's eye. If only I had remembered Harry tumbling on top of me; or the trip to the zoo; or having tea with Mum's old aunts; or meeting our relative, the writer Ethel Anderson and her daughter, Betty Foott; or Mum collecting the gold ring set with three fabulous diamonds that she had inherited from Granny M, Mum might have believed me. Apart from Uncle Edward's baggy eyes, his bald head and kind face, Aunt Margaret's beauty and their drawing room, I didn't remember anything.

I don't know how old I was when I realised that neither Mum nor indeed anyone could dictate what I did or didn't remember. And better still, I didn't have to tell them.

Crash went something hard and sharp-cornered into my head. Stars of pain jumped in front of my eyes. It was late 1955 or early 1956 – I wasn't yet three – and Harry and I had a heap of toys out on the sitting-room floor. Suddenly he hit me on the head with a brightly patterned metal spinning top. Granny was playing patience on an oval table beneath a window. She might have been dozing as she scarcely seemed to stir when I screamed in rage and pain. I flew from the room as fast as my little legs would carry me towards the staircase where I had seen Mum carrying baby John upstairs a few minutes earlier. A lump was gathering into a bruise on my head and I wanted her badly. At the end of the narrow strip of thin green carpet in the upstairs corridor at Towong Hill, I had to turn left to enter Mum's room. I slipped on the linoleum, failed to negotiate the left-hand turn and crashed in a bruised, tearful heap in the doorway.

'Off you go downstairs to Granny. I'll be down soon,' Mum said before I could take another step. She could hear but not see me, though I could see in the mirror on her wardrobe door that she was sitting, propped on pillows on her brass bed, feeding the baby. It was the first and only time I saw Mum breastfeeding. Instinctively I must have understood but, in addition to the spreading sore spot on my head, it was strangely upsetting.

Back downstairs Granny may not have been entirely aware of the incident that had propelled me to run to Mum in the first place. She began to tell me how lucky I was to have a baby brother, but I didn't feel lucky at all. She tried to soothe me by explaining that Mum and the baby needed some peace and quiet away from our more boisterous games, but her words simply added to my feeling of injustice. I was learning fast that Mum was an intensely private person, although I didn't know the word 'private' then. As a 'terrible-two-year-old' the lesson was tough.

Later Mum and Granny talked in hushed tones. I did not hear or understand much that they said, but I absorbed enough to know that neither understood what had happened nor really wanted to know. Harry had got away with it and I learned my first lesson about male privilege in our family hierarchy. The word sexism hadn't been coined then or, if it had, it hadn't crossed the threshold at Towong Hill. Granny accepted the old-fashioned hierarchy unquestioningly and she expected others – including me – to do so too. But after this incident I felt let down, though childhood memories of irritation with Harry are tempered by the vision of him breaking the ice on the horse trough and collecting the gleaming pieces for us to look at.

Dad was the local member of parliament for the state seat of Benambra for my entire childhood. In my first memories of him he was already a dyed-in-the-wool Country Party man – by the time I was born he had been a member for seven years and had already served as attorney-general and solicitor-general. Politics was in Granny M's family blood, her uncle Sir George Dibbs having served as premier of New South Wales three times towards the end of the nineteenth century. Dad was a gregarious man and, while he enjoyed the cut and thrust of politics, Granny M was undoubtedly the driving force behind him. He was often away and I didn't really know him well. It was Mum who was at home with us and she was the parent whom I knew best, or at least so I thought. She is much more present in my memories than Dad; that is not to say that Dad didn't have a role, for he certainly did.

In my next early childhood memory I am playing on a polished parquet floor, concealed behind an open door leading from the Bachelor's Room, where Granny slept when she was with us, onto the front verandah at Towong Hill. A gutter or downpipe was leaking and water was splashing in a sad rhythm in a puddle on the path just beyond the verandah. A little further away, the branches of the deodar tree on the other side of the path were drooping, trickling big tears of water onto the garden. Thick white clouds hung low over the mountains on the other side of the valley, cutting the house off from the rest of the world. When I think of isolation, this is the memory that springs into my mind.

The house was quiet. Mum was writing at her desk. Granny was gently nodding off to sleep over her book after lunch. Nobody knew I had crept past Granny's suitcases and hidden myself away. I had become absorbed in my own world of wooden farm animals, stables and farmyard. I was imagining a time when I would be old enough to go to the stables alone, saddle up a pony and gallop off across the paddocks. Indi's faithful toy hound, a whisky-coloured, long-legged terrier on wheels, stood guard close by; there was no danger of her reclaiming him as the holidays were over and she had returned to boarding school at Toorak College near Melbourne.

Suddenly a creeping feeling told me I was no longer alone. I looked up to find Dad towering above me. I hadn't heard him coming, nor did I know how long he'd been there. It is one of my earliest memories of him, a good-looking, imposing, lean figure in a dark suit, with olive skin and black hair like mine, only his was short and slicked back. If he had said anything as he approached, I hadn't heard him, and I can't remember there being a hug or a kiss. I hadn't heard him if he'd said hello. After a moment he simply turned and walked away. He might have had other things on his mind or perhaps he didn't want to interrupt me when I was playing happily. If I was a bit scared of Mum when she got cross, I was terrified of Dad.

I had once seen him chasing Harry down the drive. Harry was crying. 'The boss is chasing Harry with a big stick,' said Jack Reiners, who worked for the family and lived at Towong, and had been trying to eat a piece of crumbly sponge cake someone had given him for morning tea. Cake flew everywhere but, kind man that he was, he wanted someone to know Harry was in trouble. Playing in Granny M's room, I pondered that I too might have done something Dad didn't like; it was my first glimpse of fear and, however much I tried, I couldn't return to my safe, imaginary world in my toy stables.

Dad scared me because he was a big man with a loud voice and a quick temper, and he could make my big brother cry. I'd seen so little of him that he was almost a stranger. I don't know how old I was when I first realised that he had been an enthusiastic and highly accomplished skier, but I don't think I had an inkling then that he had won international events in Europe, Australia and New Zealand. It was tall, slim Mum in her utilitarian khaki overall in winter, or khaki shorts with a blouse tucked under a military-looking webbing belt in summer to whom I warmed more.

Scared as I might have been of Dad, I learned soon enough he wasn't always so intimidating and that he loved animals. 'I wish I could squeeze into Chikko's house too!' I pleaded to Dad when I was about five as he helped me spread some sacking to make the box comfortable for the little black cat who, quite by chance, had come to live with us. My whining pleas might have driven my older siblings mad but they seemed to work with Dad.

'It might take her a little while to get used to her new home,' Dad replied gently. I knew, of course, that there was no chance of a chubby child like me fitting into the box, but Dad had a way of bringing me around to seeing sense without being mean.

I had wanted a cat for a long time but Mum said we already had enough with the twin white cats, Tam and Oooey, who belonged to Indi and Harry respectively. One rainy evening I heard desperate mewing coming from the backyard. Thinking that one of the white cats might have been injured and in some sort of trouble, I went to look as we all loved Tam and Oooey dearly. In the damp, wintry twilight I could just see the silhouette of a black cat hopping slowly and painfully on three legs along the back verandah. Its left front paw was hanging at a strange angle and the fur had been torn revealing blood-covered red flesh, as if it had been cruelly crushed.

'Poor little thing! I think she might have been caught in a rabbit trap,' Dad suggested as he took her gently in his arms and carried her into the kitchen where there was more light. He talked to her softly as he inspected her paw.

'She might have been dumped,' Mum reckoned, but dumping did not explain why her paw was mangled unless it had been run over by a car or she had been caught in a trap between the dirt road that ran past the mailbox and our homestead. Dad took her to the vet and when he brought her home again she smelt of strange disinfectant, and her coat was dusty and rough. She was in pain and shook with fear as Dad and I stroked her coat. The vet had to amputate her paw, something that hitherto I had thought only happened to soldiers who had been badly wounded during the war that finished before I was born; now I knew it could happen to animals and people who were injured in accidents.

At Towong Hill we were cocooned from the real world. The high mountain peaks with their billowing blue-grey skirts of bush stretched down towards the Murray Valley and another long finger of bush extended behind us from Mt Elliott. Beyond the green of the Murray Valley there seemed to be layer after layer of blue hills fading into the distance well beyond my imagination. The nearest town, Corryong, was thirteen kilometres away. Although there were visitors at the homestead, there seemed to be days and sometimes weeks when we didn't see anybody who lived beyond the boundaries of Towong Hill. In the 1950s there was no television, and radio reception depended on the state of Dad's aerials, which were stretched between the house and nearby trees. Even so, reception was often distorted by a roar of static, and in any case I didn't understand the things I heard on the radio. Chikko entered my world before I could read the papers or had even begun to immerse myself properly in the imaginary world of fairytales and fiction.

Indi and Harry having their own cats had made me a bit jealous and sulky. I assumed and was determined that Chikko would be mine as I was next in line – seniority seemed to underpin most things then. It felt to me that everything from toys to cats and ponies belonged to Indi and Harry, and I badly wanted Chikko for myself. Scared as I might have been about losing her to another sibling, I had to learn not to strangle the little cat and to share her – John also loved cats and didn't have his own until later. Chikko had black fur and I had black hair so we seemed to go together, or so I reasoned. Dad suggested her name because *chico* meant 'small' in Spanish and, although that was soon to change, to begin with she was a little cat.

'She is too old to house-train,' Mum said firmly. Standing with her back to me, washing up at the kitchen sink, there was something tense in the way she was shaking her head that told me she really and truly didn't want another cat. It wasn't that she disliked Chikko; she just didn't want any more work. But I wasn't giving Chikko up for anything. 'She will have to be an outside cat,' Mum said. But more often than not it was Mum who cleaned up any messes Chikko made; I had seen and smelt cat mess and knew it was a nasty business.

The white cats, who had been at Towong Hill since they were kittens, were house-trained and so they were welcome inside. On cold days they spent a good deal of time curled up and purring in great comfort in front of the stove or a kerosene radiator. I wanted a cat that could sleep on the foot of my bed so she would purr me to sleep. Dad came up with a compromise, making Chikko a house out of a wooden fruit box and some sacking on the 'outhouse verandah'. It was only a partial solution, and I decided that if she couldn't share my bed, I wanted to share hers. Dad set me straight.

Despite her ambivalent welcome, Chikko soon found her place in the family hierarchy. She was not strictly a member of the inner circle of the family since she wasn't allowed in the house, but I think that worried me more than her. She seldom came to the front garden and remained a backyard cat. Thorny roses over trellises enclosed two sides of the backyard while the back verandah of the main house and a verandah of the outhouse where the fuel was stored enclosed the other two sides. Chikko was safe enough there, although there was only a concrete path and stony ground and no soft grass on which she could lie in the sun. She seemed to settle in and, despite her injured paw, she grew very sleek. Her rear end became disproportionately large because her hind legs had to compensate for her missing front paw. The family rather meanly but accurately suggested her figure was beginning to resemble my own dumpy silhouette! Chikko appeared not to notice the injustices in either the human or the feline worlds. Nor did she notice the able-bodied white cats coming and going. Fortunately she never went missing, which she might have done if it hadn't been for her absent paw. After all, she was a stray cat whose circumstances had changed. Even if she was never the close friend I longed for, she was a friend all the same, and Dad was very fond of her too.

When I was about six or seven I began to notice a softer, gentler and friendlier side of Dad, and at the same time I felt a corresponding tension in Mum. Dad sometimes annoyed Mum by bringing Chikko into the kitchen to sit on his lap where he settled in his cane chair in front of the Aga, though in deference to Mum's concern about cat poo Dad always put Chikko outside the kitchen door again afterwards. Mostly Dad tried not to annoy Mum, but sometimes I saw a mischievous gleam in his eye and I knew he was teasing her.

There was a sad day when Dr (later Sir James) Darling, headmaster of Geelong Grammar, and Mr Glover, a master, came to stay for the funeral of a local boy who had tragically drowned while a student at the school's Timbertop campus. Bravely I carried Chikko through the house to the sitting room where they were having tea with Mum and Dad. The distressed headmaster and schoolmaster stroked her, calling her 'the broken cat'. The combination of a dead boy and a broken cat was too much for me – I flew out of the room before I sobbed.

Chikko taught me a lot. Some of her lessons didn't occur to me until long after my little black friend had gone and I started to write about my childhood.

6

Each Item Had a Story

One of our early journeys to Melbourne to visit Granny Chauvel was not without incident. The family car, an olive-green Hudson, had a flat tyre on a dirt road in the Keelangie bush before we even reached the old town of Tallangatta. Mum and my godmother, Pat Knight, our manager's daughter, bent over in the dust behind the car as they wrestled with the wheel, trying to replace the flat tyre with the spare. With little traffic on the road between Corryong and Tallangatta, no help came and Mum and Pat had to brave the dust and the rickety jack and change it themselves. It was probably just as well that it was dust and not rain, but only Mum and Pat could have said which was worse. Only four or five years old, I sat in the shade on the side of the road crumbling gum leaves to release the scent of the bush. Harry wandered around making engine noises, scuffing the gravel and creating pretend roads for his Dinky cars.

Although I didn't hear every word, as they were getting back into the car Mum was saying something about changing a tyre while on her honeymoon in New Zealand. Mum and Dad couldn't get the spare wheel to stay on so they wrapped long strands of grass around the bolts and screwed the nuts on top, in the hope the extra packing between the nuts and bolts would help hold the wheel in place. There was a long dark crack in the back seat of the Hudson and I was always scared it would open up further and eat me up, or that I would fall through it into dusty darkness and oblivion. Worse still, I was now scared that the wheel was going to fall off and Mum and Pat were going to have to use grass to make the wheel nuts stay on. The grass beside the road was very dry and wouldn't have kept the nuts on any wheel.

It was not a good way to begin a long journey to Melbourne. We stopped at a garage in Wodonga – we didn't call them service stations then – to fill the car with petrol. In the 1950s, eucalyptus trees lined the narrow, single-carriageway Hume Highway, often forming a tunnel over the road. To me, Melbourne was a sprawling, noisy mass of houses lying somewhere a long way away at the end of that tunnel and near the sea.

Dad didn't come to see us often or to stay when we were at Granny Chauvel's and he is not part of my memories there. He was not with us on those long journeys. Invariably he was busy with political meetings and was seldom, if ever, around to help change a wheel or to deal with other mechanical issues. Pat seemed to take each flat tyre or similar inconvenience in her stride and with great humour. Her eyes twinkled over her high cheekbones when she laughed, something she managed to do when Mum found it too hard or was too tired.

Granny's place at 49 Murphy Street, South Yarra, was a Victorian house dating from the end of the nineteenth century. It was a substantial five-bedroom Hawthorn-brick home with a flourishing garden in the front and a smaller one behind, a separate brown-painted galvanised-iron woodshed, a garden shed and an incinerator at the rear. The Chauvel family moved there in the autumn of 1922, almost three years after returning from England following the end of the First World War. Grandfather had been welcomed as a hero when he arrived in Melbourne to take up his appointment as Inspector-General of the Australian Military Forces. In 1914 he had been posted to the Dominions Section of the Imperial Staff in London, and he and Granny and their first three children – Ian, Edward and Mum – were on board the *Ulysses*, a British steam passenger ship, en route to England when war broke out. During the war he rose from his command of the 1st Light Horse Brigade at Quinn's Post, Gallipoli, to Australia's first Corps Commander when he took over the Desert Mounted Corps in 1917.

The battles of Romani, Magdhaba and Beersheba were household names when I was a child staying with Granny at number 49. Grandfather died in 1945, before I was born, so my only visual memory of him was the rather stern figure in uniform that George Lambert painted. As a child I was told that Grandfather was 'famous', but I didn't know why. Granny showed me where Gallipoli, Egypt and Beersheba were in her atlas, but I still couldn't understand why he was 'fighting'. It seemed that while Grandfather had become famous for fighting, I only got into trouble for it. Grandfather was clearly part of that unfair world where grown-ups could do what they liked and children (we weren't really called 'kids' then) couldn't. Perhaps if Granny had explained that he was 'serving in the war' rather than 'fighting' it might have made more sense to me. It wasn't until I went to boarding school aged eleven that a kind teacher helped me find the location of the more obscure battlefields and explained that high-ranking officers like Grandfather planned battles in their headquarters and had a lot of administrative work to do. Only just beginning to understand Grandfather's role in the First World War, I didn't ask about it at home. It seemed as if it was something I was supposed to know and I didn't want to reveal my lack of understanding.

Initially my grandparents rented the house at number 49 from Violet and Colin Templeton, who had become close family friends and lived next door. It was Mr and Mrs Templeton who advised the Chauvels to send first Mum and then Eve to St Catherine's School. Colin Templeton's sister Flora had joined forces with the indomitable headmistress Miss Ruth Langley shortly after Miss Langley had moved St Catherine's from Castlemaine to Toorak.

In the late 1950s and early 1960s, Murphy Street felt as if it belonged more to a country town than a capital city. Residents knew and acknowledged each other in the street, albeit somewhat formally by today's standards. Each morning the milkman's horse clippety-clopped up and down the row of houses with the milk bottles rattling and clinking in his wooden cart. Granny and her contemporaries still spoke about mail and news from 'home', meaning England and Scotland.

The floor of the porch at 49 was tiled in a similar pattern to the russet and cream designs in Melbourne's St Paul's Cathedral, though simpler of course, and the long, narrow windows on either side of the front door were filled with an opaque stained glass. It was a mysterious house, ripe with damp, dusty smells and dark corners that seemed to invite exploration. There were locked doors so rarely opened that cobwebs grew in the keyholes; I knew because I peeped in them all.

On the rare and special occasions when Granny entertained, she would unlock the door to the cupboard under the stairs and emerge with some beautiful pieces of silver or glass wrapped in velvet or tissue paper. Each item had a story, as indeed did many things at Towong Hill. I could understand where Mum's love of stories and her own story-telling talents had come from. For both Granny and Mum, certain special objects had a strong power of association and often acted as catalysts stimulating fond memories.

Granny knew each of the portraits hanging in her house by name and exactly where each of the ancestors depicted fitted on the family tree. As Granny lived far from her original home in Brisbane and in an otherwise often empty house, the ancestors

Each Item Had a Story

must have given her a sense of belonging. Each time I arrived to stay at 49 I felt like I had been swept into a wider family. It was comforting, inspiring and spooky in equal measures.

Granny was tall and well built. She looked as if she could command troops as well as a large extended family, yet she was a gentle person who hardly raised her voice and moved slowly, with dignity, like a ship under full sail in her waisted dress with flowing skirts. I thought she was very beautiful.

Granny treasured her possessions, possibly most of all for the memories and associations with people and events they brought her. The treasures were the result of decades of careful collecting. As a girl, Mum used to go to sales with her mother and she was with Granny when she bought a sofa and two armchairs for the drawing room. The chairs were narrow with high arms, and Mum and Uncle Edward used to joke that some of the more amply proportioned Girl Guide commissioners visiting Granny would get wedged in the chairs and stand up with them stuck to their bottoms.

An Indian tiger skin hung on the wall above the stairs and two mounted boar heads were hanging above the sitting room and dining room doors. These rather macabre trophies scared me so much that I would not go downstairs alone at night. Mum's eldest brother, Ian, had shot the tiger in India in 1929. Luckily there was a bathroom and a loo upstairs, so I didn't have to walk past the tiger in the dark, but I could still feel its fierce presence.

Granny's house was a tribute to Grandfather's military experience in different parts of the world, and to a lesser extent Ian and Edward's military service in the 1930s in India and during the Second World War. Once she took me upstairs to the box room and proudly showed me Roman coins that Grandfather had found while bathing with his soldiers in the Dead Sea or scratching around with trenching tools in Egypt during the First World War. I had never seen anything so old, worn and battered. Unlike now, back then it was not illegal to remove small souvenirs from Egypt and Palestine. On top of a cupboard in the box room there was a pith helmet; until Granny brought it down to show me, I'd imagined helmets made of grapefruit skins turned inside out.

One afternoon when I was seven, Granny was in the pantry where she was unpacking and trying to clean some old chocolate boxes with Queen Victoria's head on them. The Queen had sent them to the troops one Christmas during the South African War. Another day during the same visit she suggested I put on my favourite blue-and-white striped party dress, with tiny pink roses on the blue stripes. Then she ordered a taxi and took me on my first visit to the Shrine of Remembrance. She asked an attendant in uniform if he would kindly unlock a glass display box with a book in it and show me Grandfather's name. He pulled on a pair of white gloves and turned the leaves of this special book until he found the page with the name 'Chauvel, Sir H.G. "K.C.M.G.," "K.C.B."'. It was written in magnificent calligraphy and seemed to be the longest name, taking up two lines in the first column on the page.

'The "H" was for Harry. George was his second name,' Granny explained before moving on to the letters following his name. I quickly forgot all she said, except that Grandfather had been a very important person. Nobody else's name in either of the columns took up two lines so either he was important or greedy – not that I would say 'greedy' to Granny. She was very proud of him and wouldn't have liked it. She said, 'Don't forget who your grandfather was.' We then went up onto the balcony so we could see St Kilda Road leading down towards Port Phillip Bay.

Granny had beautiful handwriting and she wrote in fountain pen, forming the loops and shafts of each letter carefully as if she had all the time in the world. In the afternoons she brought out letters Grandfather had written to her while he was serving in Palestine and she was living in England looking after Ian,

Edward and Mum. She was painstakingly copying Grandfather's letters into large leather-bound books. Rather like Mum, she seemed to hero-worship Grandfather; she said that during the First World War she had lived for his letters. In 1917, when they were living in Cambridge, sometimes she could hear the awful deep rumbles and booming sounds coming from the war in France. Knowing from the newspapers and from bereaved friends and relatives of the losses, she tried to ensure that the wives of Australian servicemen received newspapers too, so they would know more about what their menfolk were doing. Before she wrote on each page Granny measured and drew faint pencil lines to ensure she kept her writing tidy. She carefully pasted black-and-white and sepia photographs and drawings beside the letters they accompanied.

Grandfather's letters were only detailed in so far as censorship permitted. Both he and Granny loved flowers and he often remarked about the wildflowers he saw. Flowers he found in the Wilderness of Judea he pressed between the pages of the Bible covered with olive wood; I have Mum's illustrated copy of the New Testament and it is still filled with his now disintegrating cuttings. While Mum was not such a keen gardener as her parents, she, too, loved wildflowers and wrote about them in her diaries and books.

Granny began compiling Grandfather's letters in the 1920s. In my earliest memories she had already completed the first volume of letters covering Grandfather's time at Gallipoli and in Egypt, and was working on the second volume. In *Chauvel Country* Mum explains that she first knew she wanted to write when her mother started transcribing Grandfather's letters, when Mum was about seven. She decided, 'I too, would write a book and have it bound in calf. Mother even gave me a piece of leather, but I do not remember what was written on the pages inside the binding. I do know that, slowly and certainly, to write a book became an ambition.'[1]

Some thirty-five or more years later, Granny had almost completed what must surely be a unique collection of letters and memorabilia. It is a work of art. She had an acute sense that Grandfather and the Light Horse had contributed to a decisive period in history, but she was humble and didn't put her name to anything.

The book is now in the War Memorial in Canberra.

7

Brilliant Times and Places

It was Granny who told me, and any of her grandchildren who wanted to hear, the thrilling story of the Chauvel ancestors' escape from religious persecution in France in an open boat across the English Channel following the revocation of the Edict of Nantes on 22 October 1685. The original edict from 1598 had given full civil rights to Protestants, or Huguenots, and widespread persecution followed in the wake of the loss of these rights. At least some of the Chauvel ancestors were Huguenots.

The discovery of the story of the French side of our family was the result of a chance meeting between Grandfather and Monsieur Jean Chauvel, a diplomat who had served in China and later as French ambassador in London and at the United Nations, at a dinner on board a ship in 1923. When they realised that they shared the same surname they began to discuss their family histories, trying to find the link that would explain the coincidence. Until that meeting it appears that the Australian branch of the Chauvel family had been in effect cut adrift, having lost touch with the French branch. Indeed, until that time the Australians didn't even know if any of the French Chauvels had survived the French Revolution of 1788–89. Monsieur Chauvel told the story of all the family having been guillotined except for one little boy, who had among his meagre possessions a watch inscribed 'Chauvel de Martinière'.

Granny told another thrilling story of how an English ancestor by marriage named Captain Piercy had fought valiantly in a 1779 naval engagement off Flamborough Head on the Yorkshire coast against a superior French force under the command of John Paul Jones. Decades later when I was travelling through Dumfriesshire in Scotland, purely by chance I came across a bleak white house with dark window frames where John Paul Jones was born. Locals said he was a bit of a lad and was reputed to fly women's underwear from the mast of his ship. It was as if I had found a tangible association with my family story – not that Granny ever mentioned undergarments flying from the mast! It seemed such a small cottage for the larger than life character whose career started as a buccaneer and ended with his role as founding father of the United States Navy. It was strange that Granny thought of Jones mainly as a formidable pirate when in fact he had led a fascinating life. But even if I was discovering some inaccuracies, Granny's stories were still captivating.

While Captain Piercy's ship, the *Countess of Scarborough*, was captured and Sir Richard Pearson's ship, *Serapis*, surrendered, the convoy of forty-one merchant vessels together with its valuable cargo escorted by these two warships was able to escape. I have never seen the diamond given to Captain Piercy by the grateful British government, but my cousin Richard, who has seen it, infers that it glitters more in legend than reality. Mum wrote of this diamond in *Chauvel Country*: 'I have thought of it for years as something like a family dice [die] – if I should cast the Piercy Diamond on the chart of my life, where would it land? Which have been the most brilliant times and places?'[1]

Other tales sparkled in Granny's repertoire. It must have been upon Granny's mother-in-law that the bushranger Captain

Thunderbolt called at Tabulam, the Chauvel property on the Upper Clarence River in northern New South Wales, while the men of the family were away in Grafton. Granny told how the women showed Thunderbolt's party over the house, where fortunately there were no valuables, before directing the outlaws in the opposite direction from the one in which their men would be returning home. While the brave adventurer Captain Piercy was one of Mum's heroes, I thought she should have accorded her more direct ancestors similar accolades, but Mum preferred the male role models.

Granny wrote the story of the Chauvel family as she knew it from family papers and records and from what Grandfather learned from Monsieur Jean Chauvel. Later, I typed up Granny's notes and Mum used them as the basis for the first chapter of her book *Chauvel Country*. Subsequent researchers have suggested that the Chauvels may have come from Brittany rather than the Loire (as Granny always thought), or perhaps from both regions; so far conclusive evidence has not come to light. Those of us who grew up on Granny's version and have copies of her notes love her stories, and we admired her efforts to research and to give her grandchildren a sense of history. Granny was a great raconteur and I wish I had asked her for more stories.

For Mum, the very walls of her old home in South Yarra echoed with the tales and adventures of ex-servicemen and the stories of Chauvel ancestors who served in different parts of the world. There were swords that had been used in battles long ago, and shell cases from the Great War – one of them stood in the hall near the front door and held the standard of the Desert Mounted Corps, a red pennant with a white cross.

Philippe Batters, a resident of Murphy Street, quite accurately described the house as a 'museum'.[2] It was a much more orderly museum than Towong Hill, and when I was a child it was the best museum I had ever seen.

Before the houses in Murphy Street were renumbered, 49 had been number 33, not that this mattered to anyone. On my seventh birthday, Mum said that she thought the number seven was magic, so I wonder what she thought about the number 49 – did it indeed possess seven times the magic of seven? Whether the number 49 was auspicious or not, 49 had a special place in Mum's affections as her childhood home, and also in those of many of Granny's grandchildren.

It was from 49 that Mum had started to ride when she was about eight years old. When she was about twelve Grandfather organised for her to have riding lessons at the Remount Depot behind Victoria Barracks, but it was really Grandfather who taught her most of what she knew about horsemanship. When Uncle Ian was posted home from India in 1930 he and Mum began hunting with the Findon Harriers Hunt Club. She knew when she married Dad that hunting was a thing of the past, but I suspect there were moments when she would have given anything to have been able to return to those halcyon days. Mum said Grandfather was a shy man, but she always managed to strike a chord with him when they talked about horses and riding.

Later, in *Chauvel Country*, Mum wrote a most evocative description of an early morning in the garden at 49, when she was staying with her parents during the Second World War:

> *I could sometimes hear the distant sound of a ship's siren coming up from the Bay – that sound which we used to hear so often in South Yarra, when we first lived there after the Great War. It used to evoke in my memory the visions of limitless ocean and strange coastlines, and also the calm feeling of the family surrounding me – Mother, the boys, Nanny, and Dad no longer riding with his soldiers but back with us in the bright light of Australia. The soft ringing of Christ Church bells, too, would*

enfold me in my childhood's knowledge of certain love, and the cooing of the Indian doves murmured with peace and happiness.[3]

Mum often described her memories of those years as being bathed in brilliant sunshine.

It was difficult for any other place to usurp Mum's love of her first home. I suspect that in the early years after her marriage she often felt more at home at 49 than she did in her own home at Towong Hill, which she and the family shared with the Mitchell family ghosts. It was at 49 that she began her writing career, starting with a series of stories called 'Eve's Wood', which she wrote for her sister Eve's tenth birthday. She continued to write, sharing stories with Alice Nicholson, the cook, at the table in the dark kitchen at the back of the house. It was a humble but determined beginning to a long and successful career.

8

'Like a Wave Lifting Everything'

Number 49 was more than a museum of personal and military history. Mum loved the parties and the way of life she had enjoyed while living there before she and Dad were married. It wasn't so much that the Chauvels were particularly sociable, it was more that Grandfather's wartime service and position as Inspector-General brought with it travel and a number of official functions. Many senior military and ex-military friends and colleagues were guests at 49, and there were also special occasions to celebrate. In 1934, a year before Mum married Dad, there was the centenary of Melbourne and the visit to the city of the Duke of Gloucester for the dedication of the Shrine of Remembrance. Mum was shy, so Granny and Grandfather agreed that she could do secretarial training if she accepted the invitations to functions they wished her to attend to overcome her shyness. She must have loved every moment of the pomp and ceremony and surely missed it all acutely in the relative isolation of Towong Hill after she married Dad.

Even though Grandfather had died nine years before the royal visit in 1954, Granny was keen to rise to the occasion. While I was too young to remember anything apart from hearsay and glimpses of fabulous evening dresses hanging in wardrobes, the Queen's visit and the opening of Parliament in March 1954 provided the ideal opportunity for Mum to savour once again the high-society life she'd loved so much before she and Dad were married.

She wrote about it in detail to her younger sister, Eve, in a series of long letters describing the Queen and the Duke of Edinburgh's arrival at Essendon Airport in Melbourne and the procession at 'eight miles an hour through what is supposed to be the most tremendous welcome so far.'[1] The letter describes in thrilling detail the opening of Parliament, which Granny and Indi also attended. Mum remarked that the Queen 'read her speech very well and with less high pitch than in Sydney (that apparently being nerves)'. Mum went on to describe the Queen as wearing 'a rather ugly tiara, like a high, solid picket fence of diamonds, highly satisfactory for Indi, of course, but anyway the whole effect was of great magnificence'.

For Mum, the 'Government House Ball was really *the* party, *the* wonderful occasion of the whole time'. Mum and Dad would have been invited as Dad was a member of parliament in the Victorian government, and he had relatively recently been attorney-general and solicitor-general – both Mum and Dad were well connected in Melbourne. After a lengthy account of the people who had been invited, Mum described the Queen processing through the ballroom and then standing on the dais while the national anthem was played. 'That,' Mum remarked, 'was the most magnificent moment of the tour I think. This small, completely regal figure in either white tulle or foaming lace, all sewn with silver, a glorious tiara, and against the background of blue velvet.' Mum added, 'I realised then, much more forcefully than before, what a job she had taken on. The scene was almost unbelievable, for Melbourne, because in front of her, too, were women in the most wonderful dresses I've ever seen, and jewels, and men in uniform, and the enjoyment and excitement were like a wave lifting everything.'

Later in the nine-page letter, she mentioned that women spent about £150 or £200 on each evening dress. As Mum had seen Mrs Cain, the wife of the Victorian premier, wearing a blue organza evening dress with embroidery on the bodice very similar to one she herself was planning to wear, she dashed out to Georges and bought another far more striking dress. In her letter Mum remarked, 'I just could not appear in the same dress as Mrs Cain.' The dress she bought was made of 'oyster brocade with a pattern of gold thread roses on it, a beautifully cut skirt and the top of the bodice embroidered with gold sequins and large beads and a halter neck also embroidered'. It was the sort of dress she thought she should have had for the other evening functions during the royal visit.

As a child I had never realised how important the opening of Parliament, the ball at Government House and the many other splendid occasions were to Mum. After she died, I found carbon copies of the collection she called her 'Sister Anne' letters in the davenport desk she had bequeathed to me. (Mum and Eve wrote to each other as 'Dear Sister Anne', for reasons long forgotten.) There is a breathless, fairytale quality to these letters. In the last letter, Mum wrote: 'I can't help regretting that it is all over, it was a wonderful, wonderful time. I have put away all my good clothes with the sad feeling of "When ever again will there be quite such an occasion?"'

Anxious to maintain her own public profile, Mum sent copies of her books to the Queen. She received a formal letter of acknowledgement from Buckingham Palace and stuffed it into a drawer as she had done with the clipping announcing my birth.

The next royal visit was in 1963, but Mum and Dad were not involved in quite the same capacity. Dad's political career had already peaked a decade earlier when he was attorney-general from 1950 to 1952. They didn't attend the same number of functions in Melbourne as they had during the royal visit in March 1954. But Mum must have attended at least one reception before we returned to Towong Hill, for the story goes that one of Harry's schoolfriends, who saw her before she left the house, wolf-whistled Mum one evening as she processed slowly down the stairs at 49, splendid in a magnificent evening dress. Both Granny and Mum were slightly surprised and embarrassed, and the next day Mum said it was 'not the done thing' to wolf-whistle a schoolfriend's mother. Years later the wolf-whistler became a prominent political figure, so he was already making his mark when he came to stay for the weekend at 49.

Rather like her wild Leonie character in *Black Cockatoos Mean Snow*, Mum loved wonderful parties and beautiful clothes. Her descriptions of the official occasions, such as the dedication of the Shrine by his Royal Highness Prince Henry, Duke of Gloucester, in 1934, which she had attended with Granny and Grandfather, and of the royal visits formed a glamorous backdrop to our quiet visits to Melbourne. I could never imagine having any role to play in royal visits, let alone wearing glamorous clothes for them. I was too tomboyish and I couldn't really picture myself ever growing up.

Granny also had some glittering evening dresses she'd worn for royal visits and other important occasions in Melbourne. They were all kept in moth-proof plastic bags and the overflow from her wardrobe filled the wardrobe in the room in which I slept. I liked to unzip the gowns from their bags, and once Mum caught me taking one off the hanger to hold it against myself so I could twirl around a bit in the mirror. The next time I made sure I wasn't caught, and I had hours of fun in an imaginary world of balls in the presence of royalty as Mum and Granny had done. Granny and 49 seemed to belong to a glamorous era that reached its zenith before I was born. I found it difficult to reconcile the splendid clothes hanging in the wardrobes and what I had heard and read about the magnificent occasions with the image of

Mum in her khaki shorts or bib-and-brace overalls at Towong Hill. I think Mum found the contradictions both amusing and inspiring, and I feel that if I'd asked her about them she might have laughed, and remarked that life was all the richer for them.

I was disappointed with the Queen's 1963 visit. We went to Melbourne for the couple of functions to which Mum and Dad had been invited. A little later when the Queen visited the Snowy Mountains Authority I would have loved the sense of occasion and excitement of welcoming her at the 'site set aside for school children at Khancoban'.[2] I would also have enjoyed being on the street with masses of others waving flags in Melbourne. Instead, Mum took us to see the royal couple pass along the road from Corryong to Khancoban. From my perch on the gate near Khancoban Station I was so busy trying to take photographs with a Box Brownie that I didn't see the Queen or the Duke of Edinburgh as they passed. Worse yet, when the print came back it was too blurred to see any more than a silhouette of the royal couple and their car.

9

Where There Are Roses There Are Usually Thorns

The vacant land beside 49 was overgrown with blackberries and other weeds. Eventually a block of creamy-coloured brick flats was built there. Just after workmen had laid concrete on the next-door drive, Harry and I imprinted our sandalled feet into the grey, damp mass. 'I'll take the razor strop to you kids,' Mrs D, Granny's grumpy old housekeeper, threatened before we could cause more damage by walking concrete onto the rug in the front hall. Mrs D was the fierce live tiger at 49, her grating voice thick with the tobacco she smoked in her room. Our footmarks remained on the neighbouring drive for decades. Despite her cross words at the time, Mum always looked for our footprints whenever she returned to 49.

Not long after the footprint episode, Granny gave me a little quilted-plastic purse with a few coins in it. She must have given Harry some money too because she took both of us to Mrs Clifford's stationery and toy shop in Toorak Road to see what we could buy; it was the first time I had ever handled money. We then walked along to Chevy Chase milk bar and Granny bought us vanilla ice-cream in cardboard cups with little wooden spoons. She loved ice-cream but she didn't like being seen eating in public, so she hailed a taxi to take us and our delicious dripping dixies back up the hill.

It was from Granny's house that I was taken to the City Baths and my first swimming lessons. Miss Scott at the Baths had a secret weapon, a type of fishing rod that was really a thin pole and a line with a canvas belt on the end. After putting the belt around my chest and getting me into the water, she held me so I didn't sink and I paddled for all I was worth. The white-tiled, chlorine-strong pools were the first I had ever seen. Miss Scott was a swimming instructor who inspired confidence – one of the first people outside the family to have done that for me.

Granny's bathing towels were rough like the sandpaper from Dad's workshop back at Towong Hill. Once the towels had sand from the beach ingrained in them, they were even harder. In summer, Mum and whoever she had employed as a temporary nanny took us swimming at Elwood. I remember one occasion when Uncle Edward, who was visiting, came with us. He wore a blue towelling dressing-gown in the car to go to the beach and to stop wet sand sticking to the seats on the way home afterwards. The beach at Elwood was always chilly in the early mornings, and the sand was hard. Out in Port Phillip Bay were the silhouettes of container ships waiting to come into port, and beyond them a thin humpy line, which Mum and Uncle Edward said were probably the ridges of the You Yangs near Geelong. At the beach, Mum wouldn't let me out of her sight. She said that when I was about eighteen months old I had walked into the sea, fully clothed, and refused to come out when I was called. It must have been among my earliest bids for freedom, though it would have lasted only as long as it took the first adult to wade in and pull me out of the water.

One day Indi or Harry used one of Granny's Federation wooden beds as a trampoline and broke it. At the time Granny was visiting Eve and her family in Kenya, and Mum dreaded having to break the news when Granny returned a few days later by ship. As I was not involved in the bouncing, I can't remember if anyone got into trouble. Granny was usually surprisingly tolerant when one of us had been very naughty, but there was no guarantee. She had outbreaks of crossness.

If Granny hadn't married when she was only eighteen, and if she had been born later when it was easier for young women to pursue careers, she could have been a fabulous garden designer. At 49 she created a beautiful garden for her family, with hydrangeas, camellias and azaleas. She was always concerned that her boisterous grandchildren might damage her carefully nurtured treasures. In the middle of the front lawn there was a crabapple tree whose trunk had been scarred by masses of climbing feet. The verandah posts and wrought-iron railings provided challenging ascents for the more athletic who didn't mind getting covered with soot on the way up, or into trouble afterwards.

With her long arms and legs, Mum would have had all the attributes necessary to be a prestigious verandah-post climber when she was young. Just as she let her imagination go while she was climbing trees, she made up stories as she shinnied up and down the verandah posts. Decades later, with a family of her own, she recognised the potential dangers just as her parents had years before and spent her time trying to dissuade us from doing the same thing. Despite Granny and Mrs D's efforts to ensure we didn't even look as if we would venture up a verandah post, I did of course, and I imagine most of Granny's other grandchildren did too. But I rarely saw much of our cousins as 49 was too small for more than one family to stay there at a time.

Sometimes Granny tried to explain to Mum that her writing was coming into conflict with her family and that her children needed her too. Other times Granny simply stepped in sedately and lovingly if Mum was absent. When we were in Melbourne and Mum was busy with publishers or research, it was often

Granny who was there with us. I remember her as perfection personified, yet, as with many childhood memories, I wonder now if it is realistic.

According to a letter from Barbara Ramsay, the Chauvel family's former nanny, who had returned to her native Scotland to live, Granny had her failings as a mother too. Nanny (as her fond former protégés called her) didn't think Granny recognised Uncle Edward's abilities and insisted he go into the army rather than pursue an academic career for which, in Nanny's view, he might have been better suited. Part of the problem might have been that Nanny was fonder of Grandfather than she was of Granny, but there is nobody left now who would remember.

Granny reminded me of the soft, silky roses that grew in her garden during the summer. But where there are roses, there are usually thorns. Granny's sister Dora, our great-aunt, was beautiful in an inhibited and icy way, with her carefully permed white hair, designer clothes, elaborately beautiful hats and immaculately made-up face. During the Second World War, Dora upset Mum by suggesting she should take more responsibility for Granny and Grandfather as Granny had had pneumonia in the early months of the war and Grandfather was in his late seventies and becoming frail. Dora didn't mince her words. She told Mum that she owed her mother something. Dora continued to tell Mum that, and more, almost until she died. Aunt Dora was right, but Mum didn't like criticism and, from as early as I can remember, Mum was saying she'd had enough of Aunt Dora's pointed suggestions.

If Granny represented the gentle side of femininity, Aunt Dora was a different and pricklier role model. One Melbourne Cup day my brother John and I were playing in the garden at 49. John had made mud pies in egg boxes and was ironing them flat with a toy iron. Just as some elderly, well-dressed ladies, one of whom we thought was Aunt Dora, were walking up Murphy Street towards Domain Road on their way back from the Cup,

John stowed a couple of egg boxes full of 'pies' under his arm and climbed the tree nearest the fence. As the ladies in their hats walked beneath, John launched one of his squelchy little missiles and scored a remarkably effective hit – only it wasn't Aunt Dora. But everyone seemed to know each other then and consequences soon followed.

John as muddy missile launcher would have been temporarily blackballed from the family circle had it not been for the fact that he'd been attempting something others might have wanted to do for a long time. Although Mum could not openly admit it, she had more than a little admiration for John's audacity. Aunt Dora and Mum were opposites who did not attract. Aunt Dora was critical of Mum for 'using' Granny. Granny really enjoyed time with our family, but Aunt Dora had a point: Granny provided a home in Melbourne, family support and inspiration, and Mum made good use of them all.

Whenever Aunt Dora came to 49 the atmosphere there changed. I stopped what I was doing and watched and listened uneasily. Not surprisingly for one who didn't have children of her own, Aunt Dora didn't appear to like young people, particularly great-nieces and great-nephews from the country. Nevertheless she took an interest in Indi as she grew up as she was pretty, vivacious and a possible future social asset. Indi had far firmer career ideas, however! Dad wickedly maintained that Dora was too selfish to have children, despite the fact that her husband, Uncle Harry, would have loved a family. Even though the repartee that bounced back and forth between them was often superficially insulting, Dad secretly admired Dora, and she seemed to fancy him too.

Whatever her reputation in the family, Aunt Dora was a remarkable woman with a formidable wit and good business sense. She was renowned for her ability to make money on the stock exchange; apparently her stockbroker would dive for cover if he could before she appeared. Capital growth and her income must have helped her to buy her antiques and maintain her wardrobe – and to acquire an elaborate new hat for her friend after the mud pie incident.

'Aunt Dora's male friends ranged in age from nineteen to ninety, and there was always one available to escort her to cocktail parties at Government House or to the theatre or ballet,' Mum said. If, except for the royal visit, Granny led a relatively quiet social life after Grandfather's death in 1945, Aunt Dora made up for it as the merry widow after her own husband died.

Once, when Aunt Dora didn't have a cook, Mrs D cooked her Sunday lunch at 49. The courses were covered with lids and loaded onto trays in the boot of the taxi Granny called, then Granny, Harry and I took it around to Aunt Dora's nearby flat. By the time we had carried it upstairs and the table was laid with Aunt Dora's gleaming silver, the lunch was almost cold. Aunt Dora might have been unwell, but I don't think so. She could be a first-class prima donna. Harry and I reckoned that if she thought Mum had Granny running around after her, Aunt Dora treated her younger sister in much the same way, only a lot worse!

I reckoned Aunt Dora must have been the focus of envy for many wives in Melbourne. She was undoubtedly a domineering part of Mum's life, but she was such a powerful and scary presence that Mum never dared to write about her; Granny wouldn't have liked it and Aunt Dora would have certainly had a hissy fit. It was a pity as Aunt Dora was just the person to provide Mum with some wonderful character studies and inspiration for her novels.

Perhaps Aunt Dora was not really the ogre we thought she was. When she died, she left Mum some Kings pattern silver cutlery. Mum gave it to me as a wedding present, and every time we use it I think of Aunt Dora and the colour she added to our lives in Melbourne. From her top-floor flat on the corner of Walsh Street and Domain Road she had an excellent bird's-eye view of Melbourne society's many comings and goings.

10

A Naughty Blue Leopard with a Great Big Smile

As well as taking us to Melbourne for important occasions like royal visits, Mum regularly made the trip with us to see Granny, for Indi and Harry's exeat weekends once they were both at boarding school, and to do the family clothes shopping. Harry's Geelong Grammar school uniform came from Buckley & Nunn next to Myer in Bourke Street, while Indi's Toorak College uniform came from Ball & Welch in Flinders Street. Some of our everyday clothing came from Myer, and occasionally Mum found our smart clothes at Georges in Collins Street, where she also got her own. Mum said she could get it all done quicker without the children, so Granny looked after John and me at 49 while Mum went shopping. Also, she sometimes met friends at the Alexandra Club where children under ten years of age were not permitted. If she wasn't sure whether garments would fit us or not, she brought them back for us to try at 49, but otherwise she arranged for them to be sent to Towong Hill. I hated having very little say in the clothes that were bought for me.

Despite Granny's calm kindness and the occasional ice-cream and outing, the only game she played with us was patience, preferring her detective stories to most other things, so I was often lonely and bored. The toy cupboard in the nursery held only Mum's and Aunt Eve's old toys, including the toy iron John used to flatten his mud pies into shapes. Sometimes when Mum returned from the city we walked around to Acland Street to visit the Hay family. Once when Harry and Peter Hay were out in the garden throwing a hammer to each other, one of them didn't manage to catch it and it shattered a pane in the window by the Hays' sofa. Probably concerned about some sort of repeat incident, the Hays didn't come to see us at 49. Mrs D would have scared the bravest hammer thrower and I felt almost as isolated there as I was at Towong Hill. It would have been great if friends had been able to come and see us, but 49 wasn't a place for running riot.

Although the Stokes family was older, they kindly invited us to swim in their pool at their house in Heyington Place in Toorak. Once someone tried to teach me to ride their penny farthing bicycle on the tennis court; my legs were too short and I was so spectacularly unsuccessful that I thought the contraption was some kind of joke. But an afternoon with the Stokes gave me a feeling of freedom and fun beyond the confines of 49.

Indi, Harry, John and I were the only grandchildren who did correspondence schooling once we reached school age. Although Mum engaged a temporary governess/child-minder, Miss Montgomery (we called her Gomery), during at least one of our trips to Melbourne, I didn't do any schoolwork there. One afternoon Miss Montgomery took John and me by train out to her house in the suburbs, a little cottage with pretty leadlights by the front door, tucked away behind a high, cream-coloured wooden fence. After that journey Miss Montgomery gave me a history book on Melbourne, probably because I asked so many questions and wanted to know the story behind the things I saw.

Some other visitors to 49 were the possums that made noises like metal coathangers rattling in the wardrobe. I was convinced they actually were in the wardrobe and just waiting for Mum to turn out the light before they would come pouring out onto the bedroom floor. In my dreams, possums climbed the bedposts too. Granny didn't like sharing her house with possums and from time to time she set traps. Once the traps were full she loaded them and their inmates into a taxi and drove them over to Fitzroy Gardens where she released them. By that evening either the original possums were back, or the message had gone out that there were vacancies at 49 Murphy Street and others had rushed to fill the space.

It was at 49 that I saw television for the first time in 1959. Granny didn't have a TV set but Mrs D did, and Granny said we could go to the kitchen and watch Mum, looking smart in a suit and wearing a hat rather like a crown of sparse magpie feathers, receiving the Children's Book Council Award of 'Highly Commended' for *The Silver Brumby*. While pleased, Mum was disappointed that *The Silver Brumby* was not awarded Children's Book of the Year simply because the horses talked. Mum was always striving to do better, and 49 was a source of inspiration and support for her. With her father's military memorabilia surrounding her, his successful military career became a benchmark of achievement and excellence. She wrote about him later in *Light Horse to Damascus* (1971), *Light Horse: The Story of Australia's Mounted Troops* (1978) and the novelisation *The Lighthorsemen* (1987), from Ian Jones's film script.

I was plagued by colds, stomach upsets, violent vomiting and diarrhoea, both at 49 and at Towong Hill. When we were staying at 49, Mum called on Dr Lawrence Stokes, a well-known Melbourne doctor and an old family friend. On more than one occasion he gently pushed and prodded my cramping stomach as he tried to ascertain what was making me so ill. Medicine came from Oggs, the chemist with the large apothecary jars in its Toorak Road shop window.

With medical matters, Mum believed in going to the top as she had done with Dr Stokes. If she didn't know the top doctors personally, she usually knew someone who did. Inevitably there were appointments with other doctors and dentists during our visits to Melbourne, and we each had our tonsils out. Mum thought we would catch fewer bad colds if we didn't have tonsils, though I don't think it made much difference.

Harry and I were lucky enough to have our tonsils out at the same time. We shared an L-shaped room in the children's ward at St Andrew's Hospital where our windows looked out onto the dark, bluestone, Gothic-looking St Patrick's Cathedral. During our first evening in hospital before the operations, Harry irritated the nurse by imitating the cathedral bells long after they had finished ringing. In his short blue cotton pyjamas with brown spots, leaping in and out of his shiny, high hospital bed, he looked rather like a naughty blue leopard with a great big smile.

Being smaller and with shorter legs, I was less agile. The nurses caught me racing around and reminded me that I was in a hospital where other children felt ill and needed peace and quiet to recover. I don't suppose that Harry or I were really as happy as our mischief led the nurses to believe; I was five and couldn't remember ever having spent a night away from home or Granny's house without Mum. I was frightened of the operation, and I reckoned Harry was too. That evening I saw the sunset and then the dark, silhouetted spire of the cathedral. The next thing I remembered was waking up feeling sick and with a horribly sore throat. And Harry wasn't laughing and talking or leaping in and out of bed any more.

Fortunately, selective amnesia has spared me from other less pleasant memories. My next recollection of that time is a nurse at my bedside. 'There is another little country girl like you in the big ward,' she said. 'Would you like to see her? She hasn't got a big brother here like you have, and her mummy is in the country with her dad and brothers and sisters.' I nodded, imagining that I might meet a playmate. I hadn't thought to ask what was wrong with her. The girl's eyes were bandaged, and the bandages wound all around her head, leaving only her nose and mouth uncovered. She couldn't see me. As she tried to scratch at the bandage, she kept saying, 'It is itchy,' and then she cried for her mummy.

'My name is Honor,' I said, 'and I have a brother called Harry and we could come and play! What is your name?' The girl didn't reply. She just tossed back and forth in misery on her bed. I'd never seen anyone of my own age in such discomfort and so unhappy.

After a few minutes, the nurse returned. When she told the girl that she was taking me back to my bed but I might come again later, the girl didn't reply. I didn't see her again and neither do I remember anything else about St Andrew's Hospital, but all of a sudden my throat didn't seem to hurt quite as much. I knew instantly that I was fortunate and I never forgot it. I'd learned a little about compassion. Later, while recuperating at Granny's house, I tasted pink junket for the first time. When we arrived home at Towong Hill my jodhpurs were loose, but I soon regained the lost pounds.

11

The Bittersweet Schoolroom

In some of my earliest memories of Mum writing at Towong Hill, she sits at her desk in the front hall with her back to me, hunched over her notebooks and typewriter in a gorgeous pool of early morning sunshine. Her back spoke silently, firmly indicating that she didn't want to be disturbed, but I always wanted her to turn around and give me a hug. Above the windows in front of the desk there were magnificent Federation-style stained-glass windows with designs of trees on undulating countryside.

Mum's desk was at the east-facing window looking out past the verandah to a circular lawn surrounding a flowerbed. Beyond more flowerbeds were the large European trees surrounding the garden like a wall, separating us from the world beyond. Peeping above the treetops were the peaks of the Dargals Range, or 'one of those inextinguishable flares' or 'ice-etched symbols', as Mum frequently called them in winter. Often she would sit thinking, writing notes and doodling, preoccupied perhaps with the view and almost certainly with thoughts and dreams well beyond the boundaries of the family, house and garden – and probably even beyond Towong Hill and the Upper Murray.

The time she liked this view most was at dawn in winter, when the sun rose with brilliant spears of sunlight thrusting up behind the snow-dusted mountains. If the weather was good she had a view from the south-facing windows out over the river flats and the memory-filled, bush-covered foothills to the western face of the Alps and two of Australia's highest peaks, Mt Twynam and Mt Townsend.

These views enshrined her memories of her marvellous ski and summer expeditions with Dad before the war, some of the happiest times of her life. Then, Dad was her hero and best friend as well as her husband. Sometimes she was dreaming not only about their adventures before the war but her expeditions from the Chalet at Charlotte Pass in the winter of 1941 – back in an era before so much changed. Perhaps she also thought about her trip across the Alps in 1936, from Khancoban to the Chalet, before she could ski very much at all. Exhausted as she must have been, she must also have felt a marvellous sense of achievement. I often wondered if, during that trip, she gained the confidence and appetite for bigger challenges.

I thought of those views as being Mum's and not mine; her knowledge and experience of the mountains were so much greater than mine were ever likely to be. There was little or no room for me or any other members of the family when she was dreaming, thinking or writing. It was some years before I understood that I too could enjoy the views and going to the mountains. I could interpret them as I wished, irrespective of my level of knowledge and experience.

For me, the unusual, pentagon-shaped room we called the front hall arouses intense and bittersweet memories. I remember it best as the place where Mum clattered away on the typewriter on her desk by the window, writing letters, articles and stories. In time, many of the stories she was typing became my bedtime stories; at her desk in the front hall she wrote and typed manuscripts for *Flow River, Blow Wind*; *Black Cockatoos Mean Snow*; the early Brumby Books; *Kingfisher Feather*; *Winged Skis*; numerous articles for the magazine *Walkabout*; and a number of short stories she offered to *Southerly*, *Meanjin* and *Quadrant* and the hardback periodical *Coast to Coast*. The first four Brumby books and, to a lesser extent, *Kingfisher Feather* and *Winged Skis* became part of my imaginary world.

In the first decade of the last century, when my paternal grandparents lived at Towong Hill, the front hall had been furnished more sparsely and used as a reception room, where guests were welcomed before being taken through to the sitting room. Both rooms had beautiful parquet floors made of Murray pine. Mum said it would have made a wonderful dancing floor, although nobody used it for that. I wondered if the trees that made up the floorboards came from Walwa or Tintaldra Pine Mountain, or whether they had come from somewhere I had never heard of.

In *Black Cockatoos Mean Snow* Mum surreptitiously included her feelings about entertaining. 'All the struggle with the land during the years of War had seemed to make it impossible for [Silver] to feel much pleasure in parties, and yet lots of the men who had been to the War wanted parties more than anything, though his own brothers were not like that.'[1] Like Silver, Mum had struggled with the land, and she didn't feel she had received adequate recognition, particularly from Dad, for what she had achieved. For the most part while we were at Towong Hill, she didn't want or indeed have time for parties. Towong Hill was a work place, but trips to Melbourne were an entirely different matter.

In a changing world after the Second World War, when many visitors came to the back rather than to the front door, the family used the front hall increasingly as a study, schoolroom and family room. Mum and Dad only used it very occasionally as a reception room and then we tidied it a bit, but never as much as Dad would have wanted. It was here in the 1950s and 1960s that Mum supervised our correspondence schoolwork. The table in the middle of the room was always laden with pencils and incomplete lessons left lying about untidily; Mum was too busy running the house and garden or writing to supervise the lessons, let alone the tidying up. Mum was imagining this room when she wrote in *Kingfisher Feather*, published in 1962 when I was nine, about the twins, David and Sally Dane, doing their schoolwork. It was in a room like this that Joanna, their mother, would have read them Judith Wright's poem 'Bullocky', just as Mum introduced Judith Wright's and David Campbell's poetry to me in some of my more enjoyable lessons.

Mum was quite happy to expand the curriculum so long as it didn't include comics or books by Enid Blyton. 'They are bad literature and you mustn't read them,' she argued, thereby cutting us off from part of the culture of our generation. 'You will learn to use grammar more accurately if you read good books.' So there was no Noddy or Famous Five for us. When we were in Melbourne I could have asked my friend Steena Hay if she had any Enid Blyton books I could borrow, but I'd have landed her in trouble if her mother had told mine. Mum chose and bought our books on her Melbourne shopping expeditions; I only ever went shopping in Corryong with Mum, and we hardly ever went to the local library. The only 'bad' literature I was exposed to were the dull stories that came with our correspondence schooling, not that I read all of them. Luckily Mum found them as boring as I did.

It irritated me that the heroes of *Kingfisher Feather*, the Dane twins, enjoyed and were much better at their lessons than I was. I couldn't imagine that they spent miserable hours wondering if they would ever manage to work out long division and wishing that their mother might give them just a little bit more help, instead of writing all the time like mine did. While I knew my parents wrote masses of letters, I never saw either of them doing long division. I reasoned that if they didn't do it, what on earth was I going to use it for? I couldn't envisage living anywhere but the Upper Murray, and if Mum and Dad didn't use long division there then it seemed a waste of time.

I didn't know why everything that I found hard the twins should find easy. In fact, I was jealous of the fictional characters – I thought they were the sort of children Mum wanted me to be. I wasn't, nor was I likely ever to become, a clever-at-schoolwork goody-two-shoes (not that I knew what the expression meant before I went to boarding school). The worst of it was that I couldn't stop myself panicking when I found I couldn't do something, as Mum was an impatient teacher. While she insisted that we children should be nice to each other, she was often short-tempered with us. I would freeze in these situations and, just as Mum and Dad had said, I became unteachable, dreading her mercurial disapproval. She was quite a dab whacker with a rolled up-newspaper. 'It made an awful noise,' she later reasoned, 'but didn't really hurt.' That depended – a tightly rolled *Age* still held together with an address label pasted around the middle certainly stung my bottom and didn't help me learn how to do arithmetic.

In moments of deep frustration, I badly wanted to tip something onto the typewriter or beat up its keys, such was my craving for a bit more help. I reasoned I would get more attention if it wasn't for the dreaded bloody typewriter.

'The trouble was you wouldn't learn your tables,' Mum later complained.

'But you have to teach kids what they mean so they see the point of learning them. I didn't see the point then. It wasn't as if you and Dad seemed to use them every day,' I retorted.

'If you had tried it would have been okay!'

I didn't agree. Mum didn't understand because she didn't like maths either and found it a difficult subject to teach. Perhaps she also thought that since she had managed to get through life thus far without using maths very much, I might too.

Some of what Mum thought was mental laziness on my part was simply due to her standards being too high for the amount of time she was prepared to spend teaching. Despite wanting to write and not teach, she was largely unwilling to relinquish our education to conventional schooling. With no educational psychologists to mediate and advise, it would have taken someone fairly feisty to convince Mum that her methods of educating me and perhaps the others too were not working very well and that other approaches might be worth trying. Mum genuinely thought she was giving us the best opportunities that she could. Our way of life was one that she would have loved to have had herself when she was a child; she simply couldn't see or didn't want to admit that it wasn't working and that the world of the 1950s was vastly different from that of the 1920s. 'Many of the greatest writers and thinkers, like Bertrand Russell, never went to school,' she argued long after I went to boarding school and was taking her to task about the things I should have been taught while I was doing correspondence lessons.

Problems with arithmetic seem to crowd my memories of those days in the front hall. Mum was an imaginative English teacher and she wasn't bad at history either. She kindly and generously ensured that I had a constant supply of children's historical fiction. Dad read me stories, and lent and eventually gave me some of his much-treasured childhood history books. He subscribed to *The Illustrated London News* and we pored over the articles about archaeology. Sir Francis Drake was my hero from British history, and Captain Cook held a similar fascination. Dad brought home models of an Elizabethan warship and Cook's *Endeavour* and he helped me to make them.

Mum's informal and spur-of-the-moment lessons about the natural world were fascinating. When she was gardening or out walking or riding, she always kept a sharp eye out for birds nesting and young animals. For her, a newly born bird or beast was a miracle. Her delight in the natural world, made apparent in her early writings, was well known and respected, and people contacted her if there was something in which they thought she would be interested. Thoughtful neighbours brought dead birds for her to identify. I was scared out of my wits one day when I opened the fridge door to discover the wing of a tawny frogmouth unfolding itself from inside sheets of newspaper. Surprises were part of life and learning in that wild museum.

One spring Mum and I were sitting in the sunshine on the front verandah when Mum noticed a thrush was nesting in an old wastepaper basket on top of the cupboard where garden tools were kept. As quietly as she could, Mum fetched her binoculars from the front hall so we could have a close look at the way the nest had been carefully concealed in the wickerwork. All we could see was a little grey head with a beady, blinking dark eye and a tiny beak. From that time on, nobody was allowed to remove the wastepaper basket in case Mum's little grey friend returned to nest there once more.

Best of all was a young female platypus someone had found trapped near the Khancoban dam wall. When Mum put a bucket filled with garden worms and the platypus straight into Dad's downstairs bath, the enchanting little lady swam around with her duck-like bill vacuuming up every worm in sight. The next morning, sitting in the sun on the riverbank, we let her roll in a ball and somersault playfully from our shoulders down our front and into our laps. Then, regretfully, we let go our playmate into the Indi River.

Even more bizarre was the long-bodied, fawn-coloured creature with white spots, a pointed face and a long bushy tail. John and Jack Reiners caught it by accident in a rabbit trap in the bush, high above the house on one of the ridges of Mt Porcupine. Mum thought it was a 'tiger cat' but it was probably a quoll. Unfortunately one of its front paws was too badly damaged to release it back into the wild so they somehow managed to put it in a sack and bring it home. It was in terrible pain and very frightened. The vet came, sedated it and treated its wounds as best he could. I don't know who was brave enough to do it, but a string was tied to one of its back legs and it was released, spitting and struggling, onto the front lawn where Mum photographed it. Later it would become a unique landmark in Mum's rather chaotic but extensive photographic record of the natural world. She didn't write about it because she didn't want to bring attention to the existence of such creatures and run the risk of others being hunted and hurt in some way – the accidental injury to one had been more than enough. Eventually Mum found a home for it in a sanctuary.

Mail days brought a frisson of expectancy to the front hall when we were trying to do our schoolwork. As well as bringing the horrible corrected lessons, the mail was Mum's vital lifeline with the outside world. Its arrival three mornings a week provided a welcome distraction from Crappy Days as I called the Happy Days – or was it Merry Days? – correspondence lessons. Once I knew that the word 'crappy' was derogatory, that was the word I used to describe them.

Mum emptied and sorted the mailbag and discussed sheep and cattle and local news with 'Father' Knight, their voices rumbling and mumbling in the back corridor near the Weasel Hole. Mr and Mrs Knight were one of Mum's few sources of local news. Since the end of the war, Dad's return and the arrival of us children, Mum had all but lost her role in matters relating to stock management. During the war she had delivered lambs, footrotted sheep, learned to shear and turned her hand to any job that needed doing. At that time Towong Hill still ran sheep as well as cattle and it was also a thoroughbred horse stud. The work was tough, but Mum loved it and the active outdoor life it involved. Dad rapidly became absorbed in politics when he returned from the war and left the management of the pastoral operations to Mr Knight, who had been appointed after the previous manager, Mr Herbert, died in 1947. As Mr Knight had not worked with Mum during the war, he was largely unaware of just how much the involvement with the property meant to her. He may well have assumed that now she had children, Mum was completely absorbed in her family, but this was not the case, at least not entirely. Yearning for an escape from domesticity and small children, she either misunderstood or failed to accept the normal expectations of her situation, though perhaps she hoped that the new manager would include the owner's wife in decisions when the owner himself was absent.

'I've met a very strange Catholic priest in Corryong!' someone heard a visitor to the district remark. The priest was not a priest at all but Father Knight, who was 'Father' only because he was his daughter Pat's father! A tall, imposing, silver-haired First World War veteran who had served at Gallipoli and in Palestine, Father Knight's time as manager at Towong Hill was distinguished by his wicked sense of humour and his great character. When he came up to the homestead from the nearby manager's cottage on mail days to collect the business and his family's personal mail there would be a mumble of sotto voce voices – the jokes were not for the kids – and then a roar of laughter before Father Knight went on his way and Mum returned to the front hall with her mail under her arm.

With the mail came the welcome distraction of letters and magazines with interesting pictures of birds, animals, buildings and heads of state. These bore testimony to Mum and Dad's far-flung family members, friendships from Dad's years of travel while he was at Cambridge and studying in London, and their travels together before the war. Some of their American friends kindly sent us picture books from which I learned a bit about the Grand Canyon and what the skyline of New York was like; I mightn't have been able to do sums but I was a voracious reader. Otherwise, most of the mail was for Dad, but there were also letters for Mum from Curtis Brown, her literary agents, and Hutchinson the publishers, both of whom were later to open Australian offices in Sydney and Melbourne respectively. There was fan mail too.

As well as some of our readers and lessons, Mum's desk was often laden with lists, letters, accounts, diaries, notebooks, research notes and manuscripts. One of the three telephones in the house also sat on her desk. There, Mum first compiled and then phoned through the store order for our groceries. A van from Corryong delivered them and Mum would disappear to the kitchen at the back of the house to help and to supervise the cook unpacking and storing the groceries.

Shopping was not always so straightforward. The delivery of an order from the local chemist set the scene for one misunderstanding. Mum had requested the powdered laxative senna and was both amused and surprised when powdered henna arrived instead. The consequences of ingesting henna instead of senna might have been fairly dramatic, but fortunately she spotted the error before it was too late and the henna was returned to the chemist. It left those of us who knew the story chuckling. Mum could tell stories and laugh at herself, but I had to be careful. It was many years before I could tease her about the powdered henna and the effect it might have had on her insides.

Mum often said she had too much to do, and this was true. She would come into the front hall shaking her head with frustration and cursing something or someone under her breath. She seldom seemed to relax and was always pushing herself hard. There wasn't enough time for the things she wanted to do herself, like writing and skiing, let alone running a big house and home-educating her family. I suspect the less time she gave me, the more I demanded and the more impatient she became. Until she died she always believed she could have done it all with some more help, and if there had been fewer problems with the family and with the running of Towong Hill.

'But you said you didn't want to go to the local school,' Mum remonstrated with me years later. It was all too late when eventually Mum suggested I might go to primary school for a year before I went to boarding school. By then I didn't want to go as I knew I would be the only one in grade five who had never been to school before. If we passed the local school when the kids were in the playground I longed to join the games, but I didn't tell Mum in case she actually sent me there. The eventual realisation that I was only putting off the evil hour until I went to boarding school at the age of eleven was the stuff of nightmares. Mum blamed me again for not trying harder to learn arithmetic and told me I was not very good with people. Dad simply didn't know how scared, inadequate and unprepared I was feeling. I didn't tell him because I didn't know him well enough and didn't think he would understand.

Indi was already at boarding school by the time I began Crappy Days. I knew Harry hadn't liked the correspondence classes, but he had started in grade three at the local school by the time I began my first home lessons, so it felt like I was forging a lonely path. As the youngest, John did better in the help stakes, or so it seemed to me, although he probably felt he needed more supervision too.

'I tried to employ a governess but none of you wanted one,' Mum explained ruefully. I couldn't remember ever having been asked if I wanted a governess, and I don't know if my siblings were asked either. I never really knew what had taken place and Mum wasn't about to say any more.

'All I wanted and needed was a bit more help and attention from you,' I answered.

Mum's reply was hurt silence, then she remarked, 'You just don't know how hard I worked.' She knew what I was thinking and didn't want to admit that she really shouldn't have expected to be able to write and to teach us at the same time. Inevitably, something would suffer.

I didn't make similar demands of Dad – the role of fathers was totally different then. If I had asked him about school work he might have made decisions without further consulting me, and the outcome might have been less to my liking.

While she was very critical of others, Mum didn't take criticism well herself. With that combination it was almost impossible to have an honest, open discussion with her as there was always the risk of hurting her and thus damaging our relationship. Once someone criticised her, she never forgot it, harbouring the hurt and mentioning it again years later when others had long forgotten what it had all been about. Her memory was an extraordinary mental filing system in which she could access memories of good and bad deeds at a moment's notice.

In March 1978, Mum wrote telling me that she had just read Daphne du Maurier's 1977 autobiography *Growing Pains: The Shaping of a Writer*. She remarked, 'I hope she writes the next bit – in fact how she managed to be a successful author, and write a great number of books, and produce three children and not drive everyone else mad – or maybe she did, but I think her husband survived!' Was Mum tacitly acknowledging that an author-mother – someone like herself – might drive her children mad as well as everyone else? Did Mum realise that while she may not have written quite so many books as du Maurier, certainly I – and possibly my sister and brothers as well – wished she was less preoccupied and had more time for us collectively and individually? Had she done so we might all have got to know each other better and enjoyed each other's company more.

Despite Mum's efforts to make history, nature study and English interesting and enjoyable, it became clear that her input wasn't going to be enough to bring me up to scratch. I became aware that at least one humiliating letter had arrived from Miss B, the correspondence teacher at Crappy Days, underlining my unsatisfactory progress and suggesting that the top private schools in Melbourne may not accept me. It was a bitter blow. Even though very occasionally I had imaginary friends, I craved real friends of my own age. I lived in a very silent private world.

Many years later, while collecting and sorting out manuscripts after Mum died, I found between the pages of a manuscript of *Silver Brumbies of the South* (the book dedicated to me) a carbon copy of a letter from Mum to Miss B. In it Mum admitted that she had not apportioned her time equally between John and me and realised that I had not had the help and encouragement I badly needed. Ultimately, even if Mum never said as much to me, at least I knew she had been aware she'd let me down. This was one of those moments when I wondered if my quest to better understand my childhood with Mum was going to bring more pain. I kept most of her letters but I burned this one, although that didn't erase it from my memory.

In old age she reluctantly admitted that in many ways home education had disadvantaged her children and we would have flourished more with some professional teaching. Making some friends locally would also have helped. Since Dad was the local MP many people knew who we were, but we didn't know them.

After I went to boarding school and John was sent to the local primary school, the front hall became a family gathering place during the school holidays. In summer it was one of the coolest rooms in the house and in winter, when Mum lit the coke stove in the fireplace, it was the warmest. Thankfully Mum had evicted the vestiges of Crappy Days lessons, stuffing them into drawers and cupboards, and replaced them with a record player.

Mum had a collection of Austrian and Swiss folk tunes and she also liked classical and sixties music. She liked Simon and Garfunkel and didn't object to Johnny Cash, Neil Diamond or the Bee Gees. From what she read about their lifestyle, she was a bit uncertain about the Beatles, but she couldn't resist them and sometimes I heard her humming their tunes. She had a wonderful ear for music and occasionally played Austrian folk or skiing songs on her piano accordion. Some of our best times in the front hall were when we were talking together and listening to the record player. My memories are filled with Simon and Garfunkel's 'Sounds of Silence'; throughout my early childhood there had been a lot of silence, although my chats with silence had nothing to do with subways and tenement halls. While I didn't understand what these were, I knew without asking anyone that the song was about loneliness, and that cities could be lonely too.

Mum often welcomed me home from boarding school with a book she had ordered from Margarita Webber's bookshop in Melbourne. I particularly enjoyed Joan Phipson's *It Happened One Summer* and a number of Ruth Park's books. Mum believed that a good story gave children an opportunity to explore lives and cultures beyond the one they knew, as well as their own inner world. She was quite right, but if I felt that the legacy of Crappy Days schoolwork had been buried, I was very wrong.

12
So Many Stories

Upstairs and to my room I took the books Mum had ordered for me – and, when she let me, carbon-copy chapters of her current manuscript. I was delighted with the little library that she was building up for me – the books were windows into new worlds. First published in 1958 when I was five, by 1959 *The Silver Brumby* was my bedtime story. By then Mum was working on the manuscript of *Silver Brumby's Daughter* and it soon became my next bedtime story. For a while I had trouble moving beyond books about horses. Famous show jumper Pat Smyth's books about her heroine, Jill, became favourites, though perhaps because Mum hadn't written them and they were set far away in England, they didn't have quite the same grip on my imagination as *The Silver Brumby* and *Silver Brumby's Daughter*. I dreamed about Thowra and Storm and Kunama and Tambo, and I was forever wondering if somewhere in the Upper Murray someone had lost a beautiful white mare like Golden.

Sometimes, if she had been away in Melbourne and hadn't taken us kids with her, Mum brought home a new white china horse for me to add to the collection that had begun as decorations on my fifth birthday cake. Later Mum gave me a large bay, who became Mirri from *The Silver Brumby*, and a small bay who was Storm as a foal. Granny gave me a small collection of toy chestnut ponies to play Yarraman's herd. I never had a grey horse so a rather mean-looking, greenish-grey horse became the Brolga, Thowra's fearsome adversary in *The Silver Brumby*. On the floor in my room I discovered that I could while away many hours, safe from passers-by knocking my fragile toy horses flying.

I built the Dead Horse Gap and the Cascades huts out of building blocks and stringy bark. Stones I had collected from banks of streams and moss I had picked off rocks delineated the mountains. The Secret Valley was a crevice between two big, long grey stones. I didn't have any mounted stockmen to set up the scene of a proper brumby hunt, but I had yards that I constructed out of toy farmyard fences, and railings made from sticks. Apart from the greys, I had almost the complete brumby herd. Then, when Mum started writing *Silver Brumbies of the South* and *Silver Brumby Whirlwind*, the china horses had to play a variety of characters.

In addition to reading the books Mum gave me, and the chapters she read from her own manuscripts as bedtime stories, I spent hours composing my own stories and acting them out with my china herd. Sometimes the smudgy carbon copy of one of Mum's chapters lay on the floor beside me as I arranged the scenes to replicate the part of the story we'd just read. I felt very responsible, as Mum had emphasised that I had to be extremely careful of the manuscript. I was always thrilled to think that I was the first to hear the stories. It felt as if we had a special closeness.

One morning Mrs G, who cleaned the upstairs part of the house, came to my room and exclaimed that it was disgracefully untidy. Trying to explain the imaginary world I had constructed, I grumpily realised that all she was interested in was cleaning the floor with the roller broom, the forerunner of a vacuum cleaner, and I had to dash to rescue my treasures before she knocked them flying. Cleaning seemed a waste of time as everything would just get dusty again, and if Mum wasn't that interested in housework, why should Mrs G be? It hadn't dawned on me that I was making a difficult job even harder for her. The next time Mum went to Melbourne she returned with some toy farm fencing that must have meant more clutter for Mrs G. I can't remember her lasting very long.

Before I was born, my room had been my paternal grandparents' bedroom. Until I was about nine or ten, I didn't understand why Granny and Granddaddy M had even shared a bedroom as I couldn't remember Mum and Dad ever having done so.

'I always liked a lighter bedroom,' Mum explained. 'And Granny and Grandfather M's room always seemed so dark. I don't like the heavy Victorian furniture. Really, it is in very bad taste.' The furniture was dark, but I couldn't see why it was 'in bad taste'. I didn't really understand what the term was supposed to mean, nor was I interested.

When Granny M's name was mentioned there was that same prickly tension as when someone spoke of Aunt Hon, so there must have been more to it than just the number of 'n's in my name that had upset Mum so much. It was the beginning of my career as a minor sleuth, and I sensed the possibility of exciting and interesting discoveries about the past. I only had to wait as long as it took for me to become a fluent reader and able to decipher old-fashioned, swirling handwriting.

One wet day when I was poking around among old papers in Granny M's chest of drawers, I found a short note to Mum in Granny M's clear hand. In the quickest glance I saw Granny M had congratulated Mum on her engagement to Dad, adding she thought it was time Dad settled down. That was enough. While Granny M was doing the right thing, I knew instantly Mum would have thought that the mention of Dad's 'settling down' was the issue that mattered most to his mother, and that Mum would have perceived a slight that she wouldn't have forgotten. It was the sort of comment that Granny M might have made to anyone, but if Granny M had written something more personal, perhaps saying that Mum would make a good wife for Dad and a charming daughter-in-law too, it would have been better from Mum's point of view.

But there was more to it. In Dad's photographs, Granny M was always well dressed in practical, yet feminine, good-quality clothes. I already knew that she was a strong woman who looked directly at the camera. In an era when women were supposed to fit into their husband's family rather than the other way round, Granny M would have expected Mum to fit in with her standards and way of life.

Mum's eldest brother, Ian, had suggested to Mum and Dad that they might spend their honeymoon in late 1935 and early 1936 in India, where he was serving with the Duke of Connaught's Own Lancers. It would have made sense, as neither Uncle Ian nor Uncle Edward, who was also serving in India, could afford to return to Melbourne for Mum and Dad's wedding. Mum loved her brothers dearly and she would have enjoyed the riding and hunting enormously, plus she would have been able to see for herself the exotically exciting life that her brothers described in their letters home. It would have been the adventure of a lifetime.

Dad had planned originally that they would go to the 1936 Winter Olympics in Garmisch-Partenkirchen in Germany for their honeymoon. There was no suggestion in the family that either Mum or Dad seriously considered Ian's invitation, and yet it was such a pity they didn't. They couldn't have known that it would be their only opportunity. After the war, Ian and his wife, Jean, and two daughters ultimately settled in South Africa. Also, it was not entirely Mum and Dad's decision as to where they should spend their honeymoon.

Granny M dissuaded Dad from his plan to take Mum to the Olympics and a motoring holiday in New Zealand was booked. Mum said she hated motoring but she couldn't remember any discussion about it. It was simple. Dad and his mother decided without consulting Mum much, if at all. Understandably, by the time Mum arrived to live at Towong Hill after they were married, she wanted a say in things. One of her first decisions was to not move into Granddaddy and Granny M's bedroom. When Mum and Dad married, Granny M was living mostly in Sydney, only returning to Towong Hill on necessary occasions. After they returned from their honeymoon she settled in Sydney permanently. In making her choice, Mum threw a die in a way that rippled down the decades. That room would help to mould some of my earliest years.

Outside the two big windows in my room there was a balcony, and just beyond this were tall trees in the garden that prevented the sun coming in. The dark brown painted wooden balcony railings were rotting and needed replacement in parts, making the balcony unsafe and a bit scary. Indoors, apart from two large brass bedsteads that were occasionally polished, the room was dark and the furniture was heavy, but I thought it was dignified and not ugly. There was a dressing table and the same large wardrobe with the squeaking doors and rattling mirrors that were so central to my nightmare when I stayed at Towong Hill after Mum died. There was also a washstand with blue and white basins and jugs decorated with the maritime scenes that had been fashionable some fifty years earlier. Mum may have thought the furniture was in bad taste, but the longer I lived with it, the more I liked it.

Dark though it might have been, it was a room with its own appeal and stories. Dad was born in the brass bed closest to the window, the only baby born at Towong Hill. He described to me how, on 11 November 1906, when the house was still relatively new, his father had sat plaiting a stockwhip in the corner furthest from the window while he awaited the birth of the baby. Two years later Granny and Granddaddy M travelled to Sydney in good time before Aunt Hon's arrival. The journey to Albury must have been an epic one for a pregnant Granny M on rough tracks and roads, with few and sometimes inadequate bridges.

At some stage in the months after my birth in 1953, my cot and I were deposited in one of the lighter corners beside a window looking out onto the balcony. Once I could stand up in my cot I could just glimpse, between the garden trees obscuring my northward vision, the river winding its magical way through avenues of river red gums and willows. It was a beautiful view, but nothing like as spectacular as the one from Mum's or even Indi's bedroom on the other side of the corridor, with southward views towards the Alps. Eventually the cot vanished and Mum moved me into what had been Granny M's brass bed. It felt very grand and spacious, even if it rattled a bit when I turned over and the horsehair mattress was thin and bumpy.

One winter's evening, before Mum read my bedtime story, she spread a black and white poncho over my bed for extra warmth and said, 'Dad and I both had one of these, and we wore them when we rode through the snow as we crossed the border between Chile and Argentina. The snow was over my knees sitting on the horse and it was pouring into my boots. The bamboo and monkey puzzle trees there were all bent and humped under the weight of the snow. It looked so strange to see bamboo in the snow.'

There was no bamboo at Towong Hill, but there was a monkey puzzle tree in the garden outside my window. On moonlit nights its strange silhouette resembled spooky witches' houses under snow. That night my dreams of mountains and galloping horses were all muddled up with horses shying and rearing when they saw these strange witches' houses. In the morning I was relieved when I looked out into the garden and saw that the spooky houses had vanished and the view had returned to normal. Despite the nightmare qualities of the monkey puzzle tree, lying beneath Dad's poncho was like being covered with an extra layer of adventure. The poncho was like a magic carpet designed to take my dreams beyond my known world to steep-sided volcanoes puffing flames and smoke, deep lakes and snow-covered mountains.

Once, downstairs in the sitting room known as the Den, I had seen a leather folio of Mum and Dad's photographs of Chile, and later in Dad's Weasel Hole I saw some of the black-and-white photographs he took while he had a dislocated shoulder and was unable to ski and Mum was in bed with a broken leg in early 1939 in St Anton, Austria. Dad mentioned that he and Mum had met a ski instructor called Hannes Schneider who was in trouble with the Nazis. 'Mummy and I knew about the plot to get him to the United States,' Dad said. 'Nobody in St Anton could relax until we heard Hannes was over the border.' Fantastic though it all sounded at the time, I never forgot it. It would be a while before I found out what Mum and Dad had been doing in South America and in St Anton.

Dad spoke, and wrote in his unpublished memoir, of Granny and Granddaddy M as having been wonderful storytellers, describing how when he and Aunt Hon were children, Granny M told tales of the sea, and of her grandfather and grandmother and the adventures they had trying to evade pirates while sailing their ship, the *Lady Mary Blackwood*. He said, 'Granny M had the knack of telling a tale simply and quietly, with an unconscious choice of words that made the picture grow before your eyes,' while Granddaddy M told them about the bush birds, animals, cattle and of his early childhood at Tangambalanga, near Wodonga. 'He told us about the brolgas, the kangaroos, possums and where to find the white, leathery eggs of the walking tortoise. He made it all appear as a fairy story, a real, live fairy story that was actually happening all round us.'

Dad also always enjoyed telling the story of Neddy Wheeler, a local Aboriginal man who taught Granddaddy M and Uncle Jack all he could about the lore and language of his people. Dad also spoke about the Jai-ita-mathang or Gillamatong tribe who passed through the Upper Murray searching for bogong moths. He told us how they fought battles with other tribes as they wandered up the valleys towards the mountain source of moths for their feasts, and how they sometimes tried to steal another tribe's women. He told lively stories about Skerry, the Aboriginal stockman at Bringenbrong, whom he admired immensely for his horsemanship, his ability to find stock lost in the bush and for catching fish without a rod.

Dad also told me of his ancestor Gabriel Louis Huon de Kerilleau, who vanished in 1835 while walking from Bungonia near Goulburn to Campbelltown some eighty miles away. The only trace he left was an enigmatic note saying 'Going East' (though there is some dispute over the direction given on the note), which he had wrapped in a piece of bark. Later, only his spectacles were found by the search party. Like many unsolved mysteries, this one was never far from the surface in the family imagination. Incomplete stories teased the minds of successive generations who were always looking for fresh clues or new information. Years later, my relative and friend Jennifer Hume MacDougall took Mark and me to see the gorge in the Shoalhaven River where Gabriel Louis is thought to have perished. Gabriel Louis was the source of a dramatic family tale by getting lost, but I knew that you didn't have to get lost in the bush to *feel* lost. You could feel very lost in places you knew best.

In the winter after Dad returned from the war, when Mum was pregnant with Indi, he wrote down many of the stories that his father and mother and various station hands had told him. He called the collection 'Gillamatong' at first, and then 'Towong Tales'. In 1947, with writer and family friend Ethel Anderson's help, he tried to find a publisher for 'Midway Peak', the autobiography he had started to write in May 1942, a little more than three months after he became a prisoner of war. Unfortunately, both 'Towong Tales' and 'Midway Peak' were rejected by the Australasian Publishing Company and by Angus & Robertson. Apparently the reader at the Australasian Publishing Company remarked rather acidly that 'Midway Peak' was largely the recollections of a playboy and, while the manuscript had some merit, they doubted it would sell. The words were still stinging Dad when he told me over thirty years later. I knew from a young age that if anybody in the family had playboy tendencies it was Dad's Uncle Peter, so I thought the criticism was an insult. Later I realised that Dad could also be seen as a bit of a playboy when chatting to the ladies, even if as the local member of parliament he was only trying to be friendly.

In early 1946 Dad was appointed as one of the official historians for the Malaya campaign, but he could not complete the task because he was elected to the Victorian Parliament in June 1947. 'Towong Tales' was also put on the backburner. In the decades that followed, Dad published articles from time to time in the *Corryong Courier*, but otherwise he left writing to Mum. Fortunately he continued telling me his stories as often and sometimes more often than I wanted to hear them. In my memory I can still hear him saying, 'The tide of civilisation left this quiet, mountain-ringed corner of Australia virtually undisturbed for almost a century, and there can be few districts in which so many stories from the past still survive and have yet to be told.'[1]

On their early expeditions to the mountains in 1936, early 1937 and then again in 1939 and early 1940, immediately prior to the outbreak of war and Dad's departure in the autumn of 1941 for Malaya, Mum and Dad shared stories around the campfire as they 'talked down the sun'. Dad told stories of skiing at Kitzbühel, Austria, and of riding out to Pretty Plain with Uncle Jack and his cousins Malcolm and Colin Chisholm.

They would have planned future expeditions too. In 1936 and 1937 Dad was showing Mum the country he loved: Findlay's Lookout, Pretty Plain, Broadway Top, Geehi, Hannel's Spur and the Chalet at Charlotte Pass. By 1939 and 1940 they were making the best of the time they had together and covering some new ground on the Dargals and Mt Pinnibar. Back at Towong Hill they wrote up their winter expeditions for *The Australian and New Zealand Ski Year Book*, to which they were both regular contributors.

In 1941 and 1942 Mum continued collecting stories, recounting them to Dad in her letters and recording them in her diaries. Mr Herbert, then the manager of Towong Hill, George Lloyd, who also worked at Towong Hill, and Emily Scammell, who cooked for Mum and could weave stories out of anything, were also prolific storytellers. By the time of my first memories, Mum and Dad mostly told their stories separately.

Some of the stories 'Aunt' Emily Scammell told Mum were about Black Mag, the last Aboriginal woman to live in the district. Mum wove one of these stories into *Kingfisher Feather* and it was the Aboriginal woman's words in the opening pages that provided the catalyst for the plot. This ethereal character inspired the Dane twins to explore, to take on challenges and to try to understand the bush and the world in which they were growing up.

Years later I found out that Black Mag played a more mischievous role in *Flow River, Blow Wind* (1953), when Alice reminded her sister, Jane, 'It was Black Mag, wasn't it, that first spread the story of Mr Wilson's father riding over the river to meet Peter Austen's beautiful young wife? Surely she found them in among the willows near the Thowra boundary?'[2] Of my parents, Mum was the romantic and sometimes mischievously imaginative storyteller. But each winter when I caught bad colds and invariably ended up in bed for a few days, it was Dad, if he was home, who kept me entertained.

Except for occasional guests, my room had been empty since Mum and Dad's marriage in 1935. Sometimes during my childhood I wondered why Mum hadn't at least put up new curtains or placed a new rug on the floor prior to making it my bedroom. Was it, I wondered, because even after they had died Mum still felt a certain awe for her parents-in-law? Perhaps she didn't feel that the room or the house were hers to alter, and perhaps Dad didn't want it done. I inherited the room just as it had been left some eighteen or twenty years earlier, with the same faded curtains, the dark floral-patterned carpet, furniture and pictures. As a concession to the arrival of me and my cot, Mum placed high up on the mantelpiece a dark sepia print of a rather scantily clad woman nursing a child. I didn't like the picture as it reminded me of the circumstances of my tumble outside Mum's door, but the picture was too high for me to reach to take it down.

Apart from that picture, my room was a treasure trove. Forever the practical housekeeper, Granny M had lined the drawers with newspapers dating from the 1920s and thirties. I learned words like 'obituary' and 'unemployment' from reading those old newspapers, and that 'tender' meant something other than gentle and caring, although I wasn't entirely sure what. Surely 'Wall Street Crash' meant that a big wall had been knocked to the ground, but in the photograph there was no rubble and the streets seemed to be full of people, so the headline remained a mystery. I read and pondered the words all the same, not daring to ask for explanations in case I exposed my ignorance more than I already had with my schoolwork downstairs in the front hall. Plus I didn't want Mum and Dad to think I had been prying, which was exactly what I was doing. I had been told that the chest of drawers belonged to Granny M.

Almost all the drawers were unlocked and most were still full of my grandparents' grand-looking, old-fashioned clothes, wrapped in calico bags and filled with mothballs. It was as if Granny M and Granddaddy M had gone away, expecting to return like the immortal gods from Greek mythology. By then Granddaddy M had been dead about forty years. Dad spoke of him with loving kindness and of his mother with almost excessive deference, as if she were a great icon looking down through a hole in heaven in disappointed judgement upon my untidiness and slothful ways. From the time she died, just after my birth, Dad mourned for the rest of his life.

To begin with, I felt as if I were on foreign territory in that room. I envied Indi whose room was light and airy and had pretty pink curtains printed with circus animals. When I lay awake on winter evenings, watching the glow from the kerosene heater and the shadows of the nightlight playing on the walls and making mysterious shapes, I used to wonder if they were the ghosts of my grandparents carefully folding their clothes and putting them away as they got ready for sleep. I was terrified that they would find me in their beds and wouldn't recognise me, and I would be thrown out into the corridor with nowhere to go.

In nightmare moments, I wondered why Mum had inflicted such a spooky place on me. Maybe she thought that, being of the next generation, I was sufficiently distant from Granddaddy and Granny M not to be bothered by their legacy. Gradually the ghosts became interesting, less threatening, and ultimately I began to wish I had known my grandparents.

Just as they did in Granny Chauvel's house, possums added to my store of nocturnal fears. I heard them quark and squawk in possum language as they bustled around in the roof, the scratching sound of their claws loud against the ceiling. I was frightened that they would tumble through the ceiling above my head and land on my bed, fighting, scratching and squabbling, and then tear at me with their claws. A ladder leaning against the balcony outside my window was rather like a Jacob's ladder linking the possums' heaven and earth, and from my bed I could see their silhouettes flipping and flopping, scratching for a grip on the rungs. In my less frightened moments it was amusing to see how rude they were to each other, swinging half off the ladder as they overtook the slower ones.

One winter a mattress in my room caught fire because it was too close to the heater. Mum bravely rushed the smouldering bundle through my room and tossed it over the balcony railings onto the rose bed below. Until the house was repainted many years later, the skirting board near the door onto the balcony carried the splodgy scorch mark from the fiery cargo.

Ghosts and rowdy possums were not my only source of disquiet. One morning a kookaburra temporarily lost its balance and fell down the chimney into the fireplace. Fortunately, the fire was not lit and I was not in the room at the time as it would have been terrifying to wake to a fearsome, sharp-beaked bird madly circling the bedroom in a fruitless search for escape. Armed with a flimsy butterfly net, Mum opened the door leading onto the balcony and tried to shoo the bird out. I suspect it found its own way out in the end, but not before leaving a runny trail of droppings over carpets, furniture and those of my books and possessions I had left lying around. We discovered that kookaburra poo, like possum pee, if left untreated is fatal to the colour and texture of fabric, furniture and plaster alike.

Nevertheless, in time the room grew on me and became my favourite place in my childhood home. By then my presence had established itself sufficiently to give the room a different feeling. It was here that I first realised I was capable of learning for myself, and it was here that I began to write down some of the stories Dad told me about our family. After my nightmare in May 2002 after Mum died, these early scribbles were among the notes I bundled up from my desk and put into my luggage before returning to England.

13
The Coming of the Brumbies

Just as the Brumby stories were the inspiration for my solitary games on my bedroom floor, Thowra's kingdom of snow, wind, blizzards and secret places in the bush was inspired by the things for which Mum yearned. Mum was like Bel Bel, Throwa the Silver Brumby's dam; she was a loner and a wanderer. Even so, during the first brumby drive, Bel Bel wishes 'Mirri was still with her. Mirri was a good friend.' Having been caught as a yearling by a stockman, 'Mirri understood more about the habits of men. Mirri would know where they would build a yard in which to catch the wild horses.'[1] This loveable bay mare and her son were dependable, wise and loyal characters who did not compete on any level with Bel Bel or Thowra. They had the very qualities that Mum valued in both people and animals, and once I realised this I began to understand her better.

If Thowra was a magical silver god, Yarraman, his father, was a sun-god figure. Yarraman was a powerful chestnut stallion with a magnificent golden mane and tail whose reign supreme only lasted while his strength surpassed that of his main adversary – a young, formidable grey stallion, the Brolga. Mum wrote much of the aggressiveness that she despised in human society into the biting, kicking, bullying Arrow and his mean-spirited mother, Brownie. In *Silver Brumby's Daughter* it was Arrow's full brother Spear who inherited these unattractive characteristics.

Mum portrays man as the disciplinarian, the bully and the invader, who upsets and disturbs the bush with cracking stockwhips, fires and hidden trapyards. In the first chapter of *The Silver Brumby*, Mum writes with wonderful empathy when Bel Bel urgently advises Thowra: ' "Never go near Man, nor his huts, nor his yards where he fences in cattle and his tame horses. Man will hurt you and capture you; put straps of leather rope upon your head, tie you up, fence you in, beat you if you bite or kick." She was sweating with fear as she spoke, and the two foals' trembling increased.' [2]

In my attempts to understand Mum's ideas through the early Silver Brumby books, I traced how she drew on her own experiences and on her previous work in writing them. During the big brumby drive in *The Silver Brumby*, when Thowra was a foal, Bel Bel thinks, 'The men will have made a yard somewhere,' because this was not the first time Bel Bel had been caught in a big hunt when the stockmen came after the brumbies.

In *Australia's Alps*, Mum wrote of a trip up to the tops and riding from Dead Horse Gap to the Cascades: 'Just over the other side of this hill were the burnt remains of a round yard with two very long wings. Before the bushfires this had been the best yard in the mountains for catching brumbies.'[3] The experience gained through riding and skiing in the mountains provided her with the inspiration as well as the essential background knowledge with which to write *The Silver Brumby*.

In the winter of 1941, after Dad left to serve in Malaya, Mum skied out to the Cascades with their friends George Day, Curly Annabel and Colin Wyatt. This expedition out to the 'Brumby Run', or the Cascades, and the yarns they told around the campfire in the Cascades hut must have foreshadowed the writing of *The Silver Brumby*. In an *Australian Ski Yearbook* article of 1942, Mum wrote of the Cascades as being 'a place of which few travellers in the Alps have ever heard'. In *Australia's Alps* she describes how she, George, Curly and Colin saw a small mob of brumbies near the hut and how the three men lassoed a yearling colt.[4]

In her novel *Black Cockatoos Mean Snow* there are more clues to her experience:

> *'Been after the brumbies much this year?' asked Arthur.*
> *'Yes. It's been good sport. I got one quite good colt; but there's a beautiful white stallion running near the Cascades. Lots of us have seen him...'*
> *'He's a wonderful mover,' said Ray, 'and shining white.'*[5]

In *The Silver Brumby* the story is told from a horse's perspective:

> *There had been a time once, years and years ago, when four people had come whizzing down the snow-covered ridges with great wooden boards on their feet, and one of them had a lasso and had roped a bay colt; but they had been laughing, laughing – mad, in fact – for all they wanted was to cut off some of his tail to wear plaited and pinned on their coats. This was a legend among the wild horses, a tale every foal heard ... but it had happened a long time ago, and Man was not expected in the Cascades until the herds of cattle came for summer grazing.*[6]

The tension between the free world of wild mountain horses and native animals and the domestic world of men and their tame horses and dogs is a recurrent theme throughout Mum's writing for children. In *Silver Brumby's Daughter* this tension is still very intense, but as a solitary stockman observes of Kunama, 'she's born to be wild and free'.[7] In *Silver Brumbies of the South*, man the invader appears in a very different form, building roads and wandering around the mountains surveying. While these activities did not cause the same fear among the brumbies as the stockmen did, there was a definite feeling of uncertainty and a need to move 'South' to where there was more space for wild horses away from men.

In a similar way to *The Silver Brumby* and *Silver Brumby's Daughter*, *Silver Brumbies of the South* tells the story of the changes in the High Country. In the first chapter Thowra tells his old friend Storm that "'Along the Crackenback they make a track wide enough for six horses [...] In the daytime there is a great noise. Benni, the kangaroo, told me, so I went out one day, and heard and saw.'"[8] The track wide enough for six horses was the beginning of the Alpine Way and Thowra's description would have been based on Mum's observations in the mid 1950s. Initially Mum didn't approve of the roads. She felt that the only way to see the fauna and flora properly was from horseback or on foot. Later in the book, Thowra explains to Cloud, the rather gentlemanly light grey stallion who welcomes the silver herd to Quambat flat, "'Men make roads in my mountains [...] It is time that our herds came away – and I, I just wanted to wander like the wind from whom I was named.'"[9] As I read the books I could visualise the progress of the roads being cut through the hills.

In *Silver Brumby Kingdom*, the threat of man is largely replaced by that of the elements and of other horses, while in *Silver Brumby Whirlwind* there is evidence of man, but man is no longer so threatening to Thowra: 'When he looked downstream he could see a host of twinkling lights all scattered round the foot of Paddy Rush's Bogong. Only men could light those lights, but for some reason, he could not feel any danger.'[10] Later he sees car lights as 'two eyes' that 'seemed to follow him, blazing and seeking out his own eyes, blinding him'.

> *He stood still, beside the boulder, his eyes filled with the terrifying, aching light, unable to see anything.*

> *Above the noise of the engine a voice called, and the words flew on the wind.*
>
> *'Look! Look! There is a silver horse.'*
>
> *But the lights let go of their blinding hold on Thowra's eyes, and he bounded off.*
>
> *Thowra stopped bounding, and stood still to watch, and the thunder of his heart quietened, but far back in him memory was stirring the sounds of men's voices … the men who had owned Golden, who had hunted him.*[11]

Mum needed her refuges, her metaphorical secret valleys, not just a geographical place where she felt safe but also a private and creative area of her life. More often than not the bush and the mountains served as her secret valley or paradise. In *Silver Brumbies of the South*, Baringa and Dawn had to search for their own secure refuge; this time the threat was not so much from man but other horses – perhaps above all from the older, stronger, covetous Lightning, who was keen to have Dawn for his own herd.

Baringa and Dawn had to leave Quambat Flat and the security and company of running with other horses and strike out on their own in unknown country – not an easy challenge for two young horses. They ultimately found a deep, little-known canyon tucked away beyond the cone-shaped mountain called The Pilot. There they were to discover hints of a mystery – that of the Hidden Filly who ran with an ogre of a stallion, the Ugly One. The Secret Canyon was never quite the same paradise that Thowra found in the Secret Valley. The Ugly One knew about the Canyon, and Baringa had to fight for his life on its steep, dangerous, shale slopes. The body of another horse was washed down the stream after the fire – that horse must have known about the Canyon too. The Canyon was never strictly Baringa's preserve as the Secret Valley was for Thowra. By the time Baringa was a three-year-old it didn't provide him with the space for which he yearned.

Mum knew that not every secret place remained undiscovered by others, and that man and animal alike have to battle for their space and privacy.

Just as Thowra had to win his prize, Golden, three times, Baringa had to help his mother's brother Lightning three times before he could begin to feel that his mares were safe from the covetous stallion. Mum always believed that the reward could be rich for those who explored their environment and worked hard to create their own place in the world, and Baringa, the Silver Brumby's grandson (whom Kunama had named for light), was indeed richly rewarded. He not only found a safer place in which to hide, but he also won the silver mare he called Moon through a hard and cunningly fought fight. Since Mum was a keen mountain explorer and worked hard at everything she took on, it is little surprise that her main characters should share these qualities too. The rewards of exploration and challenge were as worthwhile for her equine heroes as they were for Mum.

In the summers of 1961 and 1962 two riding trips to the Tin Mines and Quambat Flat (now called Cowombat Flat), organised by Jean Finlay, who had a riding school near Thredbo, provided Mum with the inspiration for *Silver Brumbies of the South* and *Silver Brumby Kingdom*. I was not yet eight when Mum went on the first expedition and almost nine when she went on the second. In *Towong Hill: Fifty Years on an Upper Murray Cattle Station* she explains that 'At the head of Quambat Flat we saw two beautiful light-grey brumbies who became Cloud and Cirrus in the third and fourth Brumby books, while the deep canyon of Dales Creek became Baringa's Secret Valley.'[12] In *Chauvel Country* Mum wrote: 'I rode out to the Tin Mines – and two whole new stories seemed contained in that country.'[13] When Mum first projected the slides from those trips onto the screen in the dining room at Towong Hill, my eyes scanned the images for silver brumbies – for Thowra and Baringa, and for Cloud and Cirrus. It was a thrilling moment to be involved in a story as it was being conceived, and some compensation for the disappointment of being too young to have been included in the expedition.

Silver Brumbies of the South and *Silver Brumby Kingdom* became my new bedtime stories. I had been reading independently for almost three years by the time Mum began to write *Silver Brumbies of the South* and I waited impatiently for each chapter as it came off the typewriter, just as Indi had done with *The Silver Brumby* in earlier years. Such was my impatience for the story that sometimes I read the chapters twice as I could not wait to have the next instalment.

Despite her success with the first two Brumby books, when the moment came to send *Silver Brumbies of the South* to Miss Tomlinson, who edited children's books at Hutchinson in London, Mum was concerned about its reception. Once she had received confirmation of the publisher's acceptance of the manuscript on 11 November 1963, she wrote with relief to Miss Tomlinson, saying how glad she was that she had liked the story. Mum added, 'Honor kept assuring me that it was very exciting!' She was quite right – I thought it was thrilling. Of course I was delighted when I discovered that Mum planned to dedicate this book to me.

After lessons were finished, Mum and I would go out riding or walking and discuss the development of her latest plot. John was not as interested as me in riding or walking, nor in the Brumby books. Even when he was with us he was fairly quiet, and Indi and Harry were away at boarding school.

'Wouldn't it have been better for Baringa to fight Lightning for Dawn?' I remember asking Mum.

'Lightning would have been stronger,' Mum said. 'Anyway, it wouldn't do for members of the Silver Herd to fight each other.'

The equine characters were our friends. We talked about them as if they and their problems really existed; we discussed how they might feel in certain situations and what they might do and why. I could not have wished for a more inspiring collection of bedtime stories and reading lessons, or a better relationship with Mum at that time. She had created a magical world in which I felt I had a role.

Mum also wrote short stories and illustrated them for John and me. She sewed their pages together at the spine and made a cover out of blue corduroy so that they resembled a little book. Very occasionally she made little certificates too, to encourage us with our schoolwork.

Just as the 'faint idea flitted through Thowra's head that perhaps something had to be won three times over before it was freely owned',[14] Mum didn't put away her typewriter after her first success. Throughout her life she continued to strive to achieve more, and each book was hard work. In her diary on 11 March 1963 she mentions finding it hard to know how to finish *Silver Brumbies of the South*, and whether to leave space for another book or to close with Baringa as King of Quambat. She didn't finish it until 28 April that year, referring to it as 'the cut version for the size [the publishers] want'. She went on to say, 'I do not know whether it is a harmonious whole.' I knew that she was disappointed that she had no luck in the Children's Book of the Year awards considering how hard she had tried. Many women and mothers would have been content if they had been able to do a mere fraction of what Mum managed to achieve.

In the first four Brumby books Mum had given literary form to the inspiration that was to be her salvation. The Silver Brumby series was one of the biggest steps in Mum's effort to find her own voice, and it demonstrated how she could reach out of herself and excel, perhaps far beyond her dreams. It was the breakthrough that provided much needed fulfilment and pleasure in Mum's post-war world. I wonder if she felt that, like Kunama, she had drunk at the Pool of the Moon and dreamed of freedom, and to an extent that dream was coming true.

It was only when I was assembling Mum's correspondence archive that I realised the role Melbourne bookseller Margarita Webber had played in helping Mum achieve her dream. The Littlejohn family, who were old Chauvel family friends, had introduced Mum to Margarita, a neighbour living near Scotch College in Hawthorn. After *The Silver Brumby* was rejected by both Hodder & Stoughton and Oxford University Press, it was with Margarita's encouragement that Mum eventually sent *The Silver Brumby* manuscript to Hutchinson.

A note in Mum's papers paid tribute: 'Margarita's shop [then in Little Collins Street in Melbourne] was an oasis of civilization, during the War, a place where the value of things of the mind and spirit [were] cherished and nurtured. To Margarita Webber, I owe so much, and there are a great deal of other people who must feel that it would be fitting for her to receive recognition of the service she has done for us all.'

After the outbreak of the Second World War, Mum resolved to do something worthwhile for her country. Had she been a man she would have had the choice of taking up either the pen or the sword, or perhaps even both. Born as she was in 1913, she didn't have that choice. If she wasn't going to knit socks for soldiers, the pen was her only option, and she was desperate for the challenge. Once she remarked to me, 'If I wasn't writing, life wouldn't have any purpose.' She obviously did not understand that, for me, this comment was thoughtless and hurtful. I thought she was indirectly saying that having a family had given her little or no sense of purpose. For a sensitive person, frequently her own children's sensitivities mattered least of all.

Mum meant to continue as a novelist for adults too. 'I just want to write a cracking good yarn,' she told me on a number of occasions over three decades. But unlike her children's books, with her writing of adult fiction she was concerned about what other people, and especially initially her parents, would think. Perhaps she'd been affected by criticism of her first two novels, *Flow River, Blow Wind* and *Black Cockatoos Mean Snow*. A neighbour referred to *Black Cockatoos Mean Snow* as 'Black cockatoos fly backwards'. While she may not have admitted it, Mum was also mindful to an extent of Dad's views, and later she did give thought to how her children might react. Occasionally Dad told me that he thought Mum was doing very well with her writing. Sometimes he commiserated with us and interceded with Mum if she had been very taken up with writing and unavailable when we needed her. Otherwise he was quite silent about his feelings concerning her writing. If he said more to Mum behind closed doors, I never knew about it. Of course there were occasions when he was very proud of her.

A body of correspondence with Paul Hodder-Williams at Hodder & Stoughton Ltd indicates that Mum was worried that a proposed adult book would 'shock the children'.[15] She was very concerned about how appropriate it would be for her older children and their friends to read a book dealing with a family with some resemblance to ours, which she knew, if it were published, they would almost certainly do. Despite her tough, 'to hell with it' exterior, Mum minded criticism – explicit and implicit – very much. The book was not published. In the 1980s she wrote a ski thriller and another novel based on Mitchell family history, but neither of these were published either.

On occasions when she thought I was too young to understand or that I wasn't listening, I heard her admit to friends in jest that she found it difficult to bring up teenagers when she 'knew how to break every rule in the book'. It would have been interesting to know more about just how and why. Some of her male friends were rather close, but mostly it was impossible to tell how close. But if Mum knew how to break rules, she also kept her own secrets and mostly, if not always, those of her children too.

14
Out of Eden

Two gardens surrounded the house at Towong Hill, one cultivated, the other overgrown. A bank covered with trees, periwinkle and a fence divided the two U-shaped layers that followed the contours of the ridge around the house. Rose-covered archways and shaded stone or brick steps joined the two gardens. James Findlay, who had owned Towong Hill for about thirty years in the latter part of the nineteenth century, had been a friend of the renowned German botanist Baron von Mueller. Under the good baron's tutelage, Findlay laid out beautiful gardens and had them filled with a fine variety of European trees. Those trees gave the garden a feeling of distance from the microcosm of the front hall.

The top garden closest to the house was where we rode our tricycles, and later our bicycles, round and round the paths. We played on the lawns while Mum kept an eye on us as she read and wrote at her desk in the front hall, or worked in the garden. 'There are tiny wee gentlemen in my sandpit,' John exclaimed one hot summer afternoon. Dad had blocked off the shady corner of a path near the verandah for a sandpit. Much to John's surprise, some frogs had hopped in and were enjoying the cool shade.

From her desk in the front hall Mum was able to witness the discoveries, pleasures and tribulations of her offspring.

Indi had a beautiful garden where she had a secret tree. It was the sole surviving macrocarpa tree from what was once a hedge, some of which had been burned in the 1939 bushfires. More were damaged and uprooted in a tornado in 1954 when I was less than a year old. Apparently the family was driving back from swimming at Bringenbrong Bridge when the tornado struck. Mum said I huddled down with Indi and Harry on the back seat and she threw towels over us. The trees were uprooted by the time we arrived back at the homestead. I don't remember anything about it, but I do remember huge wreaths of wisteria covering the sole surviving tree in spring. Later, in the summer, the wisteria's flowers formed a fabulous mauve tent that was filled with bees and spread over most of the macrocarpa's branches.

When I was about five, Mum gave me a shady spot between a large hydrangea and the house so that I could have a garden of my own. The soil was rich, moist and dark, and I was very proud when I grew a small hydrangea from a cutting. Columbines grew close by and I gathered and sowed their seeds. In spring I had violets and blue irises. On the other side of the path and beneath Dad's office window there was a square bed devoted entirely to lily of the valley.

Dad seemed to be away a lot when the House was sitting and at other political functions. When he was at home, I often heard his voice on the telephone or the clink of the mail bag key on the lock of the bag as either Mum or Dad opened it. Dad always seemed to be writing to or talking to people I didn't know about things that were not part of the world I knew. Otherwise he was in the workshop. Sometimes he cut out animal shapes on a fretsaw, painted them and made them into toys.

In the mid and late 1950s, Mum took some of our happier family photographs in the top garden. Indi was probably the most athletic of us and Dad had made her some wooden hurdles. Mum photographed her leaping over them, and other pictures show Harry and me pedalling our little cars on the path round the circular lawn. The excellent quality of the colour makes these photographs look as if they were taken recently, but the clothes we are wearing tell another story. In winter we dressed in homemade corduroy bib-and-brace overalls and hand-knitted sweaters while in summer we wore bib-and-brace shorts over cotton shirts or blouses.

After the outbreak of the Second World War, lack of staff meant the lower garden had become an exciting wilderness. Tucked away among tall European trees and lilacs was an overgrown badminton court that had been used before the First World War during some grand house parties. 'Women played in flowing calf-length white dresses and the men wore white flannel trousers,' Dad explained once when we were yarning together about the old days. 'Some of those friends and relatives were injured and some bought it and didn't return from the war,' Dad added wistfully, as if he was mourning the passing of an era as well as people like his cousin Malcolm Chisholm, whom he remembered so fondly. The badminton court was like a forgotten memorial to friends who had vanished from our parents' lives.

'Don't go near the well beside the orange trees in the lower garden. There are S-E-R-P-E-N-T-S,' Harry said, purposefully and emphatically to make me shiver. In springtime the lower garden was filled with lilacs and irises that penetrated the sea of weeds and long grass. In summer it was full of crackly dry sticks, branches and grass. A tap dripped above the well; Harry and I thought that snakes drank from it and then hid between the stones in the wall of the well beneath. The oranges looked beautiful but they were dry and full of pith as nobody had watered them very much for years. It was as if the paddocks were gradually encroaching on a cultivated oasis and killing off the fruit trees and any remaining garden plants.

In spring and summer Dad – probably with help from Mum and perhaps Indi or Harry – would drive a mob of sheep into the lower garden to eat down the grass before it dried out and became a fire risk. As children it was our job to help Dad move the sheep between the lower garden, once it was eaten down, and the other small adjoining paddocks. Dad had divided the area into a number of zones, and during his spare time he made and painted wooden gates for the zones in his workshop. It was as if he was indulging himself in hobby farming on a large pastoral concern. Just as Mum lived like a guest in her own home, surrounded by her parents-in-law's possessions, in his way Dad too seemed to be slightly overawed by his inheritance. It was as if he had never managed to reconcile his political interests with his responsibilities on the property. The manager dealt with the day-to-day duties, worked with and supervised the jobs done by the station hands, kept the books and paid the accounts for the property of more than 4000 acres.

As a child I saw virtually nothing of the daily management. Dad and his manager seemed to make the major decisions without necessarily discussing them with Mum. Later I learned that a firm of trustees had always run Dad's financial affairs. Meanwhile, as a small child, I knew little about my parents' lives beyond the boundaries of the house and garden at Towong Hill. When Parliament was sitting or Dad had other political commitments, Mum was left to move the sheep as well as look after and educate us children, also to run the house and to fit in writing when she could.

'Don't touch the oleander – it's poisonous enough to kill a horse,' Dad warned me every time I went with him to the lower garden to move sheep. Dad could be counted on to warn of any danger. He didn't like the tree of heaven either and regretted planting it, but he didn't say why. Was it, I wondered, because the flowers on the male plant are supposed to be evil-smelling when crushed? The tree is rather attractive, with large ash-patterned leaves and fruits that form like bunches of keys, each one twisted like a propeller. Perhaps the fact that the tree spread rapidly was the explanation for Dad's feelings – he thought it was a weed.

While the garden around the house was shrinking, our play world moved beyond its confines and out the back to the workshop if Dad was there. We also had a series of cubbyhouses high up in Indi's secret tree where, if one or other of us was in trouble, we could climb beyond the reach of Mum and Dad for brief respite. I can't remember why Dad was so incensed the time he tried to climb up behind Harry and me. We slithered down the other side of the tree, moving much faster than Dad, still on the way up. Sirius, the 1950s short-wheelbase Land Rover, was parked beneath the tree. Harry could drive and was game for anything, so we jumped in and set off down the hill towards the milking shed. I had not closed the passenger door properly and there were no seatbelts, so when Harry turned the corner near the cowshed in the direction of the pumping lagoon, the door swung open and I fell out. Although we were not going very fast, I was a bit too shaken to laugh straightaway. If Dad was still incandescent with rage when eventually we returned to the house, I can't remember that either – Harry was so often in the hot seat. Perhaps Dad's anger subsided as quickly as it had flared.

When I was about seven or eight, a man whom Mum and Dad employed as a gardener and to milk the cows threatened to catch me and put me over his knee. I can't remember exactly what I had done; I might have been cheeky or up to mischief. Revulsion rushed up to my throat before I knew whether he was joking or serious and my legs were already carrying me as fast as I could run down the hill. Just before the cattle grid leading to the horse paddock, I fell, cutting and grazing my knee. My screams must have brought Mum running. She took me to the upstairs bathroom and gently cleaned the gravel and sand from the wound, dabbing it with gentian violet. 'It doesn't sting so badly as iodine,' she explained as I winced. Beneath the sticking plaster, a deep, dirty purple patch seeped out. Later, when Mum took the plaster off, a similar dirty-coloured scab formed.

I don't think I ever said anything to Mum about why I had been so desperately running away. The threat might have been a joke and if it wasn't I was probably getting my just deserts for being rude or too familiar. I can't really remember the events leading up to it. But suddenly I must have grown up a bit as something in me realised the sinister potential of the situation. I was terrified of the new knowledge that had dawned on me, whether the odd-job man wished me ill or not. I couldn't talk about it with Mum, or anyone.

15
Paradise for her Daughter

'Granny and her luggage and plants take up more space than the mail and parcels for the whole district!' Harry whispered to me when Mum took us to meet Granny from the service car (the bus to and from the train in Albury) in Corryong. We sniggered quietly, not wanting Granny to hear in case she gave us her pained look, her dignified white eyebrows arched and her mouth down at the corners with slight disappointment. The long-suffering driver hauled an exotic collection of large, creamy leather suitcases covered with P&O shipping labels from the bus while we helped with some of the lighter packages and plants.

I knew from an early age that Granny Chauvel was a wonderful anchor in my life. At Towong Hill she was the same quiet, dignified figure that she was in her own home in Melbourne and her routine remained much the same: if she wasn't gardening, she played cards or read detective stories. She always had a pack or two of cards in her handbag and she taught me to play racing demon. Sometimes she intervened to make peace between us children or interceded with Mum on behalf of one or other of us, though more frequently she interceded with Dad when he got cross about the mess in the house. Granny M had run a very tidy and highly organised house, and that was how Dad would have liked it to stay. Generally, for a mercurial person, Dad was fairly patient, but on occasions he flared.

Granny Chauvel started planning the Towong Hill garden in 1937, and her garden diary with some of her drawings and plans still exists. While Mum and Dad were away from late 1937 until autumn 1939 in the Americas and Europe, Granny and Grandfather Chauvel visited and gardened at Towong Hill. As Granny M died the year I was born, I never heard what she thought about Granny replanting some of the garden she had nurtured. Perhaps it was just as well she lived over five hundred kilometres away in Sydney! I have studied Granny's plans and notes and it looks to me as if she was trying to create a paradise for her beloved elder daughter in a bid to ensure that she would feel content and at home when she and Dad returned. Some thirty years later, out of sheer love for her family and of gardening, Granny was still returning regularly to Towong Hill to continue her efforts to create and maintain that paradise. Mum didn't entirely share Granny's enthusiasm – the extra work looking after the plants when Granny left meant less writing time – but she was grateful all the same.

John and I had some ducks that roamed free in the garden during the daytime, hoovering up worms and other duck delicacies. Inevitably they left their very liquid multicoloured droppings on the lawn and garden paths, so walking barefoot or sitting on the lawn could be hazardous for the unwary. We were never concerned for Granny, though, as she never walked barefoot and preferred to sit in a chair rather than on the grass.

The day Granny stepped on a nest of very rotten duck eggs concealed under the thick foliage of an agapanthus, Mum was horrified. Granny was cross because Mum wouldn't let her into the house until she had been hosed down. Granny didn't say any more about it, but Mum pressed John and me on the need to be more accountable about the eggs. I don't remember Mum's exact words but she was trying hard not to laugh too. She knew she couldn't laugh openly in case we didn't smarten up our act and something worse and even less dignified happened to Granny. 'I didn't like having to hose down my mother,' I once heard Mum telling someone on the phone. It was partially my fault so I felt guilty, but it was also funny and I started giggling like a mad jelly as I eavesdropped on Mum describing the incident.

Our ducks were not the only hazard in the garden. There was an ever-present risk that the goats that Dad had bought to help keep the grass down would get out of their adjoining paddock and wreak havoc, eating the precious plants that Granny was cosseting in the garden.

The goats had already disgraced themselves long before the incident with the duck eggs. From the washing line in the backyard, the grey and white and more personable of the two goats pulled the top of Mum's two-piece bathing suit, a forerunner and more modest version of a bikini, and was munching it steadily. In her rage, Mum hauled the purple bikini bra out of the goat's gullet. Cursing and swearing, she swiped its rump with the bra, leaving a purple streak on the goat's backside. Mum could really let rip in great style when provoked. Granny, who was sitting with us, looked mildly shocked. If she was relieved that it was only Mum's bikini that had been chewed, she didn't show it. Mum would really have been in the costly poo if it had been Granny's foundation garments!

Except for clothing for state visits and sporting requirements, Mum seldom spent much money on clothes. She had splashed out, however, on that purple two-piece and it was her fashion statement for the summer – only to be sabotaged by the goat.

16
Crucifix in the Pudding

Christmas was all the better if Granny was at Towong Hill. It would take her all afternoon on Christmas Eve to decorate the tree: she shut the dining room door so it would be a surprise for us all when we came down to breakfast on Christmas morning. One Christmas Dad played the part and took at least two of us down to the stables to collect hay and a bucket of water for Father Christmas's reindeers, though I can't recall remembering to leave any food or drink for Father Christmas. It was always Father Christmas – never Santa or Santa Claus – at Towong Hill. Santa Claus was Germanic and the Second World War was still too recent in family memory for anyone to readily adopt a German name for a beloved figure.

Our early Christmases were quite formal, the day occasionally beginning with a church service in Corryong. Later we would visit Dot and Jack Salter (who worked for us as a stockman) and sit with them in the shade on the verandah of their cottage, near the station stables and cattle yards. Dad and Mum enjoyed peacefully yarning about the old days with Dot and Jack and their family.

It was May Lloyd, Dot's mother, who said, 'Keep smiling, Mrs Mitchell,' after Singapore fell in February 1942 and Dad was listed as missing. May and her husband, George, would have known just how awful Mum felt. Their son, Dot's brother Frank, was killed on Crete, bravely refusing to surrender to the Germans in September 1941. It was over a year before his family heard the news, by which time May had already died; perhaps, fearing the worst, she died of a broken heart. Mum must have missed the brave May, and she and Dad may well have felt guilty about their relative good fortune. Dad and Mum named pine plantations in memory of Frank and also of Jack Herbert, son of Mr and Mrs Herbert (Mr Herbert managed Towong Hill until late 1946 or early 1947), who served as an officer in the RAF and was killed while training in England.

Dot was at least the second if not the third generation of her family to work at Towong Hill or earlier at Bringenbrong. Her parents, May and George, had worked at Towong Hill and had lived in the same cottage as Dot and Jack then did. Jack Salter, Dot's husband, had been working at Towong Hill since the 1930s, and had stuck Aunt Eve's head under a tap to stop her hair catching fire during the 1939 bushfires. Jack loved good stories and told them with a terrific sense of drama. Dot took a wonderfully kind interest in our family, and she grew magnificent roses that both Mum and Granny admired very much. Dot and Jack's weatherboard cottage was cream with a red galvanised iron roof. It was one of those little houses that looked like it had two eyes and a nose – the eyes being the two windows on either side of the nose that was the door. Their cottage reminded Mum of the yarns she had shared there and was a symbol of the Australian country life she loved.

By the time of my earliest memories, there was another family living in a newer cottage near the stud stables. At first all I knew about them was that the mother said she would cut their tongues out if any of the children swore. Meanwhile, Mr and Mrs Knight and their daughter, Pat (my godmother), lived in the manager's cottage between the stud stables and the homestead. At the homestead there was a cook, who sometimes lived in the servants' quarters at the back of the main house. In the cottage close to the homestead there lived a married couple, the wife cleaning and her husband milking the cows, looking after the chooks and doing some gardening. At Christmas time the Knight family was invited to our house ('the homestead') for drinks or an evening meal.

For some years Mum and Dad clung to tradition, so Christmas dinner was roast turkey followed by Christmas pudding. Mum and Granny slipped silver coins into the pudding before they served it. Dad called brandy 'gut rot' – he hadn't touched alcohol since the war – so none was poured over the pudding and there was no brandy butter. Granny always had an eye for something different and, just for a change, one Christmas she brought a packet of trinkets for the pudding. Even at her most mischievous Granny could not have foreseen what was going to happen.

Dad did not miss a trick. He saw how the little piles of coins and trinkets were growing on the sides of everyone else's plates and, counting his, he found that he had missed out. 'Poor old Dad always gets the rough end of the stick!' he grumbled from his end of the table. 'Your poor old man has only got a threepenny piece and the rest of you have got at least that and a trinket as well!' All eyes fell on Dad's plate. Sure enough, there was just one lonely silver coin.

'You should have got more than that, old Dad,' one of us said. 'Mum stuck at least a trinket and a coin into every slice! What has happened to your trinket?'

'Anyway, Dad,' Harry said, 'there was a cross amongst the trinkets and nobody else has got it.'

'He's swallowed it!' some of the younger members of the family hooted.

'No, I didn't!' Dad said, trying to maintain some dignity. But everyone else had made up their minds about the whereabouts of the crucifix, and he probably knew that the incident would become part of the family story. I don't think Granny ever brought trinkets for the Christmas pudding again.

17

Pushing the Boundaries

In the years before I went to boarding school, riding was the highlight of the chilly winter days if Mum was not taking us skiing at Thredbo. I rode Toby, a naughty skewbald pony, and I felt a nice sense of achievement when eventually Mum let me off the leading rein. Inevitably I had a few falls when my pony shied at a rabbit or a quail whirring out of the tussocks on the river flats, but Mum made me get straight back on. One May afternoon I found I couldn't remount – I'd broken my right arm. It mended quickly and shortly after the plaster was removed I ceased to notice any pain or weakness.

More often than not we rode around the bush-covered ridges and flanks of Mt Porcupine, where it was a treat to see a kangaroo, wallaby or wombat – they were much less plentiful and shyer then than they are now. Indi came along if she was at home on school holidays. Grandfather's memory was omnipresent when we were riding and Mum really wanted riding to be a family thing as it had been with her father and siblings, but it wasn't quite like that with us. Granny had been the one exception in the Chauvel family, having grown up in Brisbane and lived in cities for almost all her life; she had never worn trousers and didn't ride. In our household, Harry didn't really like riding, but with two grandfathers who were all but born in the saddle and loved horses, it would have been difficult for him to say so. Maybe he knew that Dad didn't really like riding either, something he never openly admitted. If Dad was at home, Harry went to the workshop rather than joining us on a ride. When John was old enough, Dad took him to the workshop too and taught him how to weld.

As we rode, Mum pointed out and explained things around us. Sometimes we ventured high enough to play among the acacia trees we called the wattle house. In spring, when the wattle was in bloom, the trees formed a beautiful natural enclosure of gold, with feathery green-blue leaves forming the walls. We watched, too, for wedge-tailed eagles swirling high above all worldly cares on currents of air. Their nests were large, ungainly structures of sticks and as the young eagles grew the nests looked top-heavy and insecure; it seemed a miracle that the branches supporting them didn't break in storms.

As my riding ability and confidence improved, Mum, instead of walking alongside me and Toby, would ride her bay mare Snip. Toby was really Harry's, but just as Chikko the cat didn't really belong to me, Toby didn't really belong to him. I already had a pony called Sunny that Dad had bought for me when I was five, a beautiful chestnut Welsh pony with a silvery mane and tail. He loved mustering, working with cattle and jumping but initially he was too strong for me. Mum and Indi rode him more often than I did and, rather like Chikko, he didn't seem to belong to me. I couldn't do much about that until I was stronger, so Toby was the only option. Every time we stopped he put his head down to graze, whether I liked it or not.

In *Chauvel Country* Mum explained: 'On horseback one could go a long way – not ride 10,000 days and nights, but see strange sights, melt into the seascape, the landscape. With a pony and the open country, I was a person: an explorer, a soldier, a crusader, one of Arthur's knights, or even Mowgli riding on Baloo [the bear].'[1] For Mum, horses were an important key to adventure. They were also friends whom she loved dearly, fed and spoke to every day. Including Snip, Sunny and Toby, we often had five or six horses in the paddock beneath the homestead on the north-western side and on the hill behind the house.

Some of my happiest times at Towong Hill were when Mum took one or more of us riding in the paddocks, with saddlebags and quart pots strapped onto our saddles. We hitched the ponies in the shade while we made a fire and boiled the quart pot for tea. Mum would identify bird calls and songs, and point out the ones she could see. Being slightly short-sighted, I couldn't pick out many of their distinguishing details. Later we would return home smelling of wood smoke, tired from a combination of fun, fresh air and sunshine.

If Dad was not busy or away on political business he occasionally joined us but usually he came by car, saying he was too busy to ride. Anyway, his dun-coloured horse, Moth, was too nervous to ride quietly and comfortably on family outings. He was likely to shiver and shy, dumping his rider and taking off to the other end of the paddock. Dad only fell off on one occasion that I remember, but he had many uncomfortable rides. Moth was a gift from Aunt Hon and Dad wouldn't hear anything bad about him. When I was sorting Mum's archive, I found an article in *People* in which the unidentified writer remarked that Dad 'looked as if he has been born and bred in the metropolis and would be more at home in an armchair in his club than in the saddle of a horse'.[2]

By contrast, Mum was a keen show rider and competed in the dressage events in the local agricultural shows at Corryong, Jingellic and Tallangatta. She loved the weeks leading up to the shows, patiently exercising, grooming, feeding and talking quietly to her mare and helping us with our ponies. Indi also enjoyed the shows and pony club gymkhanas, and was a keen, able and game show jumper. Mum portrayed the excitement and pleasure of those days in *Kingfisher Feather*, where the twins compete in their local show. Mum told us how her father had taught her to groom and look after her horse, and how he organised riding lessons for her at the Remount Depot in Melbourne. 'Always look after your horse first,' Mum said. 'It doesn't matter how tired, hungry and thirsty you are; having carried you, your horse will be just as tired, if not more so. Groom him and make sure he has plenty of water and food.' Mum's advice would have come straight from Grandfather.

At the 1959 Jingellic show, Mum led the final competitors' parade on Snip. I can't remember whether it was then or a year or two later that Bill Waters, the son of one of our local family friends, on his big bay horse Stanley was paired with me riding mischievous little Toby in the grand parade at the show. It was a most enjoyable case of little and large and all things great and small, with Bill saying, 'Come on, Honor, keep up!' Toby was determined not to stir his little legs beyond his own comfortable, stubborn Shetland pony pace! At least he didn't rush for the nearest tree. It would have been at the Corryong, Jingellic and perhaps even the Tallangatta shows in 1961 that Mum was preparing to show her beloved mare Snip for the last time, as she wanted to get her in foal before the next show season.

Riding in the paddocks at Towong Hill with Ossie Rixon, an old family friend and near neighbour, was another memorable treat. He had been a jockey for the Mitchell family when they had a thoroughbred stud at Bringenbrong and he had assisted with the training of Trafalgar, the family's most successful and record-winning racehorse. In 1910, and much to the family's surprise and disappointment, Trafalgar was only just beaten in the Melbourne Cup by Comedy King. There was a rumour that the jockey (not Ossie) had pulled Trafalgar, but I don't think anything was proven. Ossie had a beautiful seat on his old grey horse. Dressed immaculately in jodhpurs, a sports jacket and shirt and tie, it was as if the kindly old gentleman and his horse belonged together. He always told us that he thought he had survived the First World War's Somme battles because he was so short he could stand comfortably in a trench with his head still beneath the parapet. 'The bullets just flew over my head!' he squeaked, as if in perpetual surprise that he had not been injured and was still alive.

Dad and Mum often invited Ossie to family dinners, at which he always wore a suit with his RSL badge proudly fastened on his lapel. His conversations with Dad and Mum spanned almost a century of history, and a unique sense of wise contentment seemed to walk into the room with him. Mum and Dad were never happier than when he was around and the conversation sparkled as they yarned about the old days. He was one of the few friends who remembered both Dad's parents and many, if not all, of the people who worked for them and about whom Dad often told stories. Along with Dr Willie Littlejohn, Ossie accompanied Mum and Dad on their jeep trip in February 1948 when they drove 125 kilometres across the Alps from the Upper Murray to the Chalet at Charlotte Pass in five days, some eight years before the Alpine Way was built. It had been such a tough trip that Mum contracted pneumonia on their return home, just one of the many epic adventures that took place before I was born.

Elyne Chauvel at about twenty-one. Mum was shy but loved parties and beautiful clothes. Before she married Dad she had a busy social life in Melbourne, thanks partly to Grandfather Chauvel's distinguished service in the First World War, most famously with the Light Horse Brigade at Beersheba.

Dad was an accomplished skier, winning the Australian National Slalom five times, the National Downhill twice and the National Combined Downhill and Slalom twice. He also won titles in New Zealand and races in Europe.

Mum's hiking and skiing expeditions with Dad before the war were some of the happiest times in her life. Then, Dad was her hero and best friend as well as her husband.

Mum and Dad married in 1935. Their relationship was forged in the whirlwind of a few social meetings, and by today's standards they scarcely knew each other when they announced their engagement.

Towong Hill, tucked away on the edge of the bush and the High Country. Elyne called it 'that resonant, dream-filled house'.

Dad called his small, musty, book-lined study at the back of the house the Weasel Hole. When he and Mum returned to Towong Hill after their honeymoon, Dad had this desk installed for her.

By 1937 Mum had been selected for both the Victorian and Australian ski teams. Before she raced she used to pray, rather irreverently, 'God be in my legs and in my understanding'! Dad, her teacher and first coach, was very proud of her, especially when she went on to win championships in New Zealand, Europe and America.

St Anton, Austria: Mum's skiing days could have finished on 29 December 1938 when she broke her leg in eleven places. Six days later, Dad dislocated his shoulder while skiing. Dr Schalle and the *Schwester* from Innsbruck who expertly cared for Mum were vehemently anti-Nazi.

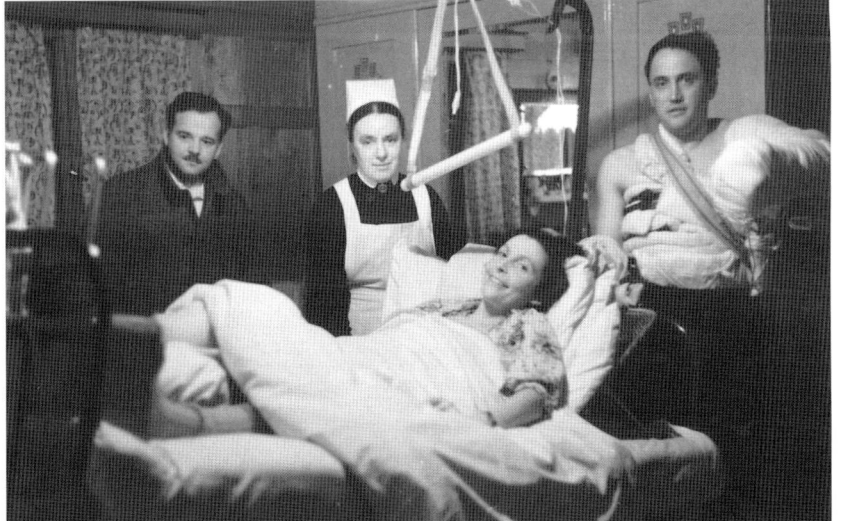

The experience Mum gained riding and skiing through the mountains provided her with both inspiration and the essential background knowledge with which to write *The Silver Brumby*. Here, family and friends (Dad is second from the left) undertake a prewar winter expedition.

Elyne saw the mountains as mysterious, little-charted lands—if you explored them you would learn something about their mystery and individuality and, more importantly, something about yourself. Here she contemplates the view from the Dargals.

An article published in February 1944 in *Pix*, accompanying this photograph, stated, 'Despite difficulties, Mrs Mitchell has been able to send about 700 fat cattle to Melbourne markets each year.' Mum had Mr Herbert, the Towong Hill manager, to help her during the war, as well as a housekeeper and cook, but with Dad a prisoner in Changi, she was exhausted from hard work and anxiety by the time he returned home.

Mum had a wonderful ear for music and enjoyed playing Austrian folk and skiing songs on her accordion. Here she and Dad enjoy a postwar picnic near Khancoban Creek. The simple pleasures of the bush helped Dad's recovery after the hardship of imprisonment.

Elyne and her four children with Granny Chauvel. Granny was a great raconteur and inspired Mum to write from an early age. Nonetheless, Granny sometimes tried to explain to Mum that her writing was coming into conflict with her family, and that her children needed her too.

Our twin white cats belonged to Indi and Harry and I longed for a pet of my own. I was jealous and sulky and felt my older siblings enjoyed privileges denied to me.

I loved my little black cat, Chikko, possessively, and had to learn not to strangle her with affection.

Some of my happiest times at Towong Hill were when Mum took me riding in the paddocks, even if my skewbald Shetland pony, Toby, would put his head down to eat as soon as we stopped.

Swimming lessons began with the fishing rod: a canvas belt attached to a thin pole was placed around my chest and I could paddle for all I was worth without fear of sinking.

Mum's favourite swimming hole was the scimitar-shaped lagoon below the house. Willows surrounded the lagoon, their shade helping keep the water deliciously cool in summer. Dad was not such a keen swimmer as Mum but he enjoyed rowing his dinghy for exercise and entertaining visitors there.

For my introduction to snow, Dad and Mum put me in a wicker pram on skis. Here, wrapped up against the elements, I resemble a glum, mummified gnome. Dad, Indi and Harry look on.

In the heavy snow year of 1960 we started skiing at Thredbo as a family. Dad never understood that others didn't necessarily find the sport as easy to master as he did. 'You've got to work hard for your fun,' he would say. By the end of each day's skiing I was exhausted and couldn't understand what Mum and Dad got so excited about.

In 1963 I was one of the youngest members of the New South Wales Junior Ski Squad. While it was nice to have been selected, particularly because it pleased Mum and Dad, I was also becoming aware that my lack of competitiveness meant ski racing didn't hold the thrill for me that it had for them.

For Mum, nothing could compete with skiing. It was both her obsession and a form of escapism. She believed that 'it was the key that let you through into unexplored places'.

I went straight from correspondence lessons at Towong Hill, with Mum a sometimes reluctant, distracted supervisor, to boarding school at Toorak College at the age of eleven. I'd had little social contact with other girls my age and at first was desperately lonely and unhappy, as well as being way out of my depth academically.

'A good talker, a good teacher, an interesting man.' As a teenager, I thought Dad was one of the most eccentric characters imaginable and found his colourful stories embarrassing. Others enjoyed them, even though they knew he exaggerated a bit. He was a well-liked and respected member of state parliament so some people called him 'the Hon Tom', while others nicknamed him 'Mr History'.

Mum with Winkle, the Australian terrier she bought for the family. He assumed an importance in her life that, as a teenager, I felt none of the family attained. Both Mum and I were inhibited and sensitive to criticism from each other, and did not have an easy relationship during my high school years.

Mum and Dad deeply wanted to rediscover their prewar happiness, but it always seemed in later years that discord far outweighed any enjoyment in each other's company. Here they have called a momentary truce.

Harry at Geelong Grammar. His cheerfulness, courage and perseverance earned him respect from all members of the school community.

Mum's face became bronzed and lined with the years; she looked like a wizened walnut and laughed like a kookaburra singing up the sun at dawn.

18
Undercurrents

The first few strokes of dog paddle I took were with Mum at the old wooden Bringenbrong Bridge over the Murray River, just a couple of hundred yards beneath the point where the Swampy Plains River and the Indi River meet to form the Murray. Jutting out from the bank on the New South Wales side of the river was a sandy willow- and scrub-covered peninsula. Downstream was a shallow backwater with very little current, an ideal place for a child to learn to swim. I had had some good lessons with Miss Scott in Melbourne, but ultimately I learned because I fell in and *had* to swim. Mum was close by and saw me take the first strokes, ready to help and full of encouragement. I never looked back. At last I had found something I could do and enjoy, and as a bonus I had also pleased Mum.

Mum also taught Bob Salter, whose parents lived and worked at Towong Hill, to swim. This was an even greater achievement as Bob's mother, Dot, was very nervous around water and most reluctant to agree to the lessons. Normally a calm, sensible person, Dot must have had good reason for concern as she didn't swim herself. Although Mum was very sensitive to her feelings, she regarded swimming as one of life's essential skills and admired

Dot for letting Bob learn, and Bob for learning. Mum also gained a sense of personal fulfilment from Bob's progress and enjoyed both his company and that of his mother.

Mum's childhood friend Edith Wood sometimes brought her youngest daughter, Ros, who was about Indi's age, to stay during our summer holidays. I enjoyed these visits, although apparently on occasion I drove everyone mad by insisting on saying the Lord's Prayer in Latin in a slow monotone! It now seems a strange tale as I have never had the distinction of being so learned, although I did know parts of the Latin grace Dad said at Jesus College, Cambridge, so perhaps I irritated them with that. Edith Wood was older than Mum but very game, cheerful and kind.

Just as our family christened our paddocks and hills, we also had names for some of our swimming lagoons, and for many years Indi Island was a favourite. A small oxbow lake at the end of a runner, or tributary, of the Murray River, the swimming hole at Indi Island swelled into a reasonable-sized pool just before the runner reached one of the old courses of the river. Indi Island itself was a little peninsula sandwiched between two lagoons in the middle of which was a graceful river red gum. When we were not there cows gathered in its shade, and there were always plenty of fresh cowpats. Some nails to which we could hitch our ponies' reins had been hammered into the gum's trunk. More than once, as I mounted or dismounted, I either landed in a cowpat or my pony nuzzled me into one. Tortoises laid their eggs among the tussocks and longer grass on the island. Dad had an empty tortoise shell that he'd found near Indi Island on the wall in his workshop.

Mum and Dad considered that one lagoon 'belonged' to Indi Island and was our swimming hole while the other one did not 'belong'. It was shallow and filled with tepid water and reeds, and there were probably snakes too. We found a fish trap filled with dead yabbies and slimy willow branches, and the smell was enough to deter me from wanting to swim there ever again. Water from the runner fed the lagoon where we swam so it was cleaner and clearer. In one corner there was a willow and in the other an overhanging river red gum branch on which we sat high above the water, and from which we could dive.

At one end of the swimming lagoon there was a short, straight channel linking it with the course of the old river. Clear water flowed through it and we built fortresses alongside it on the bank as if it were the Rhine. The shallow end of our swimming lagoon at Indi Island was oval-shaped and neatly surrounded by reeds. The shape was so perfect and the reeds grew so evenly that it looked to me as if someone had made it that way. I did not yet understand that such phenomena can be miraculously and perfectly formed by nature without humans doing anything. In the shallow end we found a plentiful supply of skipping stones. Mum could skip stones effortlessly from one side of the lagoon to the other, while my skippers nosedived a few plops away from my feet.

The old watercourse marked the state border. (A network of billabongs and runners or streams hinted at the different routes that the river had meandered in big sweeping curves across the valley floor during its long history.) In winter and early spring it ran 'a banker' – when the flood level reached the top of the riverbank – like the present river, but by midsummer it was little more than a trickle between a series of shady pools, mud, reeds, willows, sandy banks and river red gums. The remains of a tree protruded like a giant, ugly black snake from a muddy bank above a dark pool on the opposite bank from Indi Island. Once in early summer, when the river was flowing and reasonably full, a boy visiting the family climbed onto the protrusion and jumped into the pool below. Years later after I left school I saw him again, but I was too shy to tell him that I thought he'd been a show-off jumping from what Harry and I had secretly decided was a symbol of virility.

The old river divided Indi Island from the 'islands' on the New South Wales side of the border. It seemed a treat to cross the interstate border without having to get into the car or get our legs wet above our knees. The islands were like a forgotten corner of bracken-covered and willow-filled wilderness where I thought the ghost of Dad's cranky Uncle Peter might have hidden after his home at Bringenbrong was sold. And the islands had other things to offer. If we were lucky we saw a kingfisher flash among the trees, and once Mum and I saw a white kookaburra. Ossie Rixon suggested it might have been an albino, but we hadn't seen it for long enough to know for sure; one had been sighted in the 1930s at Upper Towong. Although I never saw them do so, brolgas were said to sometimes dance on the sandy banks of the runners.

The only occasion I saw Mum disciplining someone else's child was at Indi Island, when the young son of a family friend pushed me underwater and held me there for a bit too long; I could see the sun's rays shining through but I wasn't able to fight my way to the surface. Mum reacted quickly, pulling me out of the water and smacking the boy on the bottom. I had never seen her so angry; she too must have had a very bad fright. I coughed and spluttered, and thought that drowning must make you choke horribly and panic, the world spinning until you knew nothing anymore. Mum never spoke to me about it and it was as if nothing had happened, but I never forgot it.

Mum was always looking for possible new swimming spots. We often rode along the river and its lagoon banks as far as the growth of willow would allow our passage. Mum had a bird's-eye view from horseback, and safety was always the main consideration in judging a new swimming hole – it should contain no dead timber, or snags. After the spring floods she would inspect the previous year's swimming places thoroughly. Having done her Bronze lifesaving certificate in 1941, Mum took water safety very seriously. I was already frightened enough of the underwater world and didn't need Mum to instil further fear about slimy snags.

Mum's favourite swimming hole was the scimitar-shaped lagoon below the house, which at one time had been a very deep river bend in an old watercourse. Some water still flowed through it from Battery Creek and from an anabranch of the Murray River. Willows surrounded the lagoon, their shade helping keep the water deliciously cool in summer, and there was a sufficiently large clear area away from the trees to be able to swim for at least one hundred yards at a stretch. Mum swam about half a mile if she had time in the mornings, and then took the family swimming in a less challenging and safer location in the afternoons. It was one of the ways she could combine a family outing with something she enjoyed.

Sometimes she floated on her back to watch birds flying back and forth across the lagoon and among the surrounding trees. She imitated the call of a whistling eagle very well and occasionally succeeded in bringing one of the huge birds to circle over the lagoon. She kept diary records of all the kingfishers she saw and also made notes when she saw brolgas, swifts, robins, owls and bronze cuckoos, recording any differences in populations and behaviour she noticed from one season to the next. Years later I visited the naturalist Gilbert White's house and the Oates Collection near Selborne in Surrey, England, where I saw that Mum had kept her diary in a similar way to the Reverend Gilbert White, whose work she had admired for decades. Mum was a keen amateur ornithologist and botanist, and the bookcases in the front hall and sitting room were filled with volumes on birds and wildflowers. She didn't collect specimens though, preferring to view birds in their natural habitat.

Occasionally Granny came to the lagoon too and sat in the shade wearing her straw gardening hat. She belonged to a generation in which few women swam, even if they knew how.

I suspect the only swimming costume she would ever have considered would have been a neck-to-knee affair. The only time Mum saw her in a bathing costume was on a summer holiday at Bognor Regis in England in the summer of 1916. Some fifty years later there was no chance of seeing her thus clad – as ever, there was the matter of dignity to be considered.

By midsummer almost all the lagoons were filled with strands of slime intermingled with rotting logs, cowpats and other floating debris as there was often insufficient rain to flush them out. The insect life – the dragonflies, in particular – was fabulous and fascinating to look at through a magnifying glass. Although we looked for cleaner places to swim, we just accepted a certain amount of slime, duckweed and mud as being the price we had to pay for being able to cool off on a hot day. Granny didn't agree and viewed the colour and composition of the water with disapproval; she didn't have to say anything for us to know her thoughts. It probably smelt and we might have done so too, having swum in it so much. 'Don't you know, Mummy,' Mum remarked mischievously, 'cowpats are good for the complexion.' There was a faint hint in Mum's remarks that Granny might care to try it too! Granny's reply was lost in gales of raucous, naughty laughter.

About this time Granny tried to insist on everyone drinking boiled water. For a time she boiled it herself and kept it in large jugs shrouded in net covers weighed down with beads. She eventually gave up when she realised she couldn't stop Harry and me drinking from a garden hose or tap. The homestead water was pumped up from the pumping lagoon and the garden taps often coughed up bits of slime and cowpat. The quality of the water may well have been responsible for some of my tummy troubles.

Riding and swimming on these long, warm and wonderful summer days provided Mum with the inspiration to write *Kingfisher Feather;* our summer activities were very similar to those of the Dane family in that book. But we never met the Aboriginal woman driving a sulky who made tantalising suggestions about meeting the challenge of a flood and finding kingfisher feathers and dragonfly caves, though I was always looking for that elusive gleaming blue kingfisher's feather once I read the story.

Being one of the few relatively strong swimmers with a lifesaving qualification in the district, Mum offered to help teach children from the Corryong primary school to swim. One of her first tasks was to pull one of the schoolteachers out of Corryong Creek; apparently he hadn't told anyone that he could hardly swim and must have panicked in the deep, dark water. Judging by the frisson of laughter among the onlookers, Mum probably told him he was a fool, or something similar.

'Tell me what you said!' I begged Mum in the car later.

'Certainly not!' she replied, much to my disappointment.

One afternoon, the rather glamorous wife of a Snowy Mountains Authority engineer invited Mum to take the family to swim in the new pool at Khancoban. It was the best thing that could have happened to me. The pool had the highest diving board I had ever seen, and I spent the afternoon diving and trying to overcome my fear of swimming underwater. I never became very proficient but from that time on I could jump or dive from almost anything, apparently undaunted. But I never forgot what it was like to be stuck even momentarily underwater, struggling to get to the surface for breath.

Dad was not such a keen swimmer as Mum but he did spend a lot of time down at the lagoon too. He rowed his dinghy for exercise and enjoyed entertaining visitors. One winter Dad's brother-in-law Moreton Lodge helped him build two wooden boats. Dad already had a metal boat he called the *Hesperus*, which was supposedly unsinkable, and he taught us all to row in it. One afternoon James Mackinnon from Tintaldra Station and I did manage to sink the *Hesperus*. The Mackinnons' black Labrador, who was in the boat with us, swam to the shore while James and I pulled out and emptied the hitherto unsinkable vessel. We weren't popular, but I don't remember getting into trouble.

Mum was not keen on rowing and sometimes resented the amount of space Dad's boats took up in the lagoon and the clutter around the springboard. Her irritation became more acute when Dad invited the local Boy Scouts to boat on the lagoon more and more frequently. Dad was generous to a fault outside the family, and to any family member who was interested in scouting. Arguably, if ironically, while Mum wrote children's books, it was perhaps Dad who enjoyed contact with young people most. Difficulties arose when his generosity intruded or created undue demands on Mum's personal space and time. Mum felt she had already done her bit for the Scouts and Guides during the war when, along with Eve, she had accompanied a Girl Guide riding expedition into the mountains.

Dad could be dictatorial about his plans, which caused further friction and misunderstanding. Equally, Mum was unprepared to accommodate what she saw as his near-obsessive interest in Scouts and boating, and was also concerned that Dad was not a sufficiently strong swimmer and had inadequate lifesaving skills to take responsibility for other people's children. One day, Dad retaliated. 'I am going to leave the lagoon to the Scouts,' he announced to Mum's sheer horror. On other occasions he would say, 'None of you is interested so I am going to leave the whole damn place to Cranbrook [his old school in Sydney].' As children, with none of us permitted to play a real role at Towong Hill, the accusation seemed grossly unfair. Nobody had even been given a chance. When I later objected, he said, 'Granddaddy M said I could play ducks and drakes with this place if I wanted to.' He was just letting me know that he could do what he liked with Towong Hill and nobody could stop him. If it was his own inadequacy talking, it didn't sound like it to me when I was a child. It was more like a god pronouncing an edict.

I didn't really think he was serious but it was clear that there were times when he didn't think much of us kids and, on occasions, me in particular. I had no interest in Brownies or Girl Guides. 'You don't know what you are missing out on,' he said with admonishing disappointment in his voice. 'You would meet other girls and you could give so much to kids who have much less than you. You don't know how lucky you are.' He turned and went off to the workshop. His expression and body language said it all and I didn't feel in the least bit lucky.

Away from the tensions of the lagoon was Waterfall Farm, upstream on the Swampy Plains River from Khancoban township, where we could bounce our way across the swing bridge high above the swirling, rushing waters of the river flowing far beneath. A couple of hundred metres upstream from the bridge, the action of the water over thousands of years had carved perfectly circular rock pools and smooth shapes out of the rock lining some of the bank. Ti-tree, bush and tongues of fine grey sand stretched right down to the rock. Sometimes we took inflatable canoes to shoot the rapids. Afternoons at Waterfall Farm, especially when Mum brought her deliciously light homemade sponge cakes for our picnic afternoon teas, were the next best thing to heaven.

A couple of times Dad asked me to accompany him on a canoe trip from Bringenbrong Bridge to Towong Bridge. On at least one canoe trip Indi came too. Mum drove us and the canoes to Bringenbrong Bridge and then met us many hours later at the other end of our journey. The trip was eight river miles and took us all day, paddling between the river gum and willow-lined banks on the gentle stretches and then navigating the faster flowing water so we were not swept under the willows. Once we hit a tussock on the bank with a tiger snake coiled within it, and we paddled for all we were worth to get away before there was any chance of an angry snake landing in the canoe with us. I kept a keen eye out for snakes on the banks after that.

19
Beyond the Family

If Mum was often remote while she was writing and we were doing our correspondence lessons, she became more lighthearted and animated – as if a layer of worry and stress had slipped away like a restrictive, unwanted garment – once we were outside and away from the house.

Mum organised the social life we had as kids from the telephone in the front hall. We were often invited to tea with Mrs Knight, the gentle, kind, myopic wife of 'Father' Knight (who, behind his back, we sometimes called Knightie). Mrs Knight had lime juice for those who were too young to drink tea and there was always a delicious, freshly baked cake. I remember her fondly for her spoonerisms. Once instead of saying a length of cable cost a shilling a foot she said 'a fooling a shit'. Ever since the son of one of the couples who worked for us had coached me in the worst words he could think of, I hadn't heard anyone else saying 'shit'. Mrs Knight was mortified, and Mum had to suppress her giggles.

The Knights' house was surrounded on three sides by verandahs liberally laced with grapevines. We called it the bow-wow-miaow house: there were at least seventeen cats and a number of dogs of all sizes. Although it was walking distance from our homestead, the homeward journey was mostly uphill, which my short, fat legs didn't like.

On other days, either the Mackinnon family came to tea with us or we went across to see them at their property, Tintaldra Station, about ten kilometres away. In the early 1960s, when the Chisholm family arrived at Khancoban Station (after Bruce inherited it), they joined our circle. Then there was Max Anderson, a Corryong solicitor, and his wife, Bessie, who had two children, Penny and David, similar in age to Indi and Harry. Sometimes we had tea with the Andersons in Corryong, where Mrs Anderson had beautiful blue hydrangeas growing in her garden, and sometimes they came picnicking with us. One afternoon, over at Tooma, I naughtily stepped on Betsy Paton's asparagus plants to hear them crunch under my shoes, and tried to encourage her twins to do so too, until our parents stopped me. The Paton family might have gone without asparagus that season, thanks to my thoughtless mischief.

At pony club, which was sometimes held at Towong and sometimes on the sports ground near Tintaldra township, I saw Bill and Susie Waters and their cousins. We also saw the Herbert family, who lived on the other side of the river. The local policeman, Mr Ibetson, and Joan Boardman, who lived near Khancoban, came to club meetings and Mr Herbert instructed. All the Waters family were keen riders who helped and encouraged us all, making the pony club meetings into wonderfully enjoyable occasions.

For a short time the Mackinnon children also did correspondence schooling, although I think they were too polite to ever refer to it as Crappy Days like I did. James and I told each other many things, sometimes sitting behind an agapanthus in the front garden at Tintaldra, but I didn't dare tell him what I called the lessons until we were much older in case his parents heard about what I had said. The routines of our two families were similar, even if we were at slightly different stages due to our age differences. I suspect Ronnie and Jenny Mackinnon saw the weaknesses in the correspondence schooling, with the result that James and Annabel were soon sent to the primary school in Corryong. There they made some new friends and seemed to grow up while John and I were stuck in the same old lonely rut.

I loved visiting the Mackinnons. The weatherboard homestead at Tintaldra seemed serene and light, more relaxed and less spooky than Towong Hill. It fascinated me that in the 1950s the kitchen at Tintaldra was a separate building at the back of the main house, just like the one Dad had described at the original Khancoban House. The early stoves were fuelled with wood and fire was a constant fear. The logic was that if a fire broke out, only the kitchen would burn and not the whole house.

The children in our small social network went to each other's birthday parties, and as we grew up our circle widened, as did the variety of our activities. Sometimes we barbecued on fine days in the autumn and winter holidays and, if there was no fire danger, in spring. Other times we went into the bush for picnics. One year, after a big storm had left a huge hole on the edge of the lawn at Tintaldra, the Mackinnons put in a swimming pool where we spent many happy hours. Annabel and I got into trouble when I persuaded her to go for a swim before her aunt's wedding. Mrs Mackinnon was concerned that the chemical in the water would turn her daughter's blonde hair a lurid green colour; understandably, Annabel's aunt didn't want her bridesmaid to have even a hint of green hair. Later the Mackinnons built a tennis court too. In retrospect those days we spent with the Mackinnons at Tintaldra seem so companionable and so much fun compared to our family life at Towong Hill. They were indeed the very experiences upon which we all built deep, lifelong friendships.

At our own home, whether it was Scouts or family visitors, Dad loved to organise activities. If he could, he ran everything, telling people what to do and how to do it. He was all noise and action. While guests seemed to enjoy it and thought he was a character, which indeed he was, within the family his dominance of social activities began to pall, and by the time I was a teenager I found it embarrassing on the few occasions I had school friends staying. I was very relieved that when the Governor of Victoria and his wife, Sir Rohan and Lady Delacombe, visited in 1966 I was at boarding school. I had already found, when the British High Commissioner to Malaya and his wife, Lord and Lady Selkirk, stayed some years earlier, that it was all too easy to put a foot wrong.

20
War Secrets

One January in the early 1960s, Dad took Harry and me to stay with Aunt Hon and Uncle Moreton at Blowering Station, near Tumut. It was one of the very few occasions that I went there. Mum hadn't been to Blowering much since the war and this time she went to Thredbo where there was still sufficient snow to ski on some of the drifts. There had been heavy snow the previous winter and it had taken a long time to melt. Indi and John must have gone with her too.

Aunt Hon had a lily pond shaped like a rectangular swimming pool, only nobody swam in it; if they swam at all they went down to the river.[1] Among the lilies in the pond there was a bronze frog that squirted water from its mouth. 'Your aunt designed and made the frog!' Dad told Harry and me proudly. Like the weathervane on the stable roof at home, that she had also designed, depicting a silhouette of a coach and horses with the coachman's whip flying, curling in the air above the horses, to him it was another example of her wonderful talent.

My attention had already left the frog and wandered to the vista of sweeping lawns separating well-tended and colourful flowerbeds. European trees just outside the garden fence enclosed the scene, which subsequently became my vision of the biblical garden of Eden. The only things missing were the trees of good and evil and apples, though usually there were plenty of snakes in the paddocks. I reasoned that Aunt Hon and Uncle Moreton were too old and wise to succumb to temptation, so apples, serpents, and good and evil were irrelevant. Had I been older and confident enough to articulate my thoughts in a comprehensible manner, I might have received a bit of a dusting down from Dad about my interpretation of the scriptures.

Aunt Hon gave me a deliciously cool room that had a hat-shaped chimney set into one corner. The window looked out onto a shaded courtyard where vines grew on a pergola. The room was immaculately clean and tidy and the bed was beautifully made without a wrinkle beneath the bedspread. My bed at Towong Hill seldom looked so tidy and on the afternoon of our arrival I was worried that I wouldn't be able to make my bed at Blowering well enough the next morning. It was not just the bed but the entire room that looked very different from my room at Towong Hill; instinctively I knew that I couldn't construct scenes from *The Silver Brumby* on the bedroom floor here. In fact I hardly dared move for fear of destroying Aunt Hon's perfect handiwork. I had to be more grown up.

To my surprise, the following morning I discovered that my concerns about folding my clothes and making the bed were unfounded. Aunt Hon, sensing my disquiet, came to help me, patiently showing me how to tuck in the sheets with neat hospital corners. She was pleased when I did it for myself.

Uncle Moreton took us down to a bend in the Tumut River, which ran a short distance away in the valley below the house. There we shot the rapids on his aircraft wheel's inner tube called Tweedle Dee, bouncing and spinning in the spray away from the rocks. (He had another called Tweedle Dum.) Nearby, Uncle Moreton paddled his army disposals canoe vigilantly but sedately, pursing his lips and chuckling, puffing and grunting beneath his floppy towelling hat.

One afternoon, Dad took us to Tumut to meet Maggie Wilson, who in 1909 had won the Ladies' Ski Championships at Kiandra. Harry had not wanted to go, perceptively suspecting that Dad was using us as a foil for what was really going to be an interview with photographs for an article for the *Ski Yearbook*. Maggie was a sprightly old lady, with hair tied back in a grey bun. She welcomed us with a spontaneously warm smile and didn't seem to mind my questions about whether the Chinese miners skied with pigtails hanging down their backs or if snow clung to her skirts and if they got in the way. Maggie chuckled away and was happy to talk about skiing and the old days at the turn of the century in Kiandra. Her stories were tinged with hints of tales from the Orient and Europe, and of places her parents told her about when she was a child. I'd have loved to ask her more but Dad wanted to hear about ski racing. Maggie had an ample bosom and I wondered how she managed to remain upright long enough to win a race, though I didn't dare ask.

While she was humble about her own achievements and much keener to talk about her elder sister's feats on the slopes, she proudly brought out the silver butter dish she had won in 1909. Dad cajoled us into posing while he photographed Maggie showing us the trophy. Over a year later the photograph was published together with the article in the *Ski Yearbook*, just as Harry had predicted.

That evening, back at Blowering, Aunt Hon had made a floating island pudding for our dessert. Before serving it she tapped the floating island's thin toffee covering with the back of a spoon, making a soft echoing sound and adding her own magic touch to a memorable, interesting and enjoyable day.

Although we were honoured guests, the palpable generation gap at Towong Hill replicated itself at Blowering, and was probably amplified as Aunt Hon and Uncle Moreton's daughter, Suzanne, was grown up and had already left home. I can't remember being included or taking part in many of the conversations. There I was a child who was to be seen and not heard and, for the short time we were there, I managed to play the role. And how the grown-ups talked! There was an excited and almost breathless quality to their conversation. Apart from being brother and sister, there was a friendship between Dad and Aunt Hon that I had never seen before and didn't believe could exist between a brother and sister. Blood was definitely thicker than water with those two. Many conversations were about people and places Harry and I didn't know and that were difficult for us to imagine. If I had been scared of putting a foot wrong, I couldn't imagine Mum feeling relaxed here. And yet I knew that once, during the war and before I was born, she and Aunt Hon had been close friends who wrote letters, telephoned and visited each other. Mum even dedicated her book *Soil and Civilization* to Aunt Hon, but their relationship had become strained.

Why on earth had they argued about the spelling of my name and the musical designs Aunt Hon had drawn so carefully and beautifully for my christening robe? While I could easily imagine Aunt Hon getting cross, I couldn't imagine her having a 'tongue like a fishwife' as Dad said she did when she was annoyed. Possibly the christening robe designs were only part of a deeper problem. I suspected Dad was stoking the fires of difference between the two by comparing Aunt Hon's efficiency to Mum's relative lack of interest in domestic matters. Dad would have preferred the house at Towong Hill to have been clean and tidy, like Blowering! And the fact that Aunt Hon was not only Dad's beloved sister but had always been his best friend too couldn't have helped.

Dad later told me that Granny M had written to him at Brisbane when he was returning from the war on the hospital ship SS *Largs Bay*, warning him that Mum had become 'swollen-headed'. He added that Aunt Hon had had 'a harder war than Mum' as she had a child to look after and only had one stockman, Potter, to help with the running of the pastoral operation at Blowering. Uncle Moreton had enlisted in the Royal Australia Navy in October 1941, and while he had not been a POW like Dad, he had been away for much of the war. Aunt Hon not only had outdoor work but also had the books to keep, while Mum was fortunate enough to have the manager, Mr Herbert, to look after those tasks and to make major decisions. The loneliness and sense of isolation must have been all the more intense for Aunt Hon. Dad said she always kept a rifle handy, and after the news of the breakout of Japanese prisoners of war at the camp in Cowra she armed herself with a revolver and wore a cartridge belt.

In 1942 Aunt Hon also looked after Granny M, or Fido as Mum and Aunt Hon called her, when she was staying at Blowering and fell ill with pneumonia. Aunt Hon hadn't had time to go out in the mountains or write books or paint, as indeed she too might have wished: she had to put chores first. Before the end of the war Mum had two books published and the third was almost complete. She could not deny that she had written a lot. But to be fair, Mum had given credit where it was due and wrote to Dad on 19 August 1945 saying, '[Honnor] has done an incredibly good job managing Blowering all the time [Moreton] was away.' In the early war years, Mum and Aunt Hon had kept in close contact by letter and telephone, and at that time it seemed that there was almost nothing they didn't discuss, from farming matters to philosophy. Mum even said that Aunt Hon was an oracle about contraception – perhaps she had Marie Stopes' books and Mum hadn't.

But exposure to publicity had already sown some seeds of discontent. An article published in February 1944 in *Pix* stated, 'Despite difficulties, Mrs Mitchell has been able to send about 700 fat cattle to Melbourne markets each year.'[2] It was unfortunate that after the war Mum allowed remarks such as, 'she had coped during the war at Towong Hill single-handedly'[3] to persist; even if sometimes she corrected them it was often inadequately. Dad mentioned the hurt this had caused him and the loyal employees who had helped her through those difficult and uncertain years. Once, in a bitter moment, Dad told me that for most of the war 'there would have been eight people employed at Towong Hill in addition to Mr Herbert and including Mrs Scammell [who frequently cooked at the homestead] and Mrs Davis'. It could only have added insult to injury when Mum claimed that Aunt Hon had 'brought Uncle Moreton home' before the end of the war because she couldn't cope. 'One just didn't do that sort of thing,' Mum told me.

Undoubtedly, the two women coped differently. Understandably, at a time when Mum was scarcely even receiving letters from Dad, it must have upset her that not only was Aunt Hon able to communicate with Uncle Moreton, she was able to ask him (thanks to exemptions from service granted to primary producers) to come home. All Mum knew was that Dad was alive. In February 1944 she would not have known how many really tough months she had to endure before the end.

Whatever really happened, it is easy to understand why Aunt Hon might have needed her husband at home. Perhaps Aunt Hon was wise to recognise that she was not coping and the steps she took to rectify the situation were therefore sensible. Whatever happened between the two sisters-in-law, Uncle Moreton's arrival home in November 1944 must have had some impact on their relationship.

Meanwhile, Mum had her own sad difficulties towards the end of the war that Dad and his family appeared not to understand fully. Nevertheless, in 1950, before Harry was born, Mum wrote to Aunt Hon outlining her wishes about Indi's upbringing in the event that Mum didn't survive childbirth. Then, over subsequent years, it seemed that the friendship cooled. It was a complex situation. The mystery of this change haunted me throughout my childhood and later, until after Mum died and I inherited her davenport desk containing correspondence that shed light on her experience of the final year of the war.

What I discovered was that 1945 was a very testing year for Mum. In the summer of 1944 and early 1945, concerns about bushfires were running so high that Mum remained alone at Towong Hill rather than spending Christmas with her family in Melbourne. It was to be her father's last Christmas.

In a telling letter to Dr Euan Littlejohn, her parents' family doctor and great friend in Melbourne, she asked, 'Did I say I behaved like an over wound clock when I talked to you [...] I seem to have in this letter too!' By June 1945 Mum was utterly exhausted and must have reached the nadir of her loneliness. Quite apart from the anxiety and strain of war, by that time she had packed in an amazing amount of work at Towong Hill and a huge amount of writing and reading, as well as some skiing, bush walking and riding in the mountains when possible.

A month after Singapore fell on 15 February 1942, Mum typed in her wartime notes, 'Tonight I feel that all this is going to take something more than I have got.' But Mum had what it took – she simply demanded too much of herself, just as she continued to do throughout her life. Strangely, she seemed to think that her work at Towong Hill was so important that she couldn't be spared to help Granny and Eve nurse Grandfather in his last illness. Even though Dad and Aunt Hon never mentioned it, at least not to Mum, Mum's prioritising Towong Hill over her own father must have been something they noticed.

Grandfather died on 4 March 1945. In a letter written to Dr Littlejohn on 9 April of that year, Mum admitted, 'You were awfully right about missing Daddy. At the moment things seem to be more in perspective and the haunting images gone but the missing him is going on.' Just as I was born relatively late in my parents' lives, Mum was born late in her father's life – when he was forty-eight. Almost until the end of his life, a shyness between them somewhat blighted their otherwise warm father–daughter relationship. Mum felt that she had missed out on something because their relationship was so inhibited. Perhaps Aunt Eve, who was living at 49 until Grandfather died, had a closer, warmer, more open and relaxed relationship with her father.

Mum always said that her parents were delighted when her books were published. As Granny and Grandfather had very traditional views about marriage, I often wondered if they were bothered about the amount of time Mum spent writing and whether she would have space in her life for Dad if and when he came home. I could wonder all I liked, because even if I had asked Mum or even Granny it was unlikely I would have received a satisfactory answer.

Later in the same letter to Dr Littlejohn Mum wrote, 'You do see, don't you, that I don't want to turn into the sort of ruddy neurotic that can't keep on an even keel without medicine.' Mum often spoke of her regret that her father did not live long enough to see peace. It must have pained her deeply that he wasn't there to share the war victory with her. Dr Littlejohn was trying very hard to help Mum through a difficult time, perhaps one of the greatest troughs that she had yet encountered. Perhaps few would have understood better than him: not only was he a close family friend but Brefny, one of his own two sons, had just been shot down over Holland. He had also lost a nephew, Ross, a commando who was killed on the Brenner Pass. If anyone knew something of the sorrow of bereavement, Dr Littlejohn and his wife, Mary, certainly must have done so.

Dr Littlejohn told Mum to write to him when she felt 'blue'. Mum was quick to acknowledge and express her gratitude for his help. In her letter dated 5 May 1945 Mum wrote, 'You were a dear to say that you don't think I should worry about the future. Your letter arrived on the fourth anniversary of the day Thomas left, and it helped to smooth out some of the bumps – and some of the unevenness of the travelling of the last few days.' In her letter of 25 June 1945 Mum explained to Dr Littlejohn that, 'It seemed so silly to sit there quietly listening to you saying that I might have to get worse before I got better, when I so desperately don't want to burst. The getting near to bursting point has the awful effect of seeming to take away from me all I have tried to create for Tom.' Although in some of the correspondence Mum treats her health concerns as a mere nuisance, it seems that she was anxious she wasn't going to be able to last the distance until the end of the war. Dr Littlejohn tried to persuade her to have a break, which she did when she went to the Chalet at Charlotte Pass for a fortnight's skiing during July 1945.

As a child in the 1960s I was too young to understand the complexities of the relationships between grown-ups. I thought Mum was prickly and critical of Aunt Hon for tidying and cleaning the house rather than using her talents for drawing and painting. On the other hand, I thought Dad was trying to encourage Aunt Hon to gang up on Mum a bit with him. I wished they were still friends, then I might have seen more of Aunt Hon.

I suspect Mum's decision to name me after Aunt Hon was intended as an olive branch and that Mum was disappointed and irritated when it backfired. It was a great relief to find that my name and the designs for my christening robe were probably not the only reasons for the fallout; war can be a great maker and breaker of friendships. While Mum told me part of her story, Dad said little and Aunt Hon was utterly silent on the subject. Aunt Hon and Uncle Moreton visited Towong Hill when I was about five after they had returned from an overseas trip. I recall Aunt Hon giving Dad a huge pair of scissors for cutting out press clippings and me some turquoise beads that I have to this day. I can't recall Aunt Hon coming to our home again. But she always seemed delighted to see me if I visited her and I suspect she would have liked to have seen more of all her nieces and nephews.

At the end of our visit to Blowering in the early sixties, we returned via Batlow and Tumbarumba to Towong Hill. Tweedle Dee accompanied us, which thrilled me, as I knew that an aircraft tyre would be ideal for shooting the rapids at Waterfall Farm. I also looked forward to lying with my bottom through the hole in the middle, my back and legs supported by the tyre, while sailing gently around the lagoon. Thoughtful Uncle Moreton had made a sort of net of rope held together with naval knots and attached to the tyre so a swimmer could catch onto it easily.

The bush was very dry that summer. Blue sky and shafts of sunshine flashed between branches overhanging the road. This must have been the route along which Mum and Aunt Eve had ridden in 1942, before Aunt Hon's and Mum's friendship was blighted, when they, like us, were returning from a visit to Aunt Hon at Blowering. Wartime fuel shortages would have been part of their reason for choosing to ride. I never heard how long it took – almost certainly it would have taken all day and perhaps part of a second. Even though Mum would have loved the adventure, they must have been brave as it would have been a long, lonely ride for two young women.

As we drove back home, Dad told Harry and me about an 'open' low-security prison near Batlow. I hoped we wouldn't have a flat tyre or break down, imagining us being robbed by modern-day bushrangers. Dad told stories about how his father had seen the Kelly gang on their way to hold up the bank at Jerilderie. 'They stuck up Jerilderie for three days, and they robbed the bank of £3000 and got clean away.' I was not certain that there were no more bushrangers in that lonely stretch between Batlow and Tooma. Somewhere along the dirt road we passed a property that

Dad said was called Willigobung. The owners who named it must have pondered the very question enshrined in the name. I never found out if anyone did go 'bung', but living miles from anywhere and trying to make a living must have been hard and lonely.

Back at Towong Hill and despite Aunt Hon's rather daunting housekeeping standards, it was difficult not to admit to Mum that staying with Aunt Hon and Uncle Moreton was pretty good fun. It had been interesting and I had learned a lot about making beds, cleaning silver, domestic perfection and Dad and Aunt Hon's friendship – nothing that Mum would have wanted to hear. That visit was one of my last to Blowering. By 1968 the property was vanishing beneath the waters of Blowering Dam. Together with Uncle Moreton, Dad battled the New South Wales government to ensure that Aunt Hon and Uncle Moreton received fair compensation for the loss of their beautiful home. Eventually they moved to Taminick Station near Glenrowan in Victoria and they never returned to the Tumut district. The new home they created, though beautiful, was not the same as Blowering.

In less than a decade, on 11 June 1976, just after my twenty-third birthday, Aunt Hon died of influenza, emphysema and pulmonary fibrosis. Perhaps part of the cause might have been a troubled heart. It was rumoured that alcohol had something to do with her health problems. Perhaps it had something to do with the rift between her and Mum, but if this were the case, Dad was too loyal to his beloved sister to discuss it. Her death pained Dad deeply. Aunt Hon had been through a lot.

If ever I am trying to improve my own domestic standards, I think of Aunt Hon. She might be rather disappointed in her niece's efforts, but her eyes might still sparkle with fun. As she grew sick in her later years, one of the things she enjoyed most was hearing news of the family, the more colourful and entertaining the better. When she asked for news of Mum, the sparkle in her eyes was replaced by a rather sad, distant look. I wondered if she was craving her old friendship and was too ill to rekindle it. On the last occasion I visited Aunt Hon, she gave me her velvet wedding dress and the baby clothes her mother had embroidered. Because of the bulk of the wedding dress, I left it wrapped in my room at Towong Hilll when I went overseas in 1976 and I never saw it or her again.

I used a small bequest Aunt Hon left me to study French Civilization for three months in Paris. While she would have approved, she might have been saddened that I didn't become a talented French speaker. I would have needed much longer for that, but I was grateful for the time I had.

21
War Friends and Waterskiing

'Uncle Ken was the only brother I ever had,' Dad said. 'He saved my life and looked after me in Changi.' Dad was paying tribute to 'Uncle' Ken Burnside's abilities as a doctor and his extraordinary and wonderfully loyal kindness as a friend. In *Chauvel Country*, Mum wrote, 'If it had not been for Dr Kennedy Burnside's care, he [Dad] might never have survived imprisonment in Changi.'[1]

In February 1943, a year after Singapore fell to the Japanese and when he and Dad were prisoners of war in Changi, Uncle Ken managed to send a message to their families via a Singapore Radio broadcast. Apparently the words ran: 'Thomas Mitchell and self well.' A short time before, on 17 January 1943, Mum had received a telephone call from the Red Cross informing her that Dad was officially a prisoner of war. Uncle Ken's message on Singapore Radio was confirmation. Usually when Changi was mentioned, Mum shook her head as if the very name hurt and she didn't want to discuss it. Dad said little beyond expressing his gratitude to Uncle Ken.

Uncle Ken was thus an honorary part of our extended family, but far more so for Dad than for Mum. As with other honorary family members, the title 'Uncle' was used as a measure of respect in that more formal era, when people shied away from letting their children call their friends by their first names.

For at least a couple of summers in the early 1960s, Uncle Ken brought his family from Melbourne for holidays on the shores of the Hume Weir at Tallangatta, about an hour's car journey from Towong Hill. Nobody could have looked forward to their arrival more than Dad, and presumably Uncle Ken too. Both men shared a passion for boats, and Uncle Ken brought a speedboat with him, as well as a large collection of tents and deckchairs. Dad called the little metal tub he had at that time *Ena*, after Great Grandfather Dibbs' *Ena* that he took out on Sydney Harbour before the First World War. Even with an outboard motor *Ena* was no match for Uncle Ken's boat – not that Dad was worried because *Ena* had a versatility that Uncle Ken's boat didn't have in being small, so Dad could load and unload it by himself.

As a longstanding local member of parliament, Dad was well known and well liked. He was easily recognisable driving around the electorate with *Ena* on the homemade boat trailer behind his car, or with a kayak on the roof. On the way home from the various party meetings in major centres in the electorate he would stop at Boathaven or Tallangatta and relax for an hour or so in his little watercraft. Dad was quite content to putter around and explore the nearby inlets and peninsulas where dead trees stuck up out of the water while Uncle Ken took the younger generation of Burnsides and Mitchells waterskiing. I don't think I would have had the courage to ski if there had not been a large area clear of dead trees. Standing up out of the water of the Hume Weir, those dead trees were as spooky as ghosts even in daylight, and approaching them in the speedboat scared me out of my wits.

When we were not waterskiing, Dad and Uncle Ken sat in deckchairs, talking quietly at the water's edge while Ken's wife, Wendy, prepared meals in the mess tent. I'd probably been asked to call her 'Aunt Wendy', but I didn't feel I knew her well enough to do that so I avoided, if possible, calling her anything. I remember sometimes calling her Mrs Burnside, and that didn't feel right either.

Dad and Uncle Ken talked a lot about Malaya in 1941, the Australian Imperial Force, Singapore, their anti-malarial work while in Changi and, most importantly, swapped news of their mutual friends and acquaintances who had been through so much with them. I remember Wendy sitting with them once or twice and that it seemed those times were for the grown-ups only, particularly for the two men. I heard very little of the detail of the conversations. The mood was serious; the two men were totally absorbed.

Eventually I found Malaya and Singapore in the atlas at Towong Hill but I couldn't see where the Causeway was, knowing as I did from Dad that it was over this link between the Malay Peninsula and Singapore Island that the Allies had to retreat in the face of Japanese advances in January and early February 1942. The map in the atlas simply wasn't big enough to show the necessary detail. It was confusing that both the island and the city were called Singapore at a time when I thought nations had to have different names from their capital cities like Australia did. Only when I went to school did I find out where on the map Changi was. It was strange that I had to go away to learn more about the world in which my parents had lived. Their world affected me too and I wanted to understand more about it.

I didn't swim much at Tallangatta. The water near the shore smelled and tasted of motorboat fuel fumes, and I was too frightened of the dead trees to want to swim from Uncle Ken's boat, or even Dad's *Ena*. In my camp stretcher I had nightmares about snakes swimming out from the dead trees to the shore and crawling into the tent I was sharing with Indi and Jenny Burnside. I wouldn't go to the loo at night for fear of stepping on a snake.

The mirror that either Jenny or Indi had attached to our tent pole was too high for me, not that it mattered as I was too much of a scruff to be interested in looking at my reflection. With Mum not around I could get away with not brushing my hair until I became so dishevelled that even Dad noticed. All the same, I watched with interest as Indi and Jenny did their hair and put on creams. I was the kid sister who was a bit of a nuisance, curious about things I had seldom seen, like bras. Even when we changed to swim at Indi Island, Mum modestly concealed herself with a towel and kept her back to curious eyes.

While we were at Tallangatta, Mum stayed at home with Granny – if she was at Towong Hill – to water the garden and feed the cats and dogs. John stayed back to feed his chooks. Sometimes Mum and John came down to Tallangatta for the day, so I was able to go back and forth with them. Harry enjoyed boating and the waterskiing, but as he slept in the boys' tent I didn't see much of him.

I can't remember Mum enjoying those trips as much as Dad did. There seemed to be a distance between Mum and the Burnsides, just as there seemed to be between Dad and Wendy. It was as if the two wives were outside the friendship, not having shared the years as POWs. It must have been difficult for both women. While the men were great friends and always hoped that their friendship would radiate out through their families, the week or two at Tallangatta was never sufficient for me to bridge age differences and cement relationships. Uncle Ken became one of those special people I wished I had known better. He was a saviour and a giver, and I thought I had nothing to give back to such a great man. At the very least I should have said thank you for looking after Dad, but Uncle Ken died before I had gathered sufficient adult confidence to get in touch with him again.

During one of those summer holidays Mum fell and broke her ribs while waterskiing. She had already broken her right leg badly in late 1938 when she and Dad were skiing in Austria, and then again in 1940. Broken ribs sounded the death knell for housework in the weeks that followed. It didn't matter until the Archbishop of Melbourne unexpectedly called at Towong Hill. Having surveyed the mess of toys and games on the sitting room floor, he remarked, 'I wish my wife could take everything in her stride like this.' Mum was horrified. Appearances belied the reality – beneath a relaxed, welcoming façade, Mum hadn't taken it in her stride at all! To make matters worse, when she showed the Archbishop to the upstairs bathroom, a pair of lacy knickers was stretched out to dry across the screen on the window. After recovering from her embarrassment she recounted the story at her own expense with wry amusement.

The filling of the Khancoban Dam in the late 1960s added another venue to the possibilities for summer outings. Jenny Mackinnon kindly used to phone Mum to invite us to go waterskiing with them and other friends. While Mum was always happy for us to join the Mackinnons, she had become more selective about her own risk-taking, saving it for alpine skiing, which she enjoyed much more than waterskiing. Broken ribs had been quite enough. Mum was also too busy to sit and talk to other parents who didn't waterski, preferring instead to take advantage of the peace and quiet back at Towong Hill to do a few chores or continue with some writing. She had sufficient belief in what she was doing to feel she could pick and choose when she wanted to be sociable, but I believe I would have enjoyed our family outings more if she had regularly joined in.

22
Another World

In 1963, when I was ten, the parents of a friend I had met while skiing the previous September invited me to stay with them in Sydney. In their modern, new-smelling brick house, I saw through a chink in the bedroom door a double bed and realised to my amazement that my friend's parents shared the same room and the same bed. I couldn't imagine Mum and Dad sharing a bedroom, let alone a bed, without arguing. What was more, it was the nicest bedroom in the house. Men, I thought, had sharp toenails and you might be scratched if you shared a bed with them. This family used a different brand of shampoo to us – we used Tarfoam at Towong Hill – and they had toothpaste rather than the tooth powder that we had.

With my friend and her parents a whole new world started to unfold from the moment they picked me up at Thredbo. They couldn't believe that I had never been to Canberra or even heard of Lake George. I was fascinated when I saw the fence posts and vehicle tracks vanishing into the ghostly rippling waters of Lake George for the first time on the way to Sydney. I was beginning to feel like a real country bumpkin who knew absolutely nothing, or like someone who had been asleep for a hundred years, completely unaware of what had been happening in the world.

I knew enough not to let on that I hadn't realised that most parents slept together, but generally I felt too shy and gauche even to pretend I knew anything much at all. If I felt inadequate at Towong Hill, in Sydney I felt it even more acutely. But there was no denying a surge of excitement when I saw the Sydney Harbour Bridge and other Australian landmarks that everyone else seemed to know well. One day we looked for starfish and shells in the rock pools near Bondi Beach. When we chucked ugly lumps of seaweed at a boy who was following us, I found I wasn't very good at throwing any distance; I had never tried any ball sports at Towong Hill. The boy walked off laughing, and I wouldn't have minded wiping some of his smirk off with seaweed.

On another day Aunt Margaret asked me to spend the afternoon at her house in Bellevue Hill. I wore my best pink gingham shorts with a matching blouse. I can't remember how I travelled there, but I remember my sense of relief when I found that the house looked much the same as I remembered it from when Mum took me there some nine years earlier. Aunt Margaret didn't give me much time to note the changes in the house as she had invited relatives to meet me and they were all gathered by the swimming pool, waiting to be introduced. Despite their warm smiles I felt they were all studying me for family likenesses and that they would ring Mum to report their observations as soon as the visit was over. What would they say, I wondered?

Later on I went looking for linen to make Mum a handkerchief, to take home as a present for her. 'The best present you can give is one you have made yourself,' Mum had told me before I left for Sydney. 'I was about your age when my grandmother told me that.' Around Bondi, all I could buy were ready-made handkerchiefs. When I tried to explain what I wanted, shop assistants looked at me as if I was from another world – apparently not many girls my age made handkerchiefs for their mothers. I was too naive to know that I needed to start with a fabric shop selling fine linens or go to a department store in the city, so it seemed a handmade gift was not to be. Not only was I finding out that married people slept together; life beyond the boundaries of Towong Hill was overwhelmingly different.

By the end of the week I was feeling the magnetic pull of home, and I was happy to return. Feeling quite grown up, I flew to Albury where Dad met me. Back at Towong Hill I set to work, drawing in lead pencil the outline of a skier that I then inexpertly embroidered in plum-coloured thread on a pale blue linen handkerchief I had made from Mum's stock of material. I tried to hem it on the treadle sewing machine but, not knowing how to adjust the tension, the cotton knotted up. I was able to cut the handkerchief loose without damaging the material, but I couldn't unravel the cotton knotted around the spool. I was unaware of the trouble and time it later took Indi to sort out the mess I had made until Mum called me in to the front hall to speak to me. She told me I was not to use the sewing machine until I was older and knew how to do so properly. I knew that I would be in more trouble if I asked her how I was supposed to learn to use it properly if I wasn't to touch it. I didn't tell her I'd been trying to make her a present, as I'd wanted it to be a surprise.

I had forgotten all about the incident when I found the handkerchief in Mum's cupboard in the linen room after she died. I kept the handkerchief even though the memory of Mum's displeasure still hurt. The embroidery wasn't bad for a ten year old.

23

Visitors to Our World

There were some visitors of whom I have no recollection except the family talking about them. In the early 1950s Dad took an interest in helping a European family come to Australia. As I was a newborn baby at the time, it wasn't initially convenient to have them at our place so they stayed first with Aunt Honnor and Uncle Moreton at Blowering before coming on to Towong Hill. Much later Mum told me that after they had left, Aunt Honnor phoned and warned her that Dad might need to 'keep his trousers welded on'. I never discovered what had happened to provoke such a remark, but the vision of Dad being permanently stuck in his trousers struck a note of irreverent amusement.

Among the few other relations to visit during the 1950s and early 1960s were Mum's brother Edward Chauvel and his wife, Aunt Margaret. Mum said Edward was her dearest brother, and after Edward and Margaret spent part of their honeymoon with Mum at Towong Hill in 1944 they all became close friends. While out riding with them during that 1944 visit, Mum said she saw a Spectre of the Brocken – 'the shadows of figures standing on a clear summit, thrown on the mist by the level rays of the sun as it rises or sets'[1] – for the first and only time in her life. The moment was magic, she said: 'Projected on to the mist, circled in colour, were three shadowy horsemen ... the rainbow nimbus, the solar "Glory", transformed the image to something utterly strange.'[2] Uncle Edward and Aunt Margaret's engagement and wedding and the sighting of such a rare and thrilling natural phenomenon were the high points during the war for Mum, and she both talked and wrote about them.

For Edward and Margaret's visit in the summer holiday early in 1960 a treat – a day out in the mountains – was arranged. Dad and Mum loaded the family into Sirius, their old short-wheelbase Land Rover, and took us up to Dead Horse Gap. (By then the US army disposals jeep called Iris in which they had crossed the Alps was largely a farm vehicle.) Sirius was named after one of the ships in the First Fleet. Not aware of the historical association, Harry, then aged almost ten, mispronounced the name as Serious. In a sense he was quite right. It was a serious vehicle with a serious role in our lives, for it enabled us to extend the boundaries of our daily routine – up into the hills and further afield into the mountains as it carried our supplies and picnics. Sirius had a canvas canopy and in summer it was dusty if well ventilated, while in winter it was seriously draughty and shockingly cold.

Once Harry unlaced part of the canvas canopy as we climbed the hairpin bends on the Geehi Wall. We were lucky not to lose some of our supplies down the precipitous, bush-covered hillside towards the Devils Grip Gorge. Even Dad and Mum were serious about this episode. But they were less serious when they heard that Jack Hobbs, a distinguished former RAAF pilot who owned the local store in Corryong, had been changing a wheel on the Geehi Wall when he lost his grip and the wheel went leaping and bouncing down the steep hillside between the trees before it vanished, never to be seen again. It was just as well that Jack, who was very rotund, didn't bounce down the hillside in its wake. I never heard how he got home afterwards.

During Edward and Margaret's visit another outing – a bushwalk – was planned. It was one of the most organised walks in which I have ever taken part. Our expedition was top-heavy with Big Knobs, or grown-ups. Aunt Margaret was a keen, very competent Girl Guide leader (she later became Girl Guide Commissioner for New South Wales), and from Dad's perspective the war had ended only the day before and might well start again tomorrow, so we had to keep up with military-style drills where he was the officer commanding. He was keen on issuing orders and found it hard to understand that his enthusiasm was met with equal quantities of bemusement and reluctance. Providing us with maps and whistles, just in case we got lost over the ridge top, Dad drummed into us the danger of a sudden mist coming up and losing our way, despite the fact that there was not a cloud in the brilliant blue summer sky. He then divided us into groups with a parent leading each. Dead Horse Gap, Paddy Rush's Bogong, the Brindle Bull, the Ramsheads and Crackenback River were all known to us, not only from our reading and chats with Mum about *The Silver Brumby* but from our winter ski trips to Dead Horse Gap. It was easy for me to imagine Thowra galloping across that eerie, snow- and grass-covered landscape and vanishing into the weird, wind-shaped snow gums.

'Where is the Secret Valley?' I wanted to know. Mum just pointed in the general direction. Secret meant secret, even to close family.

'Can we go to the Cascades?' I pestered.

'It is too far. We'll go when you are older.'

Even though I was only six at the time, I was already fed up with adults using my age as an excuse for not doing things and going places. At the time I was disappointed not to see any other landmarks from *The Silver Brumby*. Above all, on that day trip with Uncle Edward and the family, I wanted to see a real, live brumby, but my legs were short and the white bread and strawberry jam I had indulged in for too long finally caught up with me. I huffed and puffed along behind everyone else, and I would never have made it to the Cascades.

Meanwhile, Mum had gone rather quiet and was bristling with irritation. She didn't like being organised, least of all by Dad and particularly in front of her beloved brother and sister-in-law. Dad's military-style orders appealed even less to Mum than they did to us children; as a general's daughter she had her own views about leadership. Despite his military training and highly disciplined life in the army and as a POW, Dad's style with lots of noise just didn't wash with her.

Mum's sense of humour came to the fore when the adults began exchanging Morse code messages. Judging by the gales of laughter following each 'message', Mum's input was mischievous and rather cleverly defused the over-serious atmosphere. Recognising the possible uses of Morse code in the bush, Dad had taught Mum all he could before he went to Malaya in 1941. Little did he know that his careful instruction might one day backfire on him, but he would have enjoyed the repartee nonetheless.

In the early 1960s Mum's sister, Eve Maberly, brought her family to stay at Towong Hill. Up until then she had been a shadowy figure of whom Mum and Granny often spoke fondly, but who was never around. Eve was nine years younger than Mum and their resemblance was striking. They both had high cheekbones, dark brown wavy hair and were a similar height. There were differences, too. After living in Kenya for a time, Eve's speech had become a little more clipped. Her face spread into an easier smile, she had a fuller, more comfortable-looking figure, she was chatty and she had a very mischievous laugh. The sisters were close to a point, but Eve had her own views. While she was always careful not to cause upset, she was strong and stood by her opinions.

During the Maberly visit I caught whooping cough. James, the eldest of Eve's boys, kept surprising me by putting frogs of every size, and the slimier the better, in my pocket or down the back of my neck to make me cough. Then I would thrill all the children by coughing till I was sick, so James kept the supply of frogs flowing thick and fast. It certainly didn't make me feel any worse, and I don't think I minded if I was sick or not – up and out it came on a cough and it was all over. Mum minded very much: she followed me with a spade to remove the vomit and got cross with James when she found him with more frogs in his hand.

Once an extraordinary woman with a deep, booming voice came to lunch at Towong Hill and said, 'I see you only have white bread on your table. Your children would be healthier if they ate brown bread.' Mum looked sheepish. We often ate the vegetables Mum had grown in the vegetable garden and, understandably, she thought our diet was healthy. She didn't really like bread, except for the crusts, which she baked in the oven and then ate instead of toast. Perhaps she hadn't noticed that I ate too much bread liberally spread with butter and strawberry jam. Mum did notice, however, that I was overweight for my age.

I had never tasted brown bread and thought it, along with a healthy diet, sounded scary and horrible. I can't remember Mum's reply to the woman with the booming voice and I don't think we had any brown bread afterwards. Until I was about ten, white bread and butter and strawberry jam was about the only thing I liked. I didn't like mutton chops or roasts with over-cooked vegetables, and sometimes I had to sit alone at the huge oak dining table until I ate or found some other solution for the increasingly unappetising meal in front of me. If they were around, the twin white cats were always willing to help with a little bit of meat.

One good thing about having a mother who was a writer was that she soon lost interest in supervising a reluctant eater. A rose bed had been recently dug over outside the dining room window and, providing the noisy dining room door was open and the flywire door didn't scrape and squeak, it was easy to bury some unwanted pieces of meat and vegetables with a knife and fork. The only risks were that someone might see and tell tales, or that Mum or Dad might spot a magpie or kookaburra in search of an easy meal digging up the evidence.

'All food is good food,' was Dad's maxim. 'You just don't know what it is like to starve. Our mouths watered when rats ran along the rafters. We ate everything – snakes, cats – anything we could get hold of in Changi, and it was good, too!'

'If all food is good food, Dad,' Harry said during breakfast one morning, 'you could eat my fried egg!' Harry was holding his plate of fried egg and bacon beside Dad's chair at the head of the table. By mistake he tipped the plate and the egg slithered onto Dad's lap. Dad was lost for words, and he bounded from the room. It might have been funny if Harry hadn't been in a bit of trouble once Dad had changed his trousers. We never heard how hot the egg was – Harry would have liked it to have been scorching and I didn't blame him!

24

Typical Upper Murray Fun

Fire danger prevented many a summer expedition into the bush. Dad and Mum dreaded the north-wind days – we all did. I remember Dad called it 'the fire wind, the wind that hits you in the face like licks of red-hot sandpaper'. He was quite right. When the north wind was blowing, he used to sit in his office, grim with anxiety, listening for the phone, or he would be in the wireless shack in case a message came over the bushfire radio. Occasionally he would tap the barometer in the front hall and then go outside to check for any change in the wind direction and strength.

Dad and Mum were acutely conscious that in 1939 they were overseas and not at home to fight the fires and help save the house. That year Granny M was either at Blowering or in Sydney, so Granny and Grandfather Chauvel, Eve, her friend Madeline Barrett and Roger Dunlop, a cousin who was staying with the family at the time, fought the fires for the Mitchells. Many years later, tucked in a book in the bookcase in my room at Towong Hill, I found Granny's pencil-written list of tasks to be carried out in the house by family and guests, and her letters written to Mum after the fires. From these I was able to piece together some of what had happened.

Mosquito nets and bedding were to be brought in from the verandahs. Buckets and bedroom jugs from the washstands were to be filled and placed in the corridors. Blankets were soaked so they could be used to cover people, and all windows were to be closed. Hoses were to be 'mustered' and put 'where required', and Granny underlined the need to soak the woodpile and all the surrounding sawdust. Eve recalled Roger's big feet being useful as he stamped out the small flames to prevent the fire spreading.

The fire started on Wednesday, 11 January near Walwa. A blaze was stopped at Tintaldra, but then on Friday the thirteenth it came across from Cudgewa. At about four in the afternoon the manager, Mr Herbert, received warning that the fire was coming, and it arrived about half an hour later. The men were watching for it. On 16 January, Granny Chauvel wrote to Mum: 'I, having never seen anything but grassfires in Queensland, I could hardly believe that fire could leap so quickly – everywhere.'

Despite all the anxiety, Granny was still able to comment afterwards on what the females of the family wore to fight the fire. 'Eve and Madeline were in jodhpurs – I wore the skirt of my coat and skirt!! It being the only woollen thing I had with me, & it is now at the cleaners!! – & they went under the taps and hoses at intervals to keep wet.' Granny gave credit to all the firefighters.

On 25 January, Eve wrote a very spirited account of the fire in a letter to Mum: 'I'm still alive, my eyebrows are beginning to grow again.' Apparently Granny made Eve and Roger Dunlop tie wet towels around their heads! On a more serious note Eve wrote, 'It is amazing how quickly the sparks caught just below the horse paddock and spread up the hill like a huge wave. In a couple of minutes it was right up to the fence in the lower garden.' Later Eve reverted to a more humorous description, this time of her parents at dinner late that evening: 'You've never seen such a sight as Mummy was, she looked just like an Arab woman, and Dad had a pathway of black right down his face from his eyes. We looked rather like the bushman's tea party at Buckingham Palace.' Eve concluded, 'If it had to happen I'm glad I was there. Everyone says in amazement, "Were you really there all the time or did you sit in the river?" ' Of course Eve was there all the time, as indeed Mum and Dad would have been if they weren't overseas.

Mum often said 1939 was the year when their luck ran out. On Black Friday, 13 January 1939, while the fires were blazing through the Upper Murray, Mum was in bed with a badly broken leg on the other side of the world in St Anton, Austria. She and Dad had been away from Australia for almost fourteen months. As a result of a separate skiing accident in early January 1939, Dad had dislocated his left shoulder. War was declared on 3 September of that year. For Mum, I think the fires heralded a roller-coaster of challenges and changes that were unleashed in their hitherto extraordinarily interesting and carefree lives. Even a kind letter from Granny written on 18 January 1939 telling Mum 'there is practically no loss of stock on Towong Hill' could not really lessen her distress.

The 1939 fires burned extensive swathes of pasture and fencing, and some of the stable buildings containing buggies, harnesses, other horsedrawn vehicles and implements. The family was very lucky not to lose the house, the cottages that were home to families working at Towong Hill and the outbuildings. Granny's letter enclosed a cutting from the *Border Morning Mail* telling of the plight of Corryong and how, late on the night of Black Friday, 'two fires were burning, one sweeping over Mount Elliott on the eastern side and menacing about two dozen settlers in the Thougla Valley, and another advancing on Corryong itself from the Cudgewa end'. The article mentioned the less fortunate landowners whose houses had been destroyed, people Dad and Mum would have known.

When the fires of 1952 came, memories of the 1939 fires were reignited. Mum said that the summer of late 1951 and early 1952 were particularly ghastly. In an unpublished article she wrote, 'Summer after summer fires become a greater menace, probably owing to the constant increase in superphosphating.'[1] Presumably the fire danger was a result of better pasture as well as the hot, dry weather. In the summer of 1952 there was a lot of dry grass and a fierce north wind sprang up each day. Fearing the worst and in keeping with the recommendations of the Royal Commission after the 1939 fires, Mum and Dad prepared a dugout on the bank beneath the south-facing terrace in the garden in case the 'red steer' came.

One summer, as I was lost in my thoughts while raking up dry leaves in the lower garden, Mum came out to move the hose she had running on the strawberry patch. For a moment she stood watching me, also deep in thought. Then she said slowly, 'I raked leaves in the height of anxiety during the '52 fires. I was pregnant and lost the baby. He or she would have been born in October '52.'

Later I told Dad what Mum said and he described the situation during the fires. 'Your mother spent days raking up dry leaves while I ensured the fire engines were in working order and the fire beaters were kept soaked,' he explained. 'Seeing you raking all those leaves into piles might have reminded her of '52, and we were pretty tired after it was all over.' Dad said Mum lost the baby in April, but perhaps she simply hadn't recovered from the stress and anxiety of the preceding summer.

'It was tough,' Dad went on. We thought we might lose the place. We kept the Union Jack flying at half-mast on the tank stand not just because King George VI had just died, but to show which way the wind was blowing. At night as it grew dark, we could see fire stretching from north to west. We prowled around, checking for fires coming closer, making tea and then prowling again. Eventually at about four a.m. the wind changed to a bitterly cold southerly.'

In her unpublished article Mum also described it: 'For seventeen days we were ringed around with fires that leapt closer and closer as the mad wind blew, in spite of every man in the district being out fighting them. On 25 January Tintaldra Station was burnt out.' In a note dated 28 January Mum wrote: 'Tintaldra: "Deserts of all eternity" the bare, black ridges, the bare black right down to the river flats. Bits of fire burning everywhere. WIND.' Both Mum and Dad would have felt the Mackinnons' loss acutely; Ronnie and Jenny had been married the previous November near Holbrook. 'I think that nearly everyone who was present at that wedding lost almost everything – stock, fences, grass, and many of them their houses,' Mum told me.

In the davenport Mum bequeathed me she'd kept copies of her letters to Granny describing the strong wind, dust and lack of visibility. Mum wrote that 'it was almost pitch dark outside, dark with a sort of ruddy glow, and the sun just a nasty red ball, fierce looking, and smoke about all morning, the sky was burnished red'. Later in the same letter she remarked, 'If we hadn't been so worried it would have been rather wonderful.'[2] In a letter dated 2 February, Mum wrote: 'I can't really figure out what stopped the fire. Mr Knight says we were saved by a wind change.' Changing wind direction and good fortune also saved Aunt Hon and Uncle Moreton at Blowering Station.

'I felt very guilty that we survived the fires when others didn't,' Mum said years later. 'When we were in danger, friends who had lost so much were sympathising and offering to have Indi and Harry to stay in safety. Jenny and Ronnie Mackinnon, who just a couple of days beforehand had experienced such heavy losses at Tintaldra, were among the first to offer help.'

Stories grew from the 1952 fires. Dad missed one cabinet meeting; at the time he was attorney-general in the Victorian government. When the King died on 7 February, Dad had to travel the next day to Melbourne to swear allegiance to the new sovereign, Queen Elizabeth II. It was a difficult journey. Telephone lines were down, bridges had been burned, and Mum needed Dad's old truck in case she had to drive the family to safety. In any event, Mum gave him a 'bushfire haircut' and he set off for Melbourne, leaving Mum trying to contact the premier by phone. Eventually the telephone exchange operator got an emergency line through to Parliament House and the premier arranged to have Dad picked up at Wangaratta by the police and driven with sirens blaring to Melbourne. He scarcely had time to wash off the ash before swearing allegiance and getting straight back into the police car to be returned, at speed, to Wangaratta and the 'waiting ring of bushfires'.

For the next twenty-five years, Dad strove to ensure that he played his part in fire prevention and protection at Towong Hill. He liked to think it was one of the best-protected properties in the district, and for a while it seemed that money was no object if it meant improving fire safety. Each spring the men who worked on Towong Hill ploughed firebreaks on the north side of the house. Dad insisted on regular drills to ensure that the fire engines remained in working order and he had one of the best available bushfire radios. Mum always noted the date and location of any fires in the district as if she was keeping watch over the whereabouts of an evil spirit.

During the summer months, Dad regularly checked the radios, fire engines and the water level in the tank. The bushfire wireless 'scheds', as he called the scheduled practices, were most important, and he caught up with some district news at the same time. There was usually some humour along with the seriousness, like when Bill Lloyd rescued his bushfire wireless aerial from a horse that was trying to chew on the new and unusual tree! Bill announced that he'd solved the problem and was back on the air, 'straight from the horse's mouth'!

One north-wind day, Harry broke the silence in the sitting room like a thunderbolt when he shouted, 'The lavatory won't flush. There's just filthy water.' Mum had returned to her desk in the front hall just moments before and was on her feet before he had a chance to utter another word. Her manuscript and notebooks flew to the floor as she left the room. 'It's either the septic tank or the pump. And if it is not those it's the electric light engine,' she shouted as she rushed out of the house. It usually fell to Mum to detail stockmen or the local plumber to do the repair work. She might have added something about the Aga stove sometimes going out too! Somehow it always seemed that problems developed on weekends, and that it was a public holiday when fire danger was at its height.

Mum had inherited a difficult domestic legacy and she always remarked, rather dramatically, that if her heart should be opened when she died, 'the words septic tank, pump and electric light engine would be found engraved upon it'. At the time I was particularly interested in British history, and I didn't think that smelly things like the septic tank or rowdy engines were anything near as romantic as having the word 'Calais' engraved on your heart, as Mary I of England had claimed.

When the house at Towong Hill was built at the turn of the twentieth century, Granddaddy M said he was tired of 'camping' on a permanent basis. So Towong Hill was one of the first houses in the district to have 'water laid on'. The problem was that the plumbing had not been replaced since then, and roots from nearby trees were beginning to break and block some of the pipes. The pump had already become a topic of conversation in the family well before the war. In January 1937 Mum's aunt Lily Chauvel wrote saying, 'I hope all is well with the pumping engine now and it will remain "Okey" as the Americans say.'[3] Among Mum's papers after she died I found an envelope labelled 'Pumping Engine Business!'; given what had happened in earlier years, the envelope was strangely empty. Mum might have thrown it all out, trying to evict the problems that had plagued her for so long.

The water pump was a Southern Cross engine housed in a red galvanised-iron shed beside the pumping lagoon at the foot of the hill below the house. By the time of my first memories, station hand Billy was one of the few cheerful oracles who seemed to understand it. He proclaimed that 'those Southern Cross engines might break down for a while when you don't want them to, but they don't break'. His repair work frequently involved what he called 'a wee bit of bush mechanics and a bit o' good luck'. On a hot summer's day, this meant tinkering and swearing at it, mopping the sweat from his brow and yarning while he did so. After a while, the engine would usually, miraculously, chug into action again. If it didn't, he would try a 'bit o' brutal force'! 'Them screws and nails rattle loose down there,' he explained on one occasion before beating them down with a hammer. 'That there engine slips a bit and that'd be our problem today.' During the war Billy had been invalided home from the 9th Division in North Africa, suffering from shell shock and respiratory problems. I don't think he resorted to brutal force as often as we thought, as he didn't like much noise.

The electric light engine was housed in a single-roomed brick structure on the other side of the backyard. It sat like an angry, filthy monster in the middle of an oil-slicked floor. Around the walls were rows of car batteries. Like all monsters it had a mind of its own, and it always looked as if it was about to spray oil, fanbelts and other loose, greasy missiles at anyone who came near. Electricity was important, but not absolutely essential – except for the fact that our electric light engine also powered at least one of the fire engines. We kept an ample collection of candles and hurricane lanterns on hand to cope with those occasions when the electric light engine refused to co-operate for any length of time. Dad painted a white line to represent a tennis net on the outside brick wall of the electric light house, and while the engine was chugging away generating power inside, one member of the family or other could belt a tennis ball against the wall for practice ... and sometimes to vent frustrations!

Not long after we had mains electricity connected, we returned from Tintaldra to Towong Hill during a power cut to find Euan Littlejohn, Dr Littlejohn's grandson, sitting in the darkness in the kitchen awaiting our arrival. He seemed very relieved when Mum found torches and lit candles; Towong Hill was too spooky to be sitting there alone without light.

The stories associated with repairing and maintaining the electric light engine, pump and septic tank were almost as colourful as the characters involved in the work. Dad once lost a pair of glasses when digging up the septic tank; some years later they reappeared when the tank once again needed attention. He irritated Mum by washing them off under a tap and putting them on before she could disinfect them. In all probability they were found well away from any offensive substances, but Dad seldom missed a chance to tease.

It all came under Granny Chauvel's description of typical Upper Murray fun. Mum was frequently upset that she was the general dogsbody who had to cope while Dad pursued his political and other interests, which from her perspective always seemed to be given precedence over her work. Mum had her moments of extreme and frustrated feminism! She was not, however, a complete convert to the feminist cause. Burning bras, she remarked tersely in later years, was an urban luxury. Most country women needed them for comfort, particularly if they were doing hard physical work. Mum knew as well as anyone that the country–city divide in Australian society also found its expression in feminism. But whether you wore a bra or not didn't have any bearing on who did which jobs. Like many women, Mum wouldn't have objected to some liberation, not necessarily

Typical Upper Murray Fun

from jobs seen as traditionally female but from the treadmill of more and more chores with less and less help. That was the unacknowledged grindstone.

Typical Upper Murray fun was not confined to incidents at Towong Hill. One afternoon in the hot summer of 1957 the Mackinnons invited us to Tintaldra for a family swimming party by the river, to be followed by afternoon tea. Mum was changing me into my bathing suit when either Dad or Ronnie Mackinnon saw a column of smoke swelling up from near the homestead. Irrespective of how much or how little clothing we were wearing, Ronnie, Jenny, Dad and Mum bundled us all into the Land Rovers and departed for the scene of the fire. The older generation grabbed fire beaters and filled knapsack sprays from hoses and a tap at the tank stand. Meanwhile, we children were left in varying degrees of undress – in my case, distressing near-nakedness – with 'Aunt' Sophie, Ronnie Mackinnon's kind but terrifyingly elegant French mother. Later, once the fire had been put out and the children dressed and given tea, we heard that it was the kerosene refrigerator in the workmen's caravan that had started the fire. At the time Dad and Mum had two kerosene refrigerators in the homestead, and I don't think they ever felt the same about them again. Some of the then-modern appliances introduced new hazards and potential dangers into the postwar world.

Bushfires always strike at bad moments, and some are worse than others. In February 1966, Dad and Mum had just finished cleaning up the house prior to having Sir Rohan and Lady Delacombe stay on a private visit when a fire broke out. The slasher had hit a rock, setting off a cloud of sparks that caught fire in the dry grass, so instead of attending to the final preparations for their guests, they went out fire fighting. Dad sent Indi to intercept the Delacombes at Colac Colac with his apologies for what they were about to find. The newly cleaned windows were dirty and the house was covered in a thin film of ash by the time the Delacombes arrived. I was at boarding school at the time, but Dad wrote to me describing what a wonderful job everyone had done in fighting the fire. Indi, who had left school by then, was singled out for particular praise, and Dad and Mum were very glad to have her able hands at their sides.

If fires produced good stories, snakes produced even more. 'The snakes we saw in the old days were as thick as a man's wrist, bigger than the ones you find now,' Dad often remarked. If you listened to Dad, most of the things he described were bigger and better in the old days! Mum had her stories too, sometimes writing to tell us about her adventures while we were at boarding school. In March 1968 she wrote:

Yesterday I was hastily eating an early lunch and dressed for going to the aerodrome to meet Dad when Mrs G [our cook] came running in, breathless, and gasped out, 'Quick you take your gun, there's a snake under the dunny seat.' I got the gun and went out, laughing before I got there. There was old Tom [G] with a shovel. Couldn't see the snake. He prised up the seat a little with the shovel and after a while a snake's head came up through the right side of the hole! Couldn't shoot without breaking the bowl. Tom and I were almost collapsing with laughter. Mrs G was hopping about in the background gasping, 'Fancy having the [snake] nearly bite you on the bottom, just fancy!' Then the snake wriggled round the rim of the bowl to the other side. I could just see a small arc of scales, but could not get a hit at it. The whole place was running water from the buckets of hot water they had tried to throw on said snake already. I asked for another bucket of boiling water then I put the gun down carefully, loaded both barrels, and feeling that I had a pair of jolly long bare legs, I went in and hurled the water sideways at the snake which came down wop on to the floor. I grabbed the gun and shot. When the splashes and flying bits and pieces had subsided, I saw the snake minus most of its middle still coming towards me, so I shot again and just about took half of it off. Then I grabbed the shovel to pull it out from under the door. As I pulled, the remaining front half, spitting tacks at me, came straight for me. I pinned it to the dunny floor with the shovel and sent Tom for something to hit it with. I just wish someone had had a camera because it really must have looked funny, with the front half of that snake biting everything but me! And the old fashioned dunny as background. Tom produced a mallet and donged it. Typical Upper Murray fun.

It was not the only time someone was lucky not to have been bitten. Once I heard Mum shouting for a broom, and when I found her, a tiger snake was ready and poised to strike the dog. I grabbed the dog with one hand and passed Mum the broom with the other. She took a swipe and slightly damaged the snake's back. 'Here,' she said, passing me the broomstick, 'you finish it off!' With my left hand I held the dog that was struggling to get at the snake, while with my right I aimed at the snake's head with the broomstick. As I swung the broomstick back, the head of the broom went sailing off down the hill! I was left with just the stick to deal with what was by then an extremely angry snake. Eventually I disabled it and, twirling it on the broomstick like a reluctant and struggling bit of bloody spaghetti, flung it down the hill before there was any chance of it slithering off and putting anyone's life at risk.

'You've done a good day's work,' Mum remarked as I returned to her. 'Charlie Bingham, the old stud groom, used to say that if you killed a snake, you'd done a good day's work!'

Mum was right. Over the years we damaged numerous garden implements in tussles with snakes. Often we thought it was a 'them' or 'us' situation, and we weren't about to lay down our lives to snakes. Once Mum offered a recently dead snake to the kookaburras that she fed. Apparently they sat up a tree chuckling grumpily among themselves, as if they were insulted, then they gave the dead snake a further beating against the branch of a tree before they ate some of it. She never gave them dead snake again in case she offended their dignity.

Once when Mum was staying with Mark and me in Germany we received a call from Dad to say he had lost his false teeth and he wondered if Mum might be able to cast some light on where he could find them. Despite seeming a tall order some 20,000 kilometres and half a world away, it was a case of reality being somewhat better than fiction. At the time, Dad and Mum had a young pet magpie that lived in the garden and had become so tame that it took food from their hands. One morning, when Dad had fed the fledgling and then gone to the upstairs bathroom to shave and clean his teeth, he saw some currawongs mobbing the young magpie and stealing its breakfast. So he picked up the nearest thing to hand, an enamel mug containing his false teeth, and hurled it out of the window at the currawongs. When he went to retrieve the mug and its contents, he found his false teeth were missing. Mum suggested he might start by looking beneath the pine trees by the tennis court and in a number of other places frequented by their young feathered friend, but he never found his teeth.

Typical Upper Murray fun, with all its eccentricities and surprises, was sure to bring smiles almost right round the family. We all enjoyed reminiscing about it. Even when the fun was over, as indeed it must have been when the false teeth were replaced and paid for, Dad and Mum hugely enjoyed adding such stories to their already rich repertoire. Both of them were tough and eccentric, sometimes to extremes, and there were many more stories told than were ever written down.

Mum was often at her best when recounting an incident from the past, whether recent or not. Most of her tales ended with a roar of raucous delight, rather like a kookaburra singing up the sun at dawn. From the time he was about five years old, Alec Mackinnon could provoke further laughter among the younger generations with his extraordinarily good imitation of 'Mrs Mitchell laughing'. When Mum's face had become bronzed and lined with the years, she looked like a wizened walnut and sounded like a kookaburra!

The art of typical Upper Murray fun was to make light of some of the most anxious moments. In the event of fire, there was always an element of gratitude when nobody was hurt or property damaged. If anything continued to unite Dad and Mum, it was their courage in adversity and their shared wacky sense of humour.

25
Early Skiing

My introduction to the significance the snow held for my parents came from a series of framed black-and-white photographs hanging in the downstairs corridor at Towong Hill, depicting snowy landscapes and the Victorian and Australian ski teams. The people in the team photographs looked weird to me, as if they came from a land of make-believe where people wore strange dark clothes and did even stranger things in haunted landscapes. If someone had told me that those people in dark, flapping garments were imitating the devil, I think I would have believed them!

I had no idea that these photographs celebrated some of the pinnacles in Dad's prewar skiing career, nor that Mum had won some important ski races too, notably the Canadian Downhill in 1938. In 1937 she was selected for the Victorian and Australian ski teams. The corridor photographs depicted Dad in the Victorian ski teams in 1931, 1932, 1935 and 1937 – in fact, he had been a member of the Victorian team six times and had an impressive national and international ski racing record. He was five times Australian national slalom champion and four times national combined downhill and slalom champion. He was also the New Zealand champion four times.

Early Skiing

Except for a black-and-white photograph of both Mum and Dad taken outside the Chateau Tongariro in New Zealand, I can't remember there being framed pictures of Mum skiing or of her with other members of women's ski teams hanging in the corridor. Had I known that my initiation into that world was just around the corner, or what it entailed, I probably would have felt overwhelmed – those who claimed the Mitchell children virtually came into the world on skis were wrong where I was concerned.

Once I was old enough to ask questions and understand the stories behind the pictures, they began to represent a new and romantic world to a child who knew little beyond the familiar environments of Towong Hill, the Murray Valley and 49 Murphy Street in South Yarra. The photographs were part of Dad's memorabilia from 'the old days', as he used to refer to that golden era before the war and the arrival of children. Later I discovered that the photographs were part of a much larger collection taken in the 1930s in Australia, North and South America and Austria, and that both Mum and Dad were not only wonderful skiers but good photographers.

For my introduction to snow, Dad and Mum put me in a wicker pram on skis. While I cannot recall anything of the moment myself, it was spoken of in family circles and beyond; there is also photographic evidence showing me wrapped up against the elements and looking like a mummified and glum gnome in the pram, though in the picture there isn't much snow around.

'You were so lucky to have such an innovative father and to be take so young to the snow,' visitors to Towong Hill used to remark. I would squirm with embarrassment at being singled out for such eccentric attention from my father. While Dad was proud of the fact that twenty years earlier he had won a national slalom event on the skis on which the pram was mounted, I wished they had never been part of such a bizarre contraption as the pram.

I probably screamed, yelled and was a complete pain until Mum removed me from it and restored me to more familiar and comfortable surroundings. Later, in 1958, Mum told Elva Breen at the *Herald* in Melbourne about that escapade: 'It sounded all right in theory but in practice – "NO," said Mrs Mitchell. "The skis drifted apart and the pram – and the baby – went flying. Never again!"'[1] Dad might have told the story differently! My guess is that my parents must have photographed me before I began to yell.

In my mind I have an image of the contraption being unable to support the combination of my weight and the pram's, and the skis drawing futher and further apart! It must have been draughty, too. Dad wasn't easily going to admit defeat but I don't think that the same experience was inflicted on John – a tacit acknowledgement of the experiment's lack of success. The pram now holds a doll in the Man from Snowy River Museum in Corryong.

Just how the pram, family and ski kit were transported to a distant plateau called the Six Mile, I don't know. As the entire load would seem to have been too much for one vehicle, Mum and Dad probably took the Land Rover and enlisted Pat Knight to drive another car up to the snowline and there help with getting the family onto skis. Nobody seemed to know exactly what the Six Mile was named for; 'Aunt' Emily Scammell, who cooked at Towong Hill for Mum during the war, ventured that it was because it was six miles from anywhere! In fact it is about thirty-six miles from Corryong; the Upper Murray Ski Club had a hut there from which, Dad said, members enjoyed skiing the logging trails on the peak behind.

The pram on skis was a typical Dad invention; he was a lateral thinker and keen inventor with huge energy. He had already improvised an electric eggbeater by attaching two beaters to an electric drill, not realising that a drill would spin the beaters at too great a speed to work; family history does not relate the no doubt messy outcome. Dad was renowned in family circles for his crazy schemes, and they were greeted with ever-increasing scepticism as we grew up, though perhaps we didn't give him due credit for his successes, such as a clothes hoist suspended from the ceiling in the boiler room. Undoubtedly there were others too.

While it was a relief to be able to graduate from the humiliation of the pram to a pair of skis, I soon discovered that for me the eccentric school of hard knocks was only just beginning. The skis were wooden and dated from a Mitchell family trip to Klosters in Switzerland for Christmas 1913, just before the outbreak of the First World War. They had no metal edges and even back in the 1950s they would have made an acceptable artefact for a museum of ski history. But they weren't in a museum as Dad had thoughtfully kept them for his children to learn to ski on. At one time Granddaddy M made his own skis so that he could round up cattle when the snow had come early in the mountains. If Granny M had had any say in the matter, the wooden skis he bought for Dad in Switzerland were probably the best available at the time.

For Dad the skis evoked happy memories of his father who died when he was only eleven years old. For me they became a symbol of challenge and torture. 'It is best to learn on skis without edges because you learn to use whatever edge you have,' he proclaimed, considering himself quite an authority on the subject. 'It is character-building to have to work at it!' He never admitted that we might have been justified in feeling irritated because he was teaching us the hard way, but he always said, 'You've got to work hard for your fun.'

In 1913, on that Klosters trip, Dad's father had said, 'Go on, you little devil – ski!' And that is exactly what Dad ultimately did. Being a rather stocky and determined athlete, he never understood that others didn't necessarily find the sport as easy to master as he did. It was 1927 before Dad skied again during a university vacation from Cambridge where he had met the skier and artist Colin Wyatt and the explorer John Rymill from South Australia. These two men helped to sow the seeds of adventure and exploration for Dad.

Apart from Granny M, our Chauvel grandparents and Mum's brothers who were serving abroad, the only member of the family to escape skiing was Eve. Even she did not escape entirely, having had one day with Mum in September 1944 near Mt Jagungal. Afterwards she was so badly sunburnt that she probably worked out evasive tactics to ensure she never went again, but she also never forgot her one and only day in the snow. Unintentionally Mum may have made matters worse in her attempt to relieve Eve's discomfort by plastering Eve's face with cream from the top of the milk jug. They might have kept the extent of Eve's sunburn quiet in case Granny and Grandfather were annoyed with Mum for spoiling her younger sister's complexion.

In the 1950s it was difficult and expensive to buy children's ski clothes so ours were homemade from gabardine. They were problematic because as soon as we fell, which we did constantly on skis with no edges, we got wet and cold. At least I did. It was almost as if Dad was taking some sort of perverse delight in making things as hard as possible, particularly when we soon discovered that there were more modern skis with metal edges.

Dad ironed ski wax onto our skis with an old-fashioned iron he kept hot on the stove in his workshop. The smell of hot wax filled the workshop in winter and Dad entertained us with tales of his skiing adventures in the old days as we prepared for a ski trip. Dad had taught Mum to ski in his school of hard knocks, and he applied a similar approach to his children. In the 1950s when we started, there were no luxuries like ski lifts, at least not at the places Mum and Dad took us skiing. It took ages to climb a slope and then, if I didn't fall, it took a matter of seconds to ski down before the process began all over again. There was no slacking off and no let up.

'Your Aunt Hon could have really gone places,' said Dad, speaking as a former champion and all-action man. 'But she was lazy.' Dad and Aunt Hon had skied together during the European winter of 1933 until Aunt Hon broke her leg. While she never said as much, perhaps this was the excuse she needed to phase skiing out of her life. In any case she had already met her future husband, Uncle Moreton, and her priorities were changing. Apparently Dad didn't understand; at the time skiing was everything for him. Presumably winning the Ski Club of Australia championship and being runner-up Victorian champion in 1932, running the pastoral enterprise at Blowering Station during the war and subsequently creating a beautiful home were not really 'going places' for Dad. Perhaps he also forgot that she had played a role in founding the Australian Women's Ski Club. Dad was very ambitious for his sister as well as for himself and his family. I thought Aunt Hon had done her bit and could retire gracefully if she wished, but I didn't dare say so. If Dad's obsession for ski racing in the 1930s was fuelled by not feeling sufficiently settled at Towong Hill, or indeed back in Australia, he never admitted it.

'What you need is some *fest Trainieren* [Dad's German-style expression for hard training] to get you into good condition,' Dad told me.

By the end of each day's skiing, I was exhausted and couldn't really understand what Mum and Dad got so excited about. I can't speak for other members of the family; some of them might have been stronger and more resilient and determined than I was. Indi seemed to enjoy it most, but I think Harry felt the cold like I did. On occasion, John struck it lucky and Mum got him up onto her back, skis and all. Perhaps I have forgotten that I too at some stage may have been as lucky. Fortunately, I didn't hate it. Even if

I had, neither Dad nor Mum would have understood the reasons and there would have been sparks, possibly spanks and scenes.

I can't remember which year it was when those old skis of Dad's were first clamped to my feet. It snowed at Towong Hill in the winter of 1949 four years before I was born and again in 1956. I was only three in 1956 and all I remember of that winter is the green Hudson car being towed by a tractor through mud up the drive to the house. If Mum and Dad took me skiing in 1954 in the pram, I don't remember. Mum's rather grainy black-and-white photographs from 1949 show thick flakes falling, erasing the details of the garden with a white blanket, the branches of the trees bent down by the weight of the snow. Dad and Mum loaded skis into the jeep and went skiing on the ridge behind the house. In the masses of photographs they took to record the event they wore the off-white gabardine parkas and baggy dark-coloured ski pants that the members of the Victorian and Australian teams wore in the photographs in the corridor at Towong Hill.

I used to have a colour photograph of Harry and me dressed in dull red gabardine ski trousers and jackets at Dead Horse Gap. In it I could just make out the banks of the Alpine Way in the snow; there is blue sky above and beneath the road is the tree-lined Crackenback River. Harry was sitting in the snow and I was standing beside a white wooden sign saying 'Kosciusko 5m'. Mum or Dad took this photograph sometime in 1958 or 1959. In the heavy snow year of 1960 we started skiing at Thredbo as a family. It must have been after such a day spent skiing at Dead Horse Gap that Mum began saying, 'I knew that, once again, skis were going to be the keys of the kingdom.'

As the local member of parliament for the state electorate of Benambra, Dad was one of the prime movers for the foundation of a ski resort at Falls Creek, and he wanted to carry his entire family along in his unbounded enthusiasm. Dad's vision was to create 'the winter playground of the Pacific'.[2] The trip to Falls

Early Skiing

Creek I remember best took place in August 1963, the occasion of a vice-regal visit by Sir Rohan Delacombe, as he enjoyed skiing and had been invited to present prizes at the Victorian championships. Sir Rohan and Lady Delacombe were Mum and Dad's personal friends so, instead of arranging for Granny to come and look after John and me at home, they decided to take us along as a special treat.

The presentation was soon to begin, but there was one problem: Mum had forgotten to take suspenders for her stockings. Rather than seeking assistance from the local ladies in Mt Beauty where we were staying, the ever-resourceful Mum ensured her stockings stayed up by twisting threepenny pieces into the top of her stockings and then adding elastic bands for extra security. She practised her curtsy to ensure she could do it without the vital coins flying out from under her skirt and releasing her stockings into unsightly concertinas at her ankles – it was a wonder she didn't get pins and needles and turn her legs white through lack of circulation. Relieved that the coins did their bit, she never admitted to discomfort and relished telling the story later.

Mum and Dad enjoyed skiing with Sir Rohan and their old friend Willie Littlejohn, the governor's aide de camp and the son of Dr Euan Littlejohn. Because I was rather stout, I was the butt of Willie's mischievous remarks about rotund little girls having trouble bending down over their big tummies to lace up their boots and put on their skis!

Shy and anxious to avoid the political limelight, Mum preferred to ski in New South Wales, so I never returned to Falls Creek. The opening of the Alpine Way in 1955, followed a couple of years later by the establishment of a fledgling resort at Thredbo, gave her an excuse to go there; Thredbo was closer to Towong Hill than Falls Creek. Skiing became the keys to rather different kingdoms for Dad and Mum. Dad came to Thredbo almost only in school holidays. In 1958 he crushed his leg in a sawmilling accident and he was becoming too lame to ski very much. While he was always keen to know how we were getting on and eagerly awaited the junior race results, his role began to fade and family skiing gradually became Mum's domain. Thredbo, thrillingly situated in the Crackenback Valley, was near the heartland of the Silver Brumby stories. Although we seldom saw brumbies in those days, there was always the chance that we might spot one hiding in the scrub on Paddy Rush's Bogong or Brindle Bull. It was Thredbo and the surrounding area that captured my heart at that time rather than the Victorian Alps.

26

Skiing Is Serious

Only later in life did I realise that for Mum, beginning to ski again after having children was not easy. In a short piece of prose called 'Beginning Again' in *A Vision of the Snowy Mountains*, she describes watching the skiers through the plate-glass window of the Round House at Thredbo in the winter of 1960, realising 'that a whole new technique had been developed, as well as different skis and new boots and bindings. All those skiers looked as though they were in a graceful ballet. Legs were together, the Arlberg crouch was no longer to be seen'.[1]

Mum must have missed skiing and the camaraderie of other skiers who went to the Chalet at Charlotte Pass during the heavy snow year of 1953, the winter I was born. There was another bumper snow year in 1956. Although Mum and Dad skied when they could, Mum missed out on almost fifteen years, from the end of the war until 1960. Ski racing and overseas travel had passed her by and new champions were winning state and national titles. She missed being asked for advice about the building and development of alpine villages and ski lifts. Fashion, too, had passed her by almost completely, although she caught up quickly when she bought her first elegant, close-fitting sky-blue ski pants.

In her matching Norwegian-style pale blue sweater with its design of white snowflakes across the shoulders and the tops of her arms she looked just fabulous.

For their twenty-fifth wedding anniversary in 1960, when I was seven, Mum and Dad gave each other metal skis, the latest and best available. Even though Dad was starting to feel the effects of the sawmilling accident more severely (though he wouldn't admit it), they wanted to make a new and positive beginning for the rest of their lives. They hoped that skiing would play a bigger role than in recent years when the family was very young.

The new skis were heavy. I tried to carry a pair from the Land Rover parked in the backyard at Towong Hill about fifty metres to the ski room in the outhouse. I just about made it to the ski room door, half-collapsing with them onto the edge of the concrete verandah. 'Just put them down before you drop them!' Mum's piercingly anxious voice rang across the courtyard. From wanting to help, suddenly I wished I hadn't touched them.

Mostly, though, we were indeed lucky kids. More imported modern skis followed in 1963 for us. Blizzard skis were among our first, and then one of us – Indi, I think – was given Kneissl White Stars, with long thong bindings, which at that time were regarded as the best you could get.

In the wake of the Second World War and the increasingly prosperous years of the early 1960s, skiing surged in popularity as a winter sport. It didn't seem to occur to either of my parents, and Mum particularly, that for many people skiing was a luxury leisure activity. For Mum and Dad skiing was a necessity. Mum often said she enjoyed seeing perfectly trained physical action, and for her skiing embodied this: she loved speed on long downhill slopes and impressive technique equally. She saw the mountains as mysterious and little-charted lands and said that when you were in them, the squiggly lines on maps began to represent real geographic features. If you explored them you would learn something about their mystery and individuality and, more importantly, something about yourself. When Mum and Dad first married there were unmapped and hitherto unvisited places in the mountains above Towong Hill. They carried compasses and altimeters, took bearings and recorded the height of the peaks they climbed and how long it took them to do so. They took masses of photographs that they developed and printed in their dark room at Towong Hill. Then they wrote about their expeditions for *The Australian and New Zealand Ski Year Book* and other publications. They explored the mountains both in summer and winter, and little by little they explained what Mum described as the 'mysteries of those skylines [that] began to hold memories of splendid days'.

'The very effort of coping with rough weather gives me strength,' Mum said. During the winters in the early 1960s, Mum took John and me skiing about three days a week. Indi and Harry were at boarding school at the time and must have felt that they were missing out, which indeed they were. We had some fabulous skiing. John was not always keen and sometimes stayed at home with Mrs Knight. He was thin and felt the cold. Being rather tubbier and better insulated, I mostly enjoyed it, although skiing in all weather conditions, as Mum insisted on doing, was hard. 'Skiing is always at its best in big storms when the wind howls and the snow blasts down,' she used to say.[2] She liked the challenge. Being in a blizzard was like being in another world.

I didn't agree, but it was best not to say so; in blizzards I longed for warm, dry clothes. Mum didn't seem to feel the cold – she wore the best quality clothing available and ensured we did too, it was just that I could have worn twice the number of layers. If I didn't want to ski due to bad weather, Mum said I was being difficult. Her philosophy was that if you didn't always enjoy it, you would learn to do so, as indeed she had done. Meanwhile, I was discovering my own likes and dislikes and learning how to cope with them.

For Mum, nothing could compete with skiing. It was a tough obsession and a form of escapism that I have never witnessed to the same degree in anyone else, except perhaps Mum's wartime skiing companion Jill MacDonald. Jill, too, was a free spirit with a lively and sometimes scarily acerbic wit. Mum and Jill enjoyed both skiing and the mountains together. They made few or no demands on one another and remained lifelong friends, though as Jill had no children she had fewer responsibilities than Mum.

As well as skiing two or three days a week throughout the winter, we also skied for almost the entire winter school holidays, which then fell during the last couple of weeks of August and early September. Each year, Mum booked three bunk rooms in Leo's Lodge at Thredbo. Harry shared a bunk room with Dad; Harry slept in the top bunk and Dad in the bottom with his books and parliamentary papers on the bedside table. Their dark room looked onto the hillside, the cheap wooden panelling on the walls turning a yellow colour when the low-wattage light bulb was switched on. Dad and Harry didn't open the window enough, so it was often airless and smelled a bit mouldy and damp. Indi and I shared another room, and sometimes Jenny Burnside joined us for a week. Mum and John always had the room with the view over the valley to the chairlifts and the snow-covered slopes and peaks of Crackenback. John usually slept in the top bunk leaving Mum in the bottom.

I was jealous of the kids who stayed at the Ski Club of Australia and some of the other clubs scattered through the village. Each club seemed to have a social life of its own and the members and their kids got to know each other well. The parents cooked together, and the families ate and probably skied together. At Leo's we didn't seem to get to know others as well, though in about 1962 I met a boy named Stefie who was also staying with his parents at the lodge. Although he was profoundly deaf he was very adept at lip-reading and communicating, and I often wonder what became of him. He made skiing fun.

As I slowly began to meet other families and make friends, I realised that not many other families spent all three weeks of the school holidays at Thredbo unless they had their own lodge or a share in a club. I saw too that they had different attitudes to skiing, and that it was a holiday for them in a way it wasn't for us. Apparently there was no talk about *fest Trainieren* in other families.

Sasha Nekvapil, a former Czech Olympic skier and lodge owner at Thredbo, organised the first ski races in which I took part. They were fun and gave me and many other children a taste of competitive skiing and a tremendous sense of achievement for having participated. The first NSW Junior State Championships were held a year or two later. I raced in 1962 and pleased my parents by coming third in the girls' under-fifteen giant slalom. I still have the napkin ring I won and I was quite proud of myself too.

Dad, perhaps more so than Mum, would have liked at least one of us to have been selected for the national ski team. Indi came closest to achieving their dreams when in 1964 she won the Ski Club of Australia's Adams Cup. Her trophy was placed in Mum and Dad's trophy cabinet on the wall in the stairwell at Towong Hill.

'You mustn't look as if you are trying to win,' Mum advised me.

'Why? If you want us to race so much, why don't you want me to try to win?'

'It isn't the done thing. You race for the joy of doing your best.'

'I guess you just cover your competitiveness with lots of laughter,' I ventured.

Mum was shocked and upset by my cheek. But she must have known that as I was then around eleven or twelve, racing was becoming much more competitive and serious. All the same, I reckoned Mum's was an ambivalent message from such a fiercely competitive parent. To be fair, she believed that there was much more to skiing than racing and sometimes said that 'it was the key that let you through into unexplored places'.

It seemed as if both our parents believed that they had already given us their passions and interests through their blood, and all they had now to do was to teach us the skills we needed to enjoy them. I don't think they ever sensed the tensions that their almost obsessive passion created among their offspring, or if they did realise, they had decided to ignore any dissent. Mostly I thought it wisest to keep my ambivalent feelings to myself. 'You kids have opportunities beyond the dreams of others,' Dad often told me.

I didn't know what I wanted to do if I wasn't skiing. I hadn't seen enough of the outside world to know what I might like. All I knew was that racing would have been okay if it wasn't so serious. I would rather have been skiing with friends for pleasure, although that would have been difficult as every other girl I knew my own age went to school.

In 1963 I was one of the youngest members of the New South Wales Junior Ski Squad. While it was nice to have been selected, particularly because it pleased Mum and Dad, I was also becoming aware that my lack of competitiveness meant ski racing simply didn't hold the thrill for me that it had for them. Mum would have understood more than Dad, who would have called me a squib. It wouldn't have mattered how much I raced, I knew that all Dad would say was that I wouldn't know what real ski racing was like until I had raced in Europe.

During a ski lesson in August 1964 with Indi and my favourite ski instructor Sigi, I broke my leg. The following year I went to boarding school. Mum and Dad arranged for me to race in the winter of 1965, and I gained some respectable places in the under-fifteen category of the NSW Junior Championships and the

National Junior Championships, but my life had already begun to change. It was challenging enough trying to settle into boarding school. And it was a perfect excuse to give up racing. After that I didn't race again until intervarsity ski races in the early 1970s. Meanwhile, I began to ski for pleasure and for the thrill of doing something enjoyable with friends. Each winter before the school holidays in September, I looked forward to meeting up with the Swaney family from Melbourne with whom, over the years, an intergenerational lifelong friendship was forged.

The Mackinnon family from Tintaldra Station came to the Round House at Thredbo, and there were many others whose infectious enjoyment of the sport made it all so much more fun. Mum had also become friends with the Swaneys and other families in the village and she began to understand that above all I enjoyed meeting people and establishing friendships. Dad was disappointed that there wouldn't be any more Mitchells winning major races, or at least certainly not me. On the slopes I was finding my own direction and I loved every minute of it. Meeting other people was a big part of it.

27
The Magic of Summer Skiing

Almost every summer in the early 1960s there was a long drift of snow on Etheridge Range just above Seaman's Hut near the narrow dirt road that wound its way to the summit of Mt Kosciusko. Laurie Seaman and Evan Hayes perished in a blizzard in August 1928 and the hut was built by Laurie's parents in his memory. Inside the hut I looked at the bare floorboards and the basic metal-framed bunk beds and tried to imagine how I might feel if I had to use it as a refuge from a blizzard. Even at the age of about seven I knew I would be grateful for the shelter, but I'd also be pretty frightened and uncomfortable.

On a beautiful summer's day Laurie Seaman and Evan Hayes' story seemed to have a slightly unreal quality, but I already knew enough of how quickly the weather could change in the mountains to understand its significance. Mum and Dad had made sure of that, particularly on our trip to Dead Horse Gap with the Chauvels a summer or two before. As ever, Dad had been particularly vocal. Cold wintry winds could sweep in thick cloud and mist in seconds. You couldn't be careful enough, and Dad drove the message home as hard as he could.

The Magic of Summer Skiing

The snowdrift stretched high up among the rocky outcrops of Mt Etheridge, but closer to the road and the hut it flattened out. The granular snow slipped away easily from our skis and it was much easier to manage than many winter snow types; you didn't fall so much and, if you did, your pants soon dried in the warm sunshine. Skiing in summer was easier and far more fun than it had been the first time I went to Thredbo.

Everlastings and other wildflowers grew right to the edge of the drift. As the snow melted and retreated, gradually more flowers would burst into bloom. 'I have never seen the mountains like this, just a mass of bloom,' Mum remarked, the pleasure of winter snow having been replaced by the wildflowers. She took many colour slides and photographs of flowers growing among the granite boulders and beside the translucent, jagged and icy edges of a melting drift. If she needed to identify a flower, she took a cutting, wrapped its stem in tissues soaked in water and put it in a billy to take home.

From Seaman's Hut, Mum took us down to see and dip our fingertips into the icy headwaters of the Snowy River. The brave might have stuck in a toe too. Mum loved the wonderfully clear water through which we could see the large specks of mica glittering like gold in the summer sunshine. Another time we walked from Etheridge to Lake Cootapatamba, a shallow, oval-shaped lake. We discovered that, just like the Snowy River, it was icy cold, even in the hottest weather. There was not much paddling and no swimming there either!

For me, Lake Cootapatamba was a welcome break from skiing. Better still, it was mentioned in *Silver Brumby's Daughter*: 'Kunama trembled as she stood there with only her forefeet on the strange frozen lake with its soft carpet of snow.'[1] As at that time I had not seen it in winter, it was hard to imagine the lake covered in snow, but it was thrilling to see another landmark from the Brumby books. It was equally exciting to look down from the summit of Mt Townsend into the Murray Valley far beneath, just as the brumbies had: as they climbed, Thowra told Kunama, 'We will soon see the valley where Golden says the feed is always good.'

'"The valley of man," Kunama said distrustfully.'²

Ironically, while Lake Cootapatamba had been the scene of Kunama's wonderful taste of winter freedom with Thowra, it also lay on the route along which the boy and the man took her to Grey Mare Hut and into captivity. Nowhere could the contrast between freedom and captivity have been more acutely portrayed than the scene in which Kunama is taken, fighting the stockmen every inch of the way, past Lake Cootapatamba:

> *Kunama looked, saw Cootapatamba where Thowra had rolled in the lovely snow crystals and saw the vast, high-domed mountains rolling on and on, grey-green now, with summer's snowgrass, and seeming, even more than they did under snow, to be endless. A light wind from the north blew over them, lifting her forelock, a light wind saying: 'This was the future, and the future is now here.'*
>
> *Desperate with dread, Kunama sat back on her haunches and refused to move.*³

For Kunama, as they did for Mum, the mountains represented some intangible spiritual freedom. The valley – the Upper Murray – whence Golden, Kunama's mother, had come, meant terrifying captivity. Kunama felt that if she went there, she might never escape:

> *Now, as they went around Kosciusko, she knew that they would soon be over-looking that enormous sea, and even with the weight of the boy in the saddle on her back, even with the hated bit in her mouth, and with the terror of what lay ahead of her,*

she walked eagerly forward to look over the edge at the vast sea beyond.

Then she stopped in complete, bewildered fear, because the waters had rolled right away and gone leaving no trace. The mountains dropped down, down, down, below her, vanishing in steep forested sides, but further out, and far, far below there was a valley floor, and the shining loops of a river.[4]

'Who owned Golden?' I wanted to know as we stood on Mt Townsend looking over into Geehi and the Murray Valley. If she came from somewhere in the Murray Valley, why hadn't we heard about her, or even seen her?

Mum suddenly tensed. Presumably she was trying to work out a satisfactory answer without giving away anything that might spoil the story. Somewhere, I reasoned, there must be a man or even a family missing their magnificent silver mare, and her previous owners must go up to the mountains to look for her each summer, not knowing that she had consciously chosen the wild and was hidden away in the Secret Valley. Surely someone would have heard about it?

Wise storyteller that she was, Mum never revealed how much was based on truth and how much was fiction. She encouraged me to believe that what was important and satisfying was an exciting story, and to dream up my own stories from those I already knew.

Later, when I was older and able to walk further, Mum took Harry and me to Lake Albina. On another occasion she took Harry over to the Blue Lake where Kunama had stopped with the boy and his father. It was while they were boiling the billy by the lake that Kunama smelled smoke at close quarters for the first time.

In January 1963 we stayed at the Chalet at Charlotte Pass. In *Silver Brumby's Daughter*, it was at the Chalet that the man and his son were staying when they saw Thowra and Kunama and chased them on skis towards the Ramsheads and Dead Horse Gap. I knew the Chalet from Mum and Dad's photographs and stories; they spoke of the Chalet as if it was the only one in existence. It was where they went every winter they spent in Australia from the time of their marriage in 1935 until Dad went to Malaya in 1941. Sometimes they also stayed at the Chalet during summer riding expeditions to the Main Range. Mum continued to go there during the winter of 1941 until it closed, and she was one of the first to return when it reopened before the war ended in 1945.

We never went there in winter as children. Just like Lake Cootapatamba and Mt Townsend, the Chalet would have looked very different in the summer, and I found it hard to imagine the surrounding mountains covered in snow as Mum and Dad knew them. All the same, the Chalet had a special ambience and feeling of adventure. I remember the thrill of running in the sunshine across a deep carpet of white snow daisies interspersed with mauve eyebrights and some golden billy buttons on Mt Guthrie – for once I don't think Mum and Dad minded that frivolity. For them our visit to the Chalet was a journey into the past. We stayed in dormitories sleeping eight and slept in metal-framed bunks (not unlike those in Seaman's Hut) with thin mattresses.

At that time I was too young to realise the extent to which the Chalet was part of Mum's writing world. It was where she had been happy with Dad too. In the Chalet she wrote a good deal of *Australia's Alps* in the winter of 1941, detailing the expeditions she and Dad had undertaken together with the ones she had done with others to the Main Range, the Cascades, White's River, Grey Mare, Dicky Cooper Bogong and Jagungal after Dad left for Malaya. The Chalet and the mountains thus became Mum's first solution to loneliness and anxiety. From that time the first verse of Psalm 121 – 'I will lift up mine eyes unto the hills from whence cometh my help' – was a strong theme throughout her life. Even though she did not spend another winter there, she loved every moment she was there with us.

The Magic of Summer Skiing

On the way home from the Chalet and Mt Kosciusko that summer of 1963 there was a fire in the Land Rover. According to Mum's diary, 'The bushfire wireless shorted and the wires burst into flames. Harry and Indi [were] magnificent.' I felt a bit outnumbered by the older experts, who had done all that was necessary to put out the fire.

The alpine world into which Mum and Dad were initiating us was one they loved and knew so well from their expeditions long before we were born. I had heard Mum talking about *Australia's Alps*, but I was still too young to read it; that came later when she eventually gave me a copy of the 1962 edition. It was another few years before I read it properly.

One evening Dad and Mum were reminiscing about the Ski Club of Australia rope races and how the prizes were varying amounts of time in the drying room with your race partner – the winners of course were awarded most time. Being only ten at the time, I wasn't sure that I really understood the reason for Mum and Dad's amusement. Only later did I realise that my suspicions about it having to do with adults needing some privacy together for a kiss and cuddle were correct.

The days spent skiing on the drift at Etheridge and, when we were a bit older, on the South America drift (so named because it was shaped like that continent) on Mt Northcote, just across the headwaters of the Snowy River from Seaman's Hut, are among my happiest and most thrilling memories of skiing with Mum and Dad. Their smiles couldn't have been broader, creasing the crows' feet on their tanned faces. Mum had white-rimmed Polaroid sunglasses, their circular shape making her look like an owl wearing pirate's patches. Those were hard days, too, but not as hard as skiing in the winter blizzards.

During those summers in the early 1960s, the only ski-able snow lay well above and beyond the ski lifts at the resorts and we had to climb for our skiing. Any memories of pain or physical exhaustion were soon forgotten in the sunshine, the sense of well-being and the sheer thrill of those beautiful late spring and summer days among the wildflowers. After a west wind carrying mallee dust had left a pink tinge on the snow, there was the joy of cutting a pure white track or creating a pattern on the drift. There was a wonderful lighthearted atmosphere about out-of-season skiing. The competitors at race meetings laughed and joked, and even Dad and Mum became much less serious-minded about technique and effort in the summer! Occasionally, though perhaps tongue-in-cheek, Dad reminded us that summer skiing was good training for ski racing in winter. Just as we didn't throw snowballs or make snowmen in winter, Mum and Dad didn't particularly like frivolous fun, nor did they encourage it.

On 28 December 1964 the summer races were held on Merritts Spur at Thredbo. Charlie Anton, one of the prime movers behind the establishment of the alpine village at Thredbo, was the leading light of the summer race meetings. That day Charlie orchestrated events with the aid of a loudhailer while dressed only in a racing number (no shirt on account of the heat) and lederhosen plus-fours with red socks. The fact that he looked like a happy, smiling mountain frog added hugely to his appeal. Mum and Indi took part in the races. It was the only occasion I ever saw Mum competing and it was one of her very happy days. I can't recall whether I competed or if at eleven years of age I was considered too young – the only other thing I remember was a cry of 'Man in the creek!' When a skier emerged with blood in his hair and on his face, Mum reassured us by saying that heads and faces tended to bleed a lot and he'd be okay. I didn't really believe her.

An article Mum published in *Riverlander* in 1964 reflected the deep interest and pleasure that those summer days spent in the mountains gave her:

The Magic of Summer Skiing

In summer these mountains, with their long snow-drifts still to tempt the skier, are grown over with wild flowers, and are fragrant, at evening, with the scent of heaths. The snow daisies may be in great fields of white flowers and silver leaves, so that they do indeed look like snow in rocky couloirs beneath the twisted snowgums. There are big patches of mauve from the eyebrights, and yellow where the yellow kunzea bushes grow. Candleheath sends its tall red spike, bearing cream flowers, up out of the sphagnum bogs. Mountain marsh marigolds are exquisite below the snowdrifts' rim of ice. Pimelias flower, and white purslane; prostanthera is espaliered against the rocks. Here is thrilling, subtle loveliness for those who seek it, and the subtle enchantment of the mountains themselves.[5]

At the time I thought each summer would bring similar days in the mountains. But due to the risk of bushfires and other family commitments, we didn't have as many days as we wished and had to live on early happy memories. Other areas of the mountains also captured our interest, and we were lucky to have had those days as close as you can get to the highest point in Australia. They were special times in special places. There was also the reassuring thought that, as Dad hinted, some practice in the summer might make skiing the following winter slightly easier! Or would Dad and Mum's expectations be just that bit higher for that very reason, plus the fact that we would be a little bit older and arguably stronger and fitter?

28

Adventures on the Alpine Way

Although I didn't always want to go skiing, the trips to Thredbo were a great adventure. In the early 1960s, the Alpine Way between Khancoban and Geehi was still under construction, and there were teething problems on the stretch of road between Khancoban and the Bailey Bridge on the Swampy Plains River. Despite Mum's initial disapproval of roads being driven through her beloved untouched mountains, it was not long before she realised that the Alpine Way was her key to skiing. Mum drove it 'in blizzards or solid freeze, or in summer's heat and sometimes in the dark of the night'.[1] If the trip was free of incident it took her just under two hours to drive from Towong Hill to Thredbo.

Some of the steep-sided cuttings were plagued with rockfalls. The road was often either partially or entirely blocked and we had to wait while it was cleared. It was both thrilling and frightening when we actually saw the rocks avalanching and thundering down the cuttings and smashing onto the road; we were lucky falling rocks never landed on us. If the road was only partially blocked, Mum was frequently tempted to push on through, anxiety spurring her to put her foot on the accelerator. Sometimes it was pretty bumpy and exciting. More than once

Mum remarked that it was 'rather strenuous getting there'. It could be horribly scary too.

The earthmoving vehicles used for road, dam and aqueduct building for the Snowy Hydro Scheme that travelled on the Alpine Way were fascinating too. Some of the equipment was gigantic and we called those vehicles 'eat-you-up-o's', since they looked as if they could not just swallow and chew up a person but a whole Land Rover. There were also prefabricated houses, partial or whole, strapped to trailers behind trucks following cars with signs saying 'Danger – wide load'. We speculated as to where these houses were going and who the occupants would be – whether they would be married with families, what country they came from and if they liked skiing. It helped pass the time and Mum often had fabulously imaginative suggestions.

During the heavy snowfalls of 1960 and 1964, we were often the last to drive home down the Alpine Way before the Snowy Mountains Authority decided to close it due to the quantity of snow. There were moments when Mum wished the Authority would close the road before we left Thredbo so we could stay and ski on the marvellous fresh falls. Once the road was re-opened we were usually the first on the Alpine Way returning to Thredbo to make the best of the new snow. Mum wrote to Granny on 24 July 1964 explaining that at Thredbo, 'Everything was rationed as far as I could make out, except grog!' Even though she didn't drink much, Mum enjoyed a party and would have sparkled if we'd been snowed in: singing, playing the accordion, chatting about a marvellous day's skiing or simply playing Scrabble in front of a blazing open fire at the Ski Club of Australia.

Mum had great admiration for the men who drove the huge vehicles, and those who risked their lives on precipitous hillsides in the construction of the hydro-electric scheme. When she talked about some of those men who worked for the Snowy Mountains Authority coming from countries that then lay behind the Iron

Curtain, I imagined a giant fence made of the rusty-looking pipes I'd seen on the trailers of those big eat-you-up-o trucks taking material up into the mountains to build the pipelines. These men were often cut off from their families; in some cases they might not even know if their families were alive or where they were. The *Snowy Review* (the house magazine of the Snowy Mountains Authority) published lists of people missing in Europe since the war and subsequent political upheaval, in case some of them had turned up to work on the Snowy Mountain Authority. Seeing the lists was a sobering reminder of histories and stories of devastating loss and suffering beyond Khancoban, Corryong, Thredbo, Jindabyne and Cooma.

The chains Dad and Mum had for the Land Rover were heavy and difficult to put on the wheels, and you got pretty cold and filthy doing so. They were used only as a last resort. One August morning in snowy conditions not far from Dead Horse Gap, Mum and I didn't know that we should have put on chains until it was too late and we were almost upside down in a creek, having skidded on a corner. As we slid down into the water, there was a horrible noise like smashing glass. The vehicle came to rest partially on its side, balanced on boulders. Fortunately it was a shallow creek and we were able to clamber out the uppermost door. We soon discovered the windows hadn't shattered but that John's plastic building bricks, a forerunner of Lego, had spilt noisily as their cardboard box turned about in the back of the vehicle.

In the early 1960s there was often very little traffic on the Alpine Way; had we waited with the vehicle we might have waited all day. We walked to the nearest road camp, a collection of prefabricated huts called Siberia by the men who kept the Alpine Way open. Following the road up there from where the Land Rover lay in the creek was one of the coldest, hardest and most slippery walks I have ever done. Since then I have walked in much lower temperatures, but I imagine that I was in shock and that made the cold seem worse.

The Siberia camp had a wonderful wood-burning stove where we were able to dry off and warm up, and the men working there kindly gave us warm drinks and biscuits. Some of them spoke other languages among themselves, and when they spoke English they did so with strange accents. Once we had finished our drinks and warmed up a little, they drove us back to the bend in the road below which the Land Rover was lying ignominiously in the creek. They pulled it out with ropes hitched to a couple of graders, graciously checked to make sure that there were no mechanical problems, which miraculously there weren't, and set us on our way. We could not have been better looked after.

We didn't ski that day, we simply drove home. I was surprised but very relieved when Mum didn't persist with our plans. Both of us were feeling rather nauseated and tired from shock and cold. I can't recall how much damage there was to the body of the Land Rover or what was said between Dad and Mum after our return. I don't think Dad was very happy, but if he was angry he didn't show it in front of me. Afterwards Mum wanted to do something for the men at Siberia, so she gave them some ski lessons.

In her published memoirs, Mum described the Alpine Way affectionately as 'that road of so many adventures'.[2] I have a black-and-white photograph of the family Land Rover skirting around a landslide in a steep-sided box cutting. There was certainly a unique quality to my mother and in hindsight the maverick in her was a special part of it, even if it didn't always feel like it at the time.

Some trips to Thredbo were better than others. Having successfully survived the risks of the road, sometimes we arrived to find that the chairlift wasn't running due to high winds. We then resorted to climbing for our skiing. It was a chance to return to Dead Horse Gap, climb up towards the rocky summits of the Ramsheads and ski down through the deep, untouched snow among the twisted snowgums above Dead Horse Gap Hut. It was a tough but wonderfully wild challenge away from Thredbo. Mum loved the mysteries of untouched snow, discovering whether it was windblown powder, crusty, icy or wet and heavy. Every snow type had different challenges.

In early August 1962 we were particularly lucky not to be skiing on the day the Crackenback chairlift cable snapped. About forty people were riding on the lift at the time, and as the double chairs began to swing, some of the passengers jumped down into deep snow beneath. Fortunately nobody was hurt, but it must have been terrifying for those on the lift. It had been a day of high wind with skiers unable to take the lift as far as the top station and perhaps the lift should have been closed altogether.

For someone who had never had a formal driving lesson or taken a test, Mum really did very well on the Alpine Way. But she had had plenty of off-road experience: in February 1948, some five years before I was born, along with Willie Littlejohn and Ossie Rixon, she and Dad set off in Iris, an armour-plated US army disposals jeep across the mountains from Towong Hill to the Chalet. In the article Mum wrote in *Walkabout* she admitted, 'I wished I had not gone.'[3] It read as if vehicles would come between the bush and her enjoyment of it, and that walking, riding or skiing were infinitely better ways of exploring and enjoying the mountains. Now the Land Rover – sometimes called the Bergomeister, Mum's German for Mountain Master – had replaced Iris and Sirius and was a means of getting into her beloved mountains and experiencing adventures on the way. It was the beginning of the end of her isolation, frustration and loneliness beneath the thick winter mists in the Murray Valley.

Before the Alpine Way was built when Indi was almost a year old in 1947, Granny came to look after her so Mum and Dad could ski for a few days. But they soon realised that without a road into the mountains, the distance to Charlotte Pass was too great and it would mean too long away from the baby and from Dad's newly acquired political obligations. By 1966, only about ten years after it had been opened, the future of the Alpine Way was already uncertain and Mum lobbied to keep the road open from her hospital bed in Melbourne where she was recovering from a snapped Achilles tendon.

One of the places Mum liked best on the journey up the Alpine Way to Thredbo was the Pilot Lookout. She loved the view towards Mt Pinnibar and the tall, graceful mountain ash trees, and she photographed some of the detail on their tall trunks. One of the photographs showing sunlight streaming through the mountain ash forest under sparkling fresh snow was published, together with her poem 'Mountain Ash', in her 1988 book, *A Vision of the Snowy Mountains*. Even though the poem made its first appearance in *Riverlander*, a local journal, in 1983, the inspiration had taken form almost twenty years earlier during one of those many trips up to Thredbo.

We used to stop at Leather Barrel Creek too. Sometimes we would drink a handful or so of the beautiful ice-cold, crystal-clear mountain water, and Mum and Dad would tell stories about riding up Little Mick and Big Mick and down into the Leather Barrel on their way to Dead Horse Gap. Apart from the fact that Little and Big Mick were both steep slopes and Little Mick was reputedly steeper than Big Mick, I never really knew which they were; the route we took in the car on the Alpine Way was a little different from the one they rode. Among the yarns about the riding and skiing expeditions, they discouraged us from drinking too much snow water and warned us that it might cause tummy aches.

Mum was also fond of Tom Groggin, and when we passed the turn to the homestead, driving to or from Thredbo, she told stories about some her own riding trips and the bushmen she'd met. The station was once home to Jack Riley, who Dad reckoned was Banjo Paterson's inspiration for his famous poem 'The Man from Snowy River'. Because of conflicting evidence, for Mum 'The Man' was a composite character whom Paterson created from his knowledge of riding with a number of mountain men. As well as Jack Riley from the Upper Murray, there were the two Spencers (father and son, both called James), 'Hellfire' Jack Clarke from Jindabyne, Lachie Cochran from Adaminaby and a number of other characters.

About a decade later, in the acknowledgements in *The Colt from Snowy River*, Mum explained that Banjo had written to Dad saying that 'the idea for his poem had been given to him by stories around the hut fire when Dad's father Grand Daddy M took him on the long day's ride out to Tom Groggin, and they spent the night camped with Riley'.[4]

However, Mum went on to say that in 'August 1936 Banjo Paterson told Dad that Riley was the Man from Snowy River'.[5] Banjo Paterson used to stay at Bringenbrong homestead. Both Dad's father, Walter, and his uncle Peter knew him, as did the Dibbs family in Sydney. Mum and Dad met Banjo in 1936 at a cocktail party given by Granny M at the Australia Hotel in Sydney. Mum said Banjo looked like a shrivelled walnut.

Dad often gave a very spirited and dramatic account related to him by the late Will Findlay of Jack Riley's last journey and his death on 16 July 1914 at Surveyor's Creek. I have no doubt that Dad was convinced that Jack Riley was 'The Man'.

Geehi would have been on Jack Riley's route to and from Tom Groggin. Many other stockmen would have ridden that way with their cattle, just as Mum did in her early years after she was married and first arrived in the district. She found the descriptions of the daring mountain riding hugely exciting. As we drove to and from Thredbo past Tom Groggin and Geehi, I think she felt as if we were travelling a route paved in fabulous campfire yarns and legends.

Although Mum enjoyed the advantages of being able to drive into the mountains and up to Dead Horse Gap and Thredbo, she missed the intimacy of riding through the bush and the mysteries of Geehi on the route to Tom Groggin. She also missed seeing the Geehi Walls, the spectacular views of the Western Face and our early family trips in Sirius the Land Rover over the Geehi Wall. Quite apart from the formation of the Kosciusko National Park in 1967 and the withdrawal of large tracts of the High Country from grazing, with a growing family and a busy writing career Mum simply did not have the time to ride in the bush.

29

Skiing the World

Mum's love of skiing was in part a longing to regain her youth and at least some of the adventures she'd once enjoyed. Her experiences were all the more remarkable as she learned to ski in even tougher and more primitive conditions than my generation.

Her induction began in 1935 at Mt Buller in the winter before she and Dad were married. Like us, Mum learned on wooden skis with no edges and no safety bindings; that much was understandable as skis with steel edges were not widely available in the southern hemisphere until 1937. Harder still, apparently Dad wouldn't even show her how to put on her skis or how to stand up when she fell over. He merely gave her skis and left her to struggle to work out the basics alone while he went off and had fun. By then Dad had been skiing for eight years and had extensive experience at Europe's best ski resorts. As well as being a tough taskmaster, it seems as if he had forgotten what it was like to be a beginner.

Mum's spirits must have plummeted when Dad told her, 'This is my life', the implication being that she was expected to mould her life entirely to his. Even by the standards of the day Dad expected a lot, probably too much. It is a wonder she put up with it, particularly as she'd already had cold feet and briefly broken off their engagement in July only weeks earlier. Dad was playing with fire; perhaps he thought skiing was either going to make or break his engagement once and for all. Undoubtedly Mum was feeling ambivalent, but there was a part of her that was already rising to the challenge.

When Mum finally returned to Melbourne from Mt Buller she had a sprained shoulder, a sprained knee, a sprained ankle and was covered in bruises. Having successfully concealed her injuries from her parents, she went hunting the next day with the Findon Harriers. Unsurprisingly, she found her knee was too painful to properly grip the saddle. A fall and concussion only added to her problems. Mum had told her mother she was 'quite all right' to go out hunting! It was typical of Mum.

Granny and Grandfather were annoyed when they discovered the extent of her ski injuries and uncovered enough to divine how harshly Dad had treated their daughter. His behaviour was scarcely what they would have expected from a loving fiancé. But Mum loved physical challenge and with her grit and determination she wasn't going to let skiing beat her. Her doggedness was probably one of the essential ingredients that prevented her and Dad's relationship foundering before they even reached the altar. I have often wondered whether Granny and Grandfather were so determined that she should marry an ostensibly very eligible bachelor that they had a swaying influence.

Only when Mum and Dad went skiing in New Zealand on their honeymoon did she really begin to enjoy it. Dad insisted that they should pack ski clothes in their honeymoon suitcases 'just in case'. At the time, Mum said nothing – she was dreading it and praying that all the ski-able snow would have melted by the time they arrived. Dad didn't like 'helpless, clinging females about the place', and Mum felt very alone, wondering how she would cope. Mum said that almost the only reason she began to enjoy skiing was that George Lockwood, a solicitor from Christchurch who was a friend of Dad, was perceptive enough to realise that she could hardly ski. He invited one of his friends named Nell Lovegrove, also a relatively inexperienced skier, to join them and Mum immediately felt happier and more confident, and skiing became much less lonely.

But there were harder times to come. In the winter of 1936, almost twenty years before the Alpine Way was built, Dad decided that he and Mum would make the first journey across the Great Dividing Range, riding over the Geehi Walls and up Hannel's Spur until snow prevented them riding any further. They continued on skis around Abbott Peak and into Wilkinson's Valley between Mt Townsend and Mt Kosciusko and then on to the Chalet. Mum said it was a wonderful experience but added that they only survived by the grace of God. Apparently, she was disappointed when a few days later the weather was too bad to ski back and they had to return by road to Towong Hill.

I never thought that Dad had given Mum much credit for her tenacity until I read his book about ski technique, *Ski Heil*, the first handbook on the sport to be published in Australia. As it was published in 1937, Dad must have been writing it at the time of their marriage and he dedicated it to Mum. He explained to me that Mum had had to listen to him talking about it and helped him check the manuscript. She probably typed it for him too. If he'd ever thought Mum had been long-suffering over the book, he was wrong. She had already begun to find joys and mysteries in the world of skiing and the mountains that no map ever marks.

Indeed, by 1937 Mum was in no way a long-suffering wife but a determined young woman already reaping the benefits of a whole winter's skiing and instruction from Ernst Skardarasy, the first Austrian ski instructor at the Chalet. Fortuitously, during that same winter Dad and Mum were to meet the visiting American ski team. They were racing in what Mum referred to as 'the triangular match against USA and New Zealand', skiing off Townsend Spur into Lady Northcote Canyon. Mum's meeting with Jay (James) Laughlin IV of New Directions Publishing, who sponsored the American team, was the beginning of a lifelong and most extraordinary friendship. Among other things, Jay and his publishing house were responsible for the inspiring collection of the latest American literature that in later years was to form our loo reading in the upstairs bathroom at Towong Hill!

As early as August 1936, good fortune had begun to smile on Mum. According to *The Argus* of 12 September 1936, 'Mrs Mitchell who has only recently taken up the sport came second' in the Interdominion Slalom at Ruapehu, New Zealand. (Mum and Dad had returned there especially for the races.) Her prize was a copy of the famous British mountaineer, writer and poet Geoffrey Winthrop Young's 1927 book *On High Hills*. She valued it all her life. Along with another pioneering British ski writer, Arthur Lunn, the author rapidly became an inspiration to Mum. After the war she sent him a copy of *Soil and Civilization*.

By winter 1937 it seemed that fortune was really favouring Mum rather than Dad. As the United Australia Party candidate for the local seat of Benambra, he had the double disappointment of unsuccessfully contesting the Victorian state elections on 4 October 1937 and missing out on most of the ski racing at Charlotte Pass and Mt Buller due to his commitments to his political campaign. Meanwhile, Mum had been selected for both the Victorian and Australian teams. She won the Ski Club of Australia's Adams Cup and, racing for Australia, won the Interdominion Slalom, thus proving that she could do it without Dad's coaching. Before she raced she used to pray, rather irreverently, 'God be in my legs and in my understanding!' As Dad was not going to be in parliament that term, and also perhaps because of Mum's new enjoyment of skiing and her success in the winter championships, they decided they would travel overseas and ski the world. To Mum, 'overseas' meant Europe, all the countries that Dad and his skiing friends talked about so much. There was apparently no thought of starting a family just yet.

Granny M, who at least to an extent held the purse strings, had been told that Dad was going overseas to study farming and forestry, and international relations at Harvard. Mum, if not Dad too, had some very different ideas, and initially she didn't even want to go to Boston. To give Dad his due, he did visit ranches and agricultural ministries and ultimately he went to Harvard for a term – when they were not skiing! Dad never admitted it, but clearly skiing came first. His agricultural pursuits seemed to be a sort of foil to keep Granny M happy. Also, Dad said that by 1937 'Mummy was going places', which indeed she was. Mum had her eyes firmly on skiing and travelling in Europe, so initially she was disappointed when she discovered the plan was to go to Hawaii and North America. Her feelings about the destinations were to change.

Dad and Mum embarked on the Royal Mail Ship *Aorangi* from Sydney on 25 November 1937 and arrived at Honolulu on 10 December. Meanwhile, Jay Laughlin was making arrangements for a trip that was to far surpass their dreams. Mrs Loder, a cousin of Jay Laughlin's married to a US naval officer in Hawaii, looked after them during their stay. Mum wrote of Mrs Loder in her typed travel journal: 'Her own enormous interest and affection for the islands helped us feel so much more part of the scene.'

Dad remembered with regret that Hawaii was one of the few places they visited where they were unable to ski on account of the snow coming late that year. But on 11 December they met Charlie Martin, president of the ski club, who, according to Mum's travel journal, 'laid out maps of Moana Kea where they skied last winter and told us about it at terrific length'. He even 'spoke of the possibility of getting me into an Army bomber to see it. (By this time I was ready to believe anything as Mrs Loder had told me how the navy had sent the ships for a tour of the other islands complete with the officers' wives and children and their motor cars because the families needed a change of air and to get into the cooler and higher country!!!) Anyway we arrived back with our heads simply spinning with the plans of possible skiing we might do etc.'

Only a week later on 18 December, Dad and Mum ate a thrilling lunch at the Volcano House hotel on the rim of the crater of Moana Kea. In her journal Mum wrote: 'The pit [of the crater] is about 1000 feet deep. It was quite quiet and just looked like a floor of badly poured black asphalt but Campbell [with whom they were lunching] had seen it just molten fire and bubbling!' She had already noted that Moana Kea 'might easily provide good skiing'. Unfortunately it didn't snow on the higher volcanoes in Hawaii until after they had left for the United States.

In early January 1938 they met W. Averell Harriman at Sun Valley, Idaho. He was president of Union Pacific Railroad, and had been a founder of the fledgling Sun Valley ski resort two years earlier. Later he became US Ambassador in Moscow and then briefly in London. Mum and Dad arrived in Sun Valley on 28 December 1937 intending to stay for three days but remained there a month, thus making it possible for Averell Harriman to have them included in various exploratory expeditions. They spoke about these experiences for the rest of their lives. Mum used to say it had been *'Wunderbar'*. The excitement of being at the inception of a grand new venture, which Sun Valley was in 1938, was clear. 'Mr Harriman,' Mum explained, 'had been in Europe and he had decided that America should have a big winter sports place of the St Moritz type and that Union Pacific would run it.' They made several first winter ascents of peaks in the Sawtooth Range, often climbing on skis. Harriman's 'gentleman sportsman', Count Felix Schaffgotsch from Salzburg, who had selected the site for him, took them on the first exploring trip up Bald Mountain where Mum discovered that '[s]kiing in deep powder snow is pure joy … if the turns hold!'[1]

As Mum explained in *Chauvel Country*, they became part of Harriman's public relations campaign to promote Sun Valley with the Pathé Newsreels photographers recording their exploits – even eating lunch. According to Mum, 'Everyone was so hungry that they kept finishing lunch before the film was starting and there was a perfect wail for another hamburger on the film or "quick! another slice of bread", and we had a somewhat superior lunch as a result.'[2]

Mum's successes continued at Mt Norquay near Banff in Alberta when she won the Women's Downhill in the Canadian Dominion Championships on 5 March 1938. On the previous day when the Slalom was held, Mum recorded in her journal that she had a headache and 'an increasingly awful cough' and felt 'less like racing than a tortoise'. Fortuitously the following day she 'felt more like a hare!!' On 9 March *The Gazette* in Montreal reported: 'Surprized realization that the Canadian Rockies and the Alps have not a "corner" to Mrs E K Mitchell's great showing in the recent Dominion women's championships.' The following year the editor of the *Australian Ski Yearbook* pointed out Mum's success: 'Mrs T W Mitchell gave us, last year, Australia's first win in a major event abroad.'

In June 1938 Mum and Dad went to Chile and from there crossed through thick snow on horseback part of the way to Argentina. Later that year in the southern hemisphere winter at San Carlos de Bariloche in Argentina, Mum raced against fourteen other women and won a cup and a small gold ski brooch in the Women's Argentine International Championships. Dad said Mum 'caused a furore amongst a large crowd standing about the flag-decked finish and got a special burst of applause and a roll of drums from the Argentine military band who were drawn up at the finish'. Later during a bored moment at the prize-giving she picked up an accordion and inadvertently won the hearts of those with Nazi sympathies in Argentina when she played the Horst Wessel Song! Her audience didn't appreciate that Mum thought it was an innocent German folk song. Later, she always said that the Nazis had ruined a perfectly good German melody.

From Bariloche they returned to the Chilean ski village Farellones where they expected the national championships to be held. Dad claimed to be furious when they discovered that the race meeting had been postponed, ostensibly due to inadequate snow. In any event, back in Santiago they had 'a hell of a fine time' being entertained by the Edwards – a prominent family – and both the British and American embassies. Of this time Dad noted in his diary that the Nazi influence in Chile and South America generally was not as strong as it might be 'because they do not like either Hitler or his system'.

After Mum's performance at Bariloche, Dad might have been ruing the words spoken by a friend watching Mum skiing for the first time at Mt Buller: 'Tom, one day that girl will beat you.' Although Mum had not in any true sense beaten Dad, she was showing herself to be a very competent skier, with a useful musical talent and growing confidence and people skills of her own. She was certainly not the clingy type and had her own formidable steel. Another accolade came in December 1939 when Mum was nominated to represent Australia in the FIS (Fédération Internationale de Ski) races in Zakopane, Poland. Mum's successes in North and South America had at least in part been due to Dad's training – he must have been more than a little bit proud of her.

In *Chauvel Country* Mum wrote of a time when they were snowed in at a stone *refugio* in the tiny mountain village of Farellones, high above Santiago: 'It was a night never to be forgotten: the far away grid of lights, the heavy clouds driven by the wind, the sound of that wind in the Andes, and myself, as I had stood out there alone, swept up, almost carried away by that unleashed strength of the blizzard that was raging high above us.'³ Farellones del Cerro Colorado – or Cliff of the Red Mountain – was the full name of that fledgling ski village, and Farellones (2134 metres) is now one of Chile's main resorts. Mum and Dad felt privileged to have witnessed these resorts in their embryonic stages.

Another brilliant memory for Mum was climbing Villarrica, one of Chile's most active volcanoes, as far as they could go without crampons. In the unfinished manuscript of her autobiography she proudly claimed, 'I was the first white woman to climb Villarrica and ski down it!' Yet another was seeing the Llaima volcano 'red hot in the sky, the heat of the Llaima burning through her ice' against the southern stars of the night sky. 'This I remember as though it had burnt in an after-vision onto my eyes.'⁴

To fulfil at least part of his mother's wish, Dad finally enrolled at Harvard. By 27 August 1938 he and Mum were on board RMS *Oribita* heading for New York, having changed ships in Bermuda on their way north. Dad confirmed for me that at first Mum didn't like the idea of Boston, but he'd always thought that when they actually got there she'd have a pretty good time. From New York they went straight to Boston to arrange their accommodation in time for the autumn term, which began at the time of the Munich crisis in late September 1938. Although Dad had enrolled in international relations, more specifically he studied the German colonial question. Mum said that he'd soft-soaped his mother, saying that he 'hoped that Harvard will put him a step nearer parliament and that there was nothing like education'.⁵ It was Granny M's dream that he would go into politics. I don't think Dad was averse to it, so long as he could ski.

Mum joined a similar course at Radcliffe and, like a loyal wife of her day, she typed the lecture notes for them both. During Dad's first lecture the professor notably said: 'International law has been dee-fined as being like a Swiss chee-ese: full of holes. But, gentlemen, a chee-ese, even one full of holes, is better than no chee-ese at all, so I propose we continue our study of international law in spite of what has happened and might happen abroad.'[6]

30

Accident and Intrigue

In December 1938 in New York, Mum and Dad boarded the ocean liner *Aquitania* bound for Cherbourg, France. American skiing pioneer Alice Wolfe, with whom Mum had skied in Sun Valley, was on the same ship and they became firm friends. From Paris they all travelled on the *Arlberg Express*, arriving on 17 December at St Anton, Austria, in time for Christmas. Their plan was to ski in the Arlberg while they waited to hear from Dad's various contacts in Germany. He wanted to see for himself what was happening there. With the knowledge that following the *Anschluss* – the annexation of Austria into Germany's Third Reich – the previous March, the Foreign and Commonwealth Office in London had advised British citizens (including Australians) to leave Austria and Germany, and the term studying international relations at Harvard fresh in his mind, Dad must have known that trouble was coming. But he also liked to be near the centre of things.

Alice would have told Mum and Dad long before they arrived in St Anton that Hannes Schneider, the renowned and beloved head of the St Anton ski school from as early as 1907, had been arrested and imprisoned in the local gaol in Landeck before being sent into exile in Garmisch-Partenkirchen, Germany. On

20 December they drove across the border with Alice Wolfe to visit Hannes. It appeared that Hannes's problems with the Nazi authorities had been brought about by the village mayor, Herr Moser. Moser had once been a less than impressive instructor in the ski school, and the ski instructors held a meeting and got rid of him. Moser held Hannes to blame. After he was sacked, Moser went to Germany and spent three years hoarding information that could be used against Hannes. From Mum's journal it is clear that Moser was an ardent Nazi 'who gave the "Hitler gruss" long before Anschluss'.

Alice knew Hannes from previous winters she had spent in St Anton. With Alice's help and that of her solicitor, Dr Karl Roesen, Hannes and his family received visas in early January 1939 and were permitted to leave Germany. Virtually nobody in St Anton relaxed until they knew that Hannes was safely across the border in Switzerland and on his way to the United States. Messages about Hannes's progress were whispered between Dad and Mum's anti-Nazi visitors. Meanwhile, Frau Roesen confided to Dad her concerns about her neighbours suddenly vanishing and her anxiety, wondering if her family's turn would come too.[1] Mum and Dad were becoming aware that they were living in increasingly difficult times.

With the exception of Christmas 1936, Dad and Mum had spent every Christmas since they were married outside Australia, but no Christmas could have been more unusual than 1938 in St Anton. In a description of preparations for a party on Christmas Eve, Mum wrote in her travel journal: 'There was a slight contretemps over procuring enough fresh eggs to make Russian eggs for the party. Eggs are a commodity about which apparently the hens of the Third Reich don't know anything. They all come from Bulgaria and Holland.'

There were other anxieties. Dad told me he was surprised to hear there had been no Christmas mass in the local church,

St Jacob's, in St Anton because, it was said, 'Joseph was away on "Militardienst" (military service), Mary was doing her [...] "Arbeitsdienst" (work), the donkey had foot and mouth disease and the Morning Star was in Dachau.'[2] (Foot and mouth disease had in fact broken out in Austria just after the *Anschluss*, delivering yet another blow to the struggling economy.) The ghastly remark about Dachau bears witness to the dawning awareness in early 1939 that Jews and other people were vanishing into concentration camps. The local people would have been concerned if Hannes Schneider hadn't managed to get his permit to leave Germany since something more sinister than Landeck gaol and exile in Garmisch-Partenkirchen might have awaited him.

Mum's skiing days could have finished on 29 December 1938 when she broke her leg in eleven places. It was over lunch only the day before that an American friend Kathi Ward had been joking about a chip on Mum's ski, saying, 'Look – Elyne went so fast that her ski went up in smoke.' Much more than just her ski went up in smoke in that horrible fall. Six days later, Dad dislocated his shoulder while skiing. After the kind Dr Schalle had patched up Dad, they were all photographed together in Mum's room. Mum is in bed, Dad's arm is bandaged up and sticking straight out in a sling, and the *Schwester* (nurse) is looking stern on the other side of the bed. On the back of the photograph there is a caption: 'The break-up party'. These words were to prove truer than any of them could have known.

Within days they realised that Dad's shoulder was no simple dislocation: his left arm was partially paralysed, so the prognosis was not good. Mum's accident meant the end of her plans to ski in the FIS the following February. She received the official notification of her selection in mail that arrived from Australia on 9 January. In her travel journal she wrote: 'I can't imagine anything much bloodier than getting that when I was lying in bed with a broken leg.'

Meanwhile, back at Towong Hill, the situation was critical, but in a very different way. Black Friday, when so much of Towong Hill was burned, was only four days away on 13 January 1939. Even though Mum was able to celebrate her birthday the day after her accident with a party in her room in the Pension Bergheim (Dad bought her a chocolate cake), by 16 January she was seriously ill with an embolism.

Due to this illness and having such a badly broken leg, throughout January and February 1939 Mum became a captive audience and was visited by both Nazis and non-Nazis staying at St Anton, while others filled her room with flowers and sent their good wishes. When Mum was ill, Dr Schalle tried, often unsuccessfully, to prevent all visitors, but through them she was able at least to keep abreast of events, opinion and intrigue. Dr Schalle and the *Schwester* from Innsbruck who expertly nursed Mum through her illness were vehemently anti-Nazi.

Alice Wolfe was responsible for much of Mum and Dad's social life, and despite her championing of Hannes Schneider she introduced Herr Bergmann to Mum who, Mum remarked in her typed journal, 'is a former lieutenant of Goering and is reputed to be the only 100% Nazi there is'. The specialist who came to see Mum on 18 January must have been almost one hundred per cent Nazi too. Mum wrote a vivid account in a journal extract: 'He came in, gave his heels a resounding click together and said, "Heil Hitler!" Then he sort of marched to the bedside. If he had done the goose step, I don't think my eyes could have popped out any further. Every movement he made was sharp, in fact snappy and I was expecting after every quick action that he would say Heil Hitler.' She admitted that 'if it wouldn't have been terribly painful I think I would have probably howled with laughter'.

Local man Guido Schmidt was another of 'Goering's lieutenants' who visited Mum. In her journal she described one of his visits towards the end of January 1939 when he had 'landed himself a good job with Goering':

> *'Aach,' he said throwing himself in a chair. 'Goering is wonderful!', then he beamed round at us. 'He is not like the others, he is not just a man he is a ... Herr [lord].' His eyes were restless and snappy. 'The weather was terrible but when you have been there a few days, Berlin, it is wonderful, you wonder why you love St Anton so. In Berlin there is so much happening.' He then produced a magazine about the 'Kolonial Frage' (Colonial Question) [for Dad].*

Guido Schmidt was Austrian Chancellor Kurt von Schuschnigg's last Secretary of State before the *Anschluss*. It is quite possible he was not the one hundred per cent Nazi he made himself out to be. Later he explained to Dad and Mum that one of the worst days of his career was when he accompanied the Chancellor to Berchtesgaden and he could hear 'the Führer roaring at poor Schuschnigg behind the closed door of the study'. Even Guido Schmidt did not know what became of Schuschnigg. Soon after the war ended, Dad and Mum heard rumours that Schuschnigg had been seen in Dachau. In fact he was liberated in 1945 by the Americans.

According to Mum's journal, Otto Petzold's visit contributed more interesting details about Goering:

> *Otto Petzold came in later with stacks of photographs of Goering and his new and enormous hunting lodge Carinhall. The lodge is a wonderful place in its own forest and with its own lake. There were photos too of the furnishings of the vast rooms and several entertainments there. Tables set with miles of wonderful glass and silver. There were also many of [Goering's] lion cub. We couldn't help wondering how the poor people of Germany*

found it compatible to hear Goering, the owner of all this (and of an extremely well-covered figure too), saying that guns were preferable to butter.

Biji De Wardner, head of a department at fashion house Mainbocher in Paris, who had for some years dressed Mrs Simpson – by then the Duchess of Windsor – was also one of Mum's regular visitors. Mum remarked in her journal:

She was very interesting about the Windsors. She had been in the Riviera during the September Crisis staying where they were and had been with them a good deal. Her main impression of the Duke was that he was incredibly like a boy, a schoolboy's mentality. It was a new line to me.

Almost at the end of her Austrian journal, on 21 March 1939, Mum wrote rather tellingly, 'All the Austrians were furious with Hitler over the Czech business. Everyone had said it was too much, that soon war would come and who wanted war? There was something bitter and sad about Austria with her lost identity being rushed unwillingly forward into the European maelstrom.' Having annexed the Sudetenland following the Munich Agreement on 29 September 1938, Hitler had seized the rest of Czechoslovakia on 15 March 1939. Despite his fascination with being almost in the epicentre of the maelstrom, even Dad knew that it was time to leave.

Three months after breaking her leg, Mum was finally fit enough to catch the *Arlberg Express* back to Paris in late March 1939. It was years before either Mum or Dad had news of many of the friends from the village who saw them off at the railway station. Some they never saw again.

31
Moths in the Lamplight

With the benefit of hindsight, it is easy for me to question why my parents set off on a trip to Europe so close to the outbreak of war there. It seems that when they boarded the *Aquitania* to Cherbourg in late 1938, they were like moths being drawn towards a treacherous lamplight. Their maverick genes had leapt to the forefront once more. When Dad told me how in 1933 he had seen fire hoses being turned on the Nazis in the streets of Innsbruck, he remarked, 'How grand we thought it would be to see Oswald Mosley hosed down the Strand – and at the time I only half wondered how deep the Nazi river ran below the smooth snow surface of the Austrian valleys.'[1] By the time Mum and Dad left St Anton in the European spring of 1939, Dad must have felt that his experience had provided part of the answer to his question. Sometimes he spoke of Austria during this era as being the last dying flame of freedom.

Mum recalled discussions concerning German foreign policy when Lord Huntingfield, the Governor of Victoria, stayed at Towong Hill for the Back to Corryong events in March 1936. As Inspector-General of the Australian army in the 1920s, one of Grandfather Chauvel's main concerns then, and later during his retirement from active service in the 1930s, was attempting to prevent successive governments cutting the defence budget and troop numbers because he feared Australia would be involved in further conflict. I don't know if Grandfather ever attempted to dissuade Dad and Mum from their travel plans. He wrote to farewell them, explaining that he was unable to do so in person as he was very taken up with board meetings.

On 14 December 1937, at the start of their journey, Mum and Dad visited Pearl Harbor. They were not to know then that this would be the site of a devastating Japanese aerial attack on the US navy on 7 December 1941. In her journal for 1937, Mum wrote:

> *It is an enormous naval base, very well laid out and in the beautiful surroundings of rich volcanic lands and the Waisnai [Waianae] hills not very far off. There are enormous docks there and it must be a very good harbour. There seems to be terrific quantities of oil stored in tanks [...] One is certainly unable to stay more than a few hours in Honolulu without having it forcibly brought to one's notice that there is a very large fighting force there. Aeroplanes fly over at all hours of the day and night, bugles go, there are forts all over the place and the army always seems to be out on manoeuvres and the destroyers and submarines quite frequently too. Incidentally a great many people in the States, particularly in the Services, seem to be enraged over Japan.*

Presumably Mum was referring to disquiet about the Japanese military action in Manchuria and the capture of the Chinese city Nanking.

Of their arrival on 28 December 1937 in Wilmington Harbor about three kilometres from the centre of Los Angeles, Mum remarked in her journal, 'There was a lovely sunrise – red across the waters and, looking out of the misty light were the U.S.A. battle ships and two destroyers in the distance.'

Within days of Mum and Dad's arrival in Sun Valley they were aware that Count Felix Schaffgotsch had Nazi sympathies and only employed ski instructors who were Nazis. Mum and Dad noticed that one member of the German ski team (competing in the Harriman Cup at Sun Valley) ensured that all of the team said 'Heil Hitler' when appropriate, although most of the other members were good friends with them.[2] Returning on 10 March 1938 to Sun Valley for the Harriman Cup, Dad and Mum witnessed the elation of some members of the team when in March 1938 Austria's *Anschluss*, or union with Germany, was announced. Interestingly, Dad wrote that he wondered if 'this was not the beginning of the end? Or did the now already half-forgotten fairy-tale happiness in the world spin itself out, goldenly, till the following September?' Dad described how the prize-giving after the races 'was excellent fun and yet something of a Mad Hatter's Tea Party, as we sat singing German ski songs and wondering, sometimes, at the back of our minds, whether we wouldn't all be at each other's throats within a very short time.'[3]

Not long after that, when they were staying at Sunshine, above Banff in the Rockies, they heard a wireless announcement 'in which all British subjects were told to leave Austria'.[4] A few months later, Mum must have mentioned to her mother that they found the fortnight after the Munich Agreement on 29 September 1938 difficult, uncertain whether it was sensible to continue with their plans to travel to Europe. Years later Granny told Mum that she hadn't said very much about the crisis in her letters because she felt sure that there was going to be war and she was so bothered that she could hardly bear to mention it. Indeed she must have been afraid that her daughter and son-in-law would be caught in it.

Dad and Mum must have become even more aware of the perilous state of world affairs while they were studying international relations. While at Harvard and Radcliffe, Dad and Mum met Heinrich Bruning, the former Chancellor of Germany, who explained in detail the reasons for Hitler's rise to power and also what lay behind his own departure from Germany. Despite a clearly worsening international situation, nothing could deter them from their plans to ski in Europe; it was almost as if they heard but didn't want to heed the warning signals.

Perhaps the international turmoil and imminence of war in Europe was an attraction for them, rather than a deterrent. In St Anton, Mum and Dad found British people who had also chosen to ignore their government's warning.

As one of Austria's best resorts, St Anton was popular with both the upper echelons of the Nazis and well-to-do non-party members. Due to the slump in the tourist trade following the *Anschluss*, the local people of St Anton needed visitors and the business they brought. All the same, it must have been difficult for them to keep both sets of clientele happy. Mum and Dad had been welcomed with open arms but, like the largely anti-Nazi local community, they too had to walk the heady tightrope between Nazis and non-Nazis. They were lucky that the Nazis did not dream up some reason to prevent them leaving St Anton when they did. I don't know how much they owed their safety, and perhaps their lives, to the local people in the village who so kindly looked after them.

In January 1940 Dad and Mum received a letter from a friend who signed himself enigmatically 'A.C.'. It was written on headed notepaper from Middlesex School, Concord, Massachusetts. The letter recounts how, on 28 August 1939, A.C. headed for Germany where he 'travelled the complete length of the Siegfried Line. The Germans were crowding the forts. The barbed wire was already up. Guns, troops and men were being rushed up to the fort.' Even Dad must have known that it was time to leave when they did, but part of him probably would have liked to have stayed and travelled like A.C., right until the last moment before war was declared. They were back in Australia by then.

In family circles Mum and Dad alluded wistfully to their travels in the Americas and in Austria and often dined out on their stories and adventures. It was no secret that those days were the best in their lives. Their stories were thrilling but daunting, and even aged ten or eleven I was under no illusion that although the war had come and changed things, it was also us children who had helped spoil the fun.

Mum pointed out to me where Chile was on the map motifs decorating the curtains in her bedroom, but I had to find the other places she and Dad spoke about in the atlas and I couldn't understand why I could see names like Innsbruck but not St Anton. My parents spoke of St Anton as if it was the centre of the world, which indeed it was for them and many other world-class skiers too. In addition to the geographical complexities, Mum and Dad had created a legacy of experience and achievement that would be hard to live up to.

32
Toorak College

Indi had the unenviable job of taking me to boarding school for the first time in early February 1965. I was eleven and about to go into grade 6. If I had been scared about being exposed among my peers and not knowing anybody at the local primary school, my fears were all the more paralysing as we drove between the brick gateposts and imposing black wrought-iron gates of Toorak College near Mt Eliza on the Mornington Peninsula. Not that I told Indi, but I was praying to God that Mum hadn't mentioned to the school that she thought I was 'concrete from the ears up' and 'un-teachable'. Above all I wanted to start with a clean slate but thought I was unlikely to have it; Mum didn't always keep her opinions to herself and in all probability had already discussed her concerns with Indi and the school.

Indi had left school over a year earlier and seemed so grown-up and sophisticated in her elegant dark blue linen dress. The cheery, stooped, white-haired figure of Mrs Jones, one of the house-mistresses, met us at the top of the staircase leading to the junior boarding house. Mrs Jones recognised Indi, and I was very proud that she was my sister. I didn't say very much; my limbs felt heavy and my actions robotic. Indi helped me to unpack and showed me where to put the pressed and folded piles of clothing on designated shelves and where to hang the starched uniforms.

Miss Maclean, or Clane-um as we called her behind her back, was the mistress in charge of the junior boarding house. Her room was in the corner between two wings. A long balcony with at least ten beds ran from the corridor opposite Miss Maclean's door. Her hearing was exceptional and her room well-positioned to catch everything from the quietest whispers to the softest of scampering feet after lights out. She was unsmiling and formidable but a respected disciplinarian. On our first meeting she scared the wits out of me and she continued to do so for most of my first year.

My bed on the balcony was the second closest to Miss Maclean's door. She might have put me there as I had never been to school before and was the most likely new girl to be homesick. Shada was in the bed closest to the dreaded door; I liked her because she, like me, had an unusual name and she also had pretty platinum blonde hair. She boarded because her parents were unhappily separated. In the other bed beside mine was the short, cheerful, bouncy Susie. She had been a boarder for a long time. Her dad lived close by and she boarded because her mum had died when she was very little.

Susie and Shada reminded me of the girl with bandaged eyes in St Andrew's Hospital. Each of them told me I was lucky to have both parents still living together. Clearly both of them had more sadness in their lives than I had, so I reasoned I just needed to get on with life as they did. On my first evening at boarding school I felt anxious that things would change at home while I was away, that Mum and Dad would go their own ways more than ever, and that anxiety never left me entirely. In a way Mum did increasingly go her own way as her offspring became more independent.

Being so close to Miss Maclean's door meant we didn't talk as much as I would have liked. I was envious of the girls further along the balcony who were less likely to be heard if they whispered. Next to Shada's bed was a fire escape and on the first night before I went to bed I looked at it and thought about trying the door and creeping down the steps. But where would I go when I reached the playing fields? Beyond the playing fields was the Wilderness, a bush-covered area of school property. It was very dark down there, and when I looked out of the window behind my bed it didn't seem to be a friendly darkness. So I stayed in bed and listened to the breeze stirring the leaves of the Virginia creeper that covered the brickwork around the glassless windows. Far above on the school clock tower sounded the thwack, thwack of the lanyard hitting the flag mast.

I wondered what it was like for Harry who was just starting his year at Timbertop, the rural property in the Victorian Alps owned by Geelong Grammar. Mum said Timbertop was special because it was in the mountains and there was bushwalking and skiing. Next year he would go into Perry House, which had been designed by the same architect as Toorak College and looked just like our boarding house, except that it was built entirely of red brick while our building was clad in grey rendering, except for the cloisters.

I wasn't sure how far away Timbertop was, but I tried to imagine what Harry was feeling being back at school, having started three years earlier. Maybe he was used to it by now and felt content, not lonely inside like me. I didn't know and there was no reason why I would have – I was the kid sister. With three years dividing us, our relationship was by then often quite distant and Harry had scarcely spoken to me about Geelong Grammar or what he thought about Mum and Dad sending him away to boarding school. I knew he didn't read as much or as accurately as I did, but it didn't seem to have held him back like my inability to conquer maths had for me.

Within hours of first arriving at boarding school I knew that while I had sufficient uniform, I didn't have enough clothes to wear in the evenings and at weekends. Having the right clothes seemed so important in the mid sixties, and if I was lucky enough to be invited by friends to spend weekends with them my clothing was embarrassingly inadequate. I had no trousers except for the navy blue uniform corduroys for boarders' weekend wear; apparently Mum had been told by the school that that was all I would need. I needed at least one more pair, and some jodhpurs would have been good. A daygirl invited me riding and I really wanted to go but was embarrassed to admit I didn't have any appropriate clothes.

Mum eventually handed some of Indi's clothes on to me. As a few of the cotton dresses had no manufacturer's label stitched into them, I assume she'd had them made. She'd had a supply of cotton fabrics resourcefully stockpiled since the beginning of the war. Mostly they were pretty materials but at the time I thought they were hideously old-fashioned. Perhaps Patsy, Dot Salter's daughter, had made them at much the same time she was making my bib-and-brace corduroy overalls and shorts and gabardine ski clothes. Years later in London, Steena Hay, whom I had known since I was a child, remarked that she had admired my red cotton blouse until she realised it was part of my sports uniform. I had two or three red school blouses for sport, but except for some dresses and skirts and sweaters to wear in the evenings, I didn't have much else.

'When I first went to St Catherine's,' Mum said, 'I was teased about the unfashionable clothes Granny and Nanny made for me.' Why, I wondered, did Mum let history repeat itself? I don't know if Indi had ever asked the same question. I certainly didn't, because I knew Mum would say, 'The family allowance Dad gives me is not enough to clothe you kids.' If I knew, Dad too must have known that she saved everything so she could ski and we could all go to Thredbo for the school holidays. I didn't question it, as at the time I knew nothing different. On a couple of occasions, when I was about fourteen or fifteen, Indi kindly interceded with Mum and helped me buy some of the clothing I needed. She also came with me to shop for a long evening dress for my first school dance; except for the fact that it made me look more flat-chested than I would have wished, I was very pleased with it. I had invited Hugh Watson, who was very good-looking, and I knew that there would be no critical remarks at home as his parents were friends with Dad.

Much to my chagrin I rapidly discovered that there was little flexibility in the rather military-style routine governing boarding school life. I'd never imagined that before breakfast I would have to dress, make my bed, tidy my room and clean my shoes ready for inspection as we lined up in the cloisters – seniors on one side, middle school on the other and juniors on a shorter side of the quadrangle outside the junior common room. We stood in silence for Miss Hancock, the senior boarding house mistress, to call the roll and ensure everyone was clean and tidy.

Miss Hancock's standards were second to none and she had all-seeing eyes. If I had untidy hair or uniform, my shoes were not clean enough or I had just accidentally pushed a fingernail through my stockings when I was dressing, I was sent back to do my hair or clean my shoes or change my stockings just like anyone else – only I seemed to be sent back with monotonous frequency. Mrs Hancock was quick to give a detention if you were late and she saw you running across the beautiful green lawn in the quadrangle. I couldn't understand why we had to line up before every meal and were supposed to march in silence to the dining room where we stood by our chairs until grace had been said. Some girls seemed to find the routine discipline easy, but I hated it. And unless I was really hungry, I didn't think the food was worth lining up for. Chocolate La Monge – or Yarra Mud as we called it – was like eating faintly chocolate-flavoured slime.

There was little privacy anywhere, except in the bathrooms. Even there, the partitions between the shower and the loo cubicles reached neither the floor nor the ceiling so one's privacy could easily be disturbed. There was a junior and senior common room at each end of the cloisters where, on Sundays after lunch, we wrote our letters home. I could never think of anything to say except that the room smelled of stale food, mouldy fruit and used sports kits, so I naturally enough didn't want a teacher to read my letter.

At the beginning boarding school was lonely, strange and scary. Those who had been there longer and knew the system sometimes teased and picked on new girls simply because they were vulnerable. Mum had always stressed that if you were nice to people, they were nice to you, but it didn't really seem to work like that. Mum was unworldly but very determined that she wasn't. The letters she wrote every week and sometimes even more often were short and supportive, almost every one rather like the one she'd written the week before.

About school life Dad advised, 'Now, you watch other girls and see how they get on with each other. You can learn a lot by watching and remembering what others do and say in certain situations.' I knew Dad was quite right, but it was hard to do what he said I should. I was so scared of being teased that sometimes I imagined it happening when it probably wasn't. Before I arrived at Toorak College the only classroom I had ever seen was Harry's grade 3 room at the Corryong primary school. I can't recall ever having visited Indi while she was at school so I don't think I had seen a dormitory.

I don't know if Mum realised that, except for the daygirls arriving in kindergarten or the children beginning as boarders in grade 1 at Wardle House, I would be the only new girl who had never been to school before. It was lonely being the only one who had come from correspondence schooling, and for whom *everything* was new and strange. I now bitterly regretted not taking up Mum's suggestion that I go to the local primary school for a year before heading to boarding school.

At the end of my first term when I received an F for maths, Miss D remarked, 'You could do better than that. You could try.'

'What is the point when I'm hopeless at maths?' I replied.

'Why do you think so?' Miss D asked quietly.

'Because Mum said so,' I replied, and the story of how I couldn't remember all my times tables or do long division came tumbling out.

In return for a promise that I would really try, at the beginning of the next term Miss D began to teach me some of the skills I needed and it was not long before I was called teacher's pet. It was the gentle Miss D who persuaded me that I had the ability to learn and that, if I tried, I could do well. Learning to learn wasn't a smooth process and while she didn't manage to completely convince me about maths, at least I had begun to enjoy it. Confidence took longer, but in time a little began to develop and I was beginning to hold my own.

Miss D was much too good for us and soon, like her parents, she became a missionary. I was very sorry when a few years later we heard that she had died in South America.

Arithmetic was not my only weak subject initially. Knowing how whistling eagles built their nests or where I might find azure kingfishers was no use whatsoever when it came to nature study at school. Nor was my knowledge of some of the names of the mountains we could see from Towong Hill any use in geography lessons where we were learning about other countries. But I loved both subjects and was quick to catch up.

Although the children's books Mum had written were a salvation during my early childhood at Towong Hill, ultimately I found their legacy a bit of a burden after I arrived at boarding school. Mum became busier and busier as a writer, and it seemed some teachers and peers alike expected me to have a fabulous imagination and to be a talented, well-practised storyteller and a good English student. I had read a lot in comparison to many of my contemporaries and I could tell a reasonable yarn, but my handwriting, spelling and grammar were dire and let me down badly. Before I went to school I was under the impression that, next to history, English was my best subject. I soon discovered that while Mum had put plenty of lines through my arithmetic, she hadn't corrected much of my spelling or grammar. 'I didn't want to stifle your individuality,' she later remarked. She could be exasperatingly inconsistent.

When Miss W in second form thumped my desk in frustration until the books and pens bounced over my mistakes, I found that, at least initially, individuality had a humiliating price. I simply had to learn the rules before I could begin to break them. Meanwhile, the thumping made me quake in my shoes. I soon dreaded grammar almost as much as maths lessons, with the result I learned almost nothing except how to survive a year in Miss W's class.

I thought she got her just deserts when I heard some of the boarders in my form had put water in her petrol tank. She drove her Morris Minor out onto Old Mornington Road where it came to a spluttering stop. Clearly I was not the only one who thought she was a battleaxe, and she wasn't the only battleaxe either. In form 3 Mrs S spent a whole year teaching us English grammar. I found it deadly boring; she was humourless and she terrified me. Once again I learned next to nothing and spent time in prep teaching myself what she had tried to teach in class.

Other students who had read *Kingfisher Feather* and *Winged Skis* and realised the extent to which both books were based on our family knew too much about me, while I knew relatively little about them. Peers saw the discrepancy between me and the goody-two-shoes characters of the Dane twins in *Kingfisher Feather* and

Barry Milton in *Winged Skis*. Most of my contemporaries knew my parents were distinguished skiers, but thank goodness none of them seemed to know about the dreaded ski pram. It was a pity that *Silver Brumbies of the South*, which Mum dedicated to me, was not published until 1965 after I had started boarding school. A desire to keep it quiet tempered my delight in seeing in print the book that I had spent so many happy hours reading and talking about with Mum. I wished too that I had been at home to share some of the pleasure of its publication with her.

The history I had taught myself from reading historical fiction bore little or no relation to the history our teachers taught us during our social studies lessons. At that time history was not taught as a separate subject at Toorak College. Nonetheless, I enjoyed the lessons, and old friends relate that the stories I told helped them to pass the history questions in exams. I can't remember doing very much of that and I imagine that my knowledge of historical fiction may have distorted my grasp and interpretation of facts, but I was relieved to be able to cope with one subject and to be able to help those who had helped me in other ways.

Even though I thought I was a reasonable swimmer, when I arrived at school I found I hit the water like a whale compared to some of the slimline torpedoes in Speedos. The heats for the swimming sports were held between the jetties on the pier in nearby Davies Bay. The wooden jetties were slippery from being submerged and the barnacles were hard on the soles of our feet. Except for occasional swims at Elwood when we were staying with Granny and on my trip to Bondi Beach in Sydney, I had not swum very much in the sea and found it difficult to proceed in a straight line through the waves. I was lucky to finish the heats let alone to qualify for some races.

Nor had I learned to play rounders, baseball or basketball. I had made the useful discovery during the holiday I spent in Sydney before I went to boarding school that I couldn't throw anything with any accuracy or distance, and my ability wasn't improving much with practice. The winter after I started at Toorak College I also discovered I couldn't hit a hockey ball very far or very fast, and I was so unfit that I couldn't run for more than a few minutes. When I too often got cold and bored playing in the right-back position, I moved to right-halfback. I had to run more there, but it was more exciting.

Being able to ski wasn't any help when it came to learning about games. There was a brick practice wall nicely tucked away below the tennis courts and on the edge of the Wilderness, the bushland within the school grounds. I could practise there in some peace and, with the help of tennis lessons with Mr Guiney and later Mr Fox, ultimately was able to hold my own and enjoy tennis.

I spent time sewing. Mum had taught me to hand sew and embroider a little, and I learned how to use the Singer treadle machines that were lined up around the walls in the old weatherboard school hall affectionately known as The Elephant. Mrs Roberts showed me that it wasn't difficult to set the machine correctly and to untangle threads, and eventually I made myself skirts and even dresses for my last two school dances. Dad had brought me back a small transistor radio from a trip he made to Japan in 1965 and in the afternoons after school and on weekends I took it everywhere.

When Mum realised that I had been lonely and unhappy at boarding school, she proved to be too fierce an ally too late, and wasn't sufficiently discreet about to whom she expressed her concern. She told me how much she had hated boarding school and that she never expected any of her children to enjoy it, so when I was unhappy in the first two or three years it was like a self-fulfilling prophesy to her. Inevitably, time improved my situation and, although I still found the rigid routine difficult, I began to find friends and settle down. There was some steel developing in my personality and I wanted to break out of what seemed to be a generational cycle of being unhappy and underperforming at school. Turning things around took time.

I became a swot. With a bit of effort I found I could retain the basic maths, English, science skills and French vocabulary I needed. With a bit more work I began to realise I could be an average and sometimes a slightly better than average student. At home I thought I was capable only of reading and learning a little history, but at school I discovered that science, and in particular biology, was fascinating. I still lacked the maths skills necessary to do chemistry and physics. While I didn't have Indi's artistic talent I could draw and enjoyed art and craft. The art hut where Mrs Paxton Petty ran a relaxed but inspiring empire was a world of its own, cut off from the main school buildings by two large playing fields. I never learned to read music accurately, but I loved listening. I didn't sing at first because Mum said I was tone deaf and people who were tone deaf sounded awful. Eventually, when I tried, I loved singing.

Having eventually gained some control over my academic life, when I was in fourth form I thought I might be able to regulate my appetite and lose weight from my sturdy thighs so I would look better in bathers, and slender and elegant in sports shorts on the playing fields and tennis courts. It seemed some girls dieted successfully, but for me it did not go as planned. I lost weight from almost every area of my body except for my legs and my progress in class and on the sports field began to flag. When a member of staff intimated there might be a problem, Mum rushed down with the most delicious collection of cakes I had ever seen for a picnic afternoon tea. She didn't eat anything and I was supposed to eat much more than I was able. It was an overreaction by Mum, and during the next school holidays, and for many subsequent holidays and visits, at almost every meal Mum's eyes were on my plate. If she thought I wasn't eating enough she shook her head and sighed. I dreaded the scrutiny.

Mum was not interested in food and cooking: she ate grapefruit and dried biscuits mixed with wheat hearts and honey for breakfast, some salad or leftover cooked vegetables baked with breadcrumbs on top for lunch, and some meat and vegetables in the evening. She expected her family to eat 'normally' – meaning plenty of meat and vegetables. Sometimes when she offered me more of the dish we were eating I snapped back. In September 1969 Mum wrote to Granny saying, 'Honor was just her old, sweet self this time and it was very nice indeed,' implying that I wasn't always like that. And indeed I wasn't. On reflection, Mum and I were finding it hard to get on. I couldn't understand her attitude to food, I resented her scrutiny, struggled with some of the meals at home and the quantities that Mum thought necessary for me to eat.

At meals Mum and Dad taunted each other. Dad teased and Mum got hurt and fought back. My intestines seemed to leap and knot themselves and my appetite evaporated. It was a vicious circle, and dieting had made it worse. Just as I knew years ago after falling at Mum's bedroom door that I was being a nuisance, now I knew I was causing her anxiety on top of her having too much to do when she was trying to write. I longed for the relationship we'd had when she was writing *Silver Brumbies of the South* and *Silver Brumby Kingdom*.

At about the time *Silver Brumbies of the South* was published I suggested she might write a story about a dingo pup. She started *Jinki: Dingo of the Snows*, but for me the little dingo pup never had the charismatic appeal of Thowra or Baringa. Jinki reminded me of the Australian terrier called Winkle that Mum had bought for the family and that came to assume an importance in Mum's life that I don't think any of her family attained. Instead of bringing the closeness I craved, Jinki simply meant that Mum retreated more into her writing. Feeling hurt about being a nuisance and also guilty about not liking Jinki, I taunted her, accusing her of being taken up with 'chapter six, line two' and not having enough time for her family. Dad was quick to pick up my line and teased her even more. The following year, 1969, it was the same while she wrote *Light Horse to Damascus*. Mum retreated more into her shell, the tension increased and I felt even guiltier.

Mum and I were similar in some ways, but we were not doing each other any good. Both of us were inhibited and sensitive to criticism from the other. Both of us wanted to do well – Mum wanted continued success with her writing, while I was striving to achieve the simplest things at school and hoping for some parental approval. It seemed to me that Mum was very critical and quick to point out my flaws and to pick up on my mistakes. I began to experience stomach pains and gastric upsets, but neither the local doctor nor the school doctor could ascertain the cause. Mum had always suffered from tummy aches; during 1945 particularly she had had gastric attacks. She had suffered for far longer than I had – she just got on with it. Although she expected me to do so too, I knew she was worried about it. So was I, and suspected that stress didn't help and on some occasions even caused the cramps.

If she had been able to attend more school events and functions we might have had an easier relationship. There would have been more opportunities to see Mum and Dad if I had been sent to school in Melbourne – not that they were there together very often – and I would have been closer to Granny. Toorak College was about an hour out of Melbourne and I was out on a limb. Perhaps there wasn't sufficient time among the other things Mum had to do on each of her visits to Melbourne to drive down to Toorak College as well. And, love her as I did, when I was a teenager she was the sort of mother who embarrassed her kids. I knew that she was a bit of a rebel and liked to be different, and she wasn't fashion-conscious like many of the other mothers. What I didn't realise was that on the rare occasions she came to our swimming sports, a tennis match or speech day, it was not easy for her. She was shy, self-conscious and often sat alone as she knew few other parents. Also she was older than most of them. If she had known how I felt she would have been mortified, so I didn't say much. Guessing reasonably accurately what I was thinking from the little I did say, she said I was being mean, and I ended up feeling bad.

Once I was selected for the team to swim at the Southern Districts Swimming Sports at the Olympic Pool in Melbourne. As we were boarding the bus to return to school, the driver said to me, 'You are Honor from the Upper Murray!' He was smiling, obviously pleased to see me. I knew instantly he was the man who about six or seven years earlier had threatened to catch me and put me over his knee. Embarrassment at my memory overcame me. If I could have made myself invisible or fled, I would have done so.

During the 1968 Easter holidays, Indi made me a white empire-line Swiss voile dress for my confirmation. Her boyfriend Rick was staying and he sat reading while she fitted and pinned the dress. Both sniggered a bit, probably at my embarrassment, or my figure, or both, or simply because I was the kid sister. While I was delighted with the dress, I was relieved when the fittings were finished. Indi sewed beautifully and when the day came I had that wonderful feeling that I looked my best.

I hadn't attended many Confirmation classes as they clashed with tennis lessons, or I contrived that they did. Nor did I learn the things I was supposed to learn, although I wasn't entirely alone. As if to make up for deficiencies in my religious education, my brother John sent me his own humorous version of the Ten Commandments. Mum, Granny and Indi came to the Confirmation service at St James the Less, the simple white church in Mt Eliza where the Anglican boarders attended early church on Sundays. I emerged from being confirmed no more knowledgeable than I had been, but the Bible and prayer book that Mum, Dad and Granny gave me have travelled with me throughout my life.

Except for mentions of the flood and fires, even the Bible stories Mum had read to us seemed so far removed from Towong Hill that I hadn't really listened to very many of them. Neither I nor my siblings had been to Sunday School nor even to church very much, so I didn't know any of the hymns we were expected to practise in our music lessons. I am not sure that the idea that we would then sing them better in school assemblies worked, and some more inspired teaching wouldn't have been amiss. All the same, I eventually began to enjoy them and they formed the foundations of my growing love of choral music. Senior boarder and prefect Libby Harper read from poems by Yevgeny Yevtushenko at evening prayers and thanks to her I started looking enthusiastically to modern authors outside the school curriculum and Mum's recommendations for my reading. I was building my own reading world.

The staff at Toorak College tried their best to ensure I was happy and in many ways I am sure I benefited from the certainty of boarding house regime. For one term, when I was about fifteen, I was put into a small dorm with two others on the ground floor near the sick bay and next door to Sister's bedroom. The bathroom we shared with the girls in sick bay had no shower, and one evening after tennis one of us – possibly me – ran a bath and forgot about it. We met the water flowing down the corridor where it was already seeping under Sister's door. Strangely, she had not come out to complain about the water so we knocked. When she shouted 'Come in!' we opened the door and found her sitting on her bed in fits of laughter. We reckoned she was a bit inebriated because it made the story better. She was quite a good sort, as indeed were most members of the staff – even those I thought were battleaxes.

33
A Bid for Freedom

Soon after John went to boarding school in February 1967, aged about eleven, Mum set off to ski in Sun Valley, Idaho, and Zurs in Austria. It seemed strange that she hardly waited to see how John had settled in. Glamorgan in Toorak, a preparatory school for Geelong Grammar, was close enough to South Yarra for Granny to keep a close eye on him. To me it felt as if Mum couldn't wait to get away from our family and its problems in this her first bid for freedom. Mum's absence felt like a catalyst for more unwanted change. I became watchful, reading Mum's letters more carefully than ever for signs of other travel plans and absences.

Skiing at Thredbo the winter before, Mum had torn her Achilles tendon and I couldn't understand why she would want to take that risk again less than a year later. Instead, while in Sun Valley, she broke her leg. Surely it was not worth it, I thought. I'd just learned what a lemming was and the description seemed to fit Mum perfectly. While I knew she was also catching up with friends, some of whom she had not seen since before the war, and there would be many years' worth of news to discuss, none of my school friends' mothers seemed to go off alone on overseas ski trips. The contrast between Mum and other mothers was hard to understand.

Granny kept in touch with us all by letter and telephone while Mum was away. She also wrote to Mum at length, giving her our family news. One day Granny came down to Toorak College and took me out to lunch with friends of Aunt Eve who were visiting from South Africa. The next day I came out in measles and spent the following two weeks in bed in sick bay.

Although I was older and well settled at school by then, I found Mum's next trip to Austria and England in 1970 equally difficult to accept, and the anxiety that she mightn't return lingered at the back of my mind. I knew Dad had threatened to refuse to sign her passport application so I knew he didn't like her going either. I don't know why he eventually agreed to sign; I thought they must have struck a private bargain of some sort. But he was loyal and never said anything critical about her trips in my hearing. Outside the family Mum made light of her injuries, stressing the importance of her exercise routine to keep going. Anyone who saw her in bathers would have known how bent her right leg was in comparison with her left leg and that it was also shorter. Some of her friends made a point of telling me how marvellous she was – 'She just keeps going!' For a while I felt obliged to agree, though I thought it was remarkable rather than marvellous. That said, she wrote regularly during those two trips and her letters were among the best I ever received from her. So, true to form, I said little or nothing at all.

The 1970 trip was particularly notable for the extraordinary amounts of snow that Mum saw and described in a postcard she wrote to me in April from Lech, Austria: 'Apparently 1916–1917 was like this, otherwise nothing like it till way back in 1847.' The following day she wrote: 'This has been quite a week – the whole of Europe under blizzard and snow – terrible – and yet quite an experience.' Three weeks earlier she had described how she had been taken to see 'the biggest avalanche any of them [Zurs ski school instructors] have ever known'. It had 'huge trees in it and the wind it made knocked out trees on the other side of the valley'. I could feel her excitement in all that she saw. It was manna for Mum, who seemed to be on a perpetual quest for adventure.

The 1970 trip was not just for skiing. Mum also went to St Anton to meet Rudi Matt, with whom she had skied briefly in 1938 before she broke her leg for the first time. In a letter she wrote of her concern about recognising him and her admiration for his achievements in making films of the local wildlife. She saw Uncle Ian, her eldest brother, and Aunt Jean in London where they were visiting their two daughters and their families. In London Mum also met Dorothy Tomlinson from Hutchinson Publishing Company and Paul Langridge from Curtis Brown, her agents, thus making that leg of her trip a professional one.

I never understood why some of the money Mum spent on the 1967 and 1970 trips was not used to visit Ian and Jean at their home near Durban in South Africa, or Eve and her family who were living in what was then Rhodesia. Given Mum's interest in Grandfather's campaigns, life and achievements, I felt she might have combined visiting family with seeing some of the Boer War battlefields where Grandfather and the Queensland Mounted Infantry had fought. It would have meant that in the mid 1970s when she began her research for *Light Horse: The Story of Australia's Mounted Troops* she would already have had first-hand knowledge. But like all of us, Mum had her foibles. There was sometimes a conflict of interest between her near-obsessive love of skiing, her desire to see friends, her writing and her family.

Mum was away in Easter 1970 when John was ill with suspected appendicitis. Dad insisted that he should eat something and sent me to scramble some eggs for him, but I knew that if he ate it, he *would* be ill. Either Harry or I saw to it that most of the scrambled eggs were scraped off the plate onto some paper in a drawer so that Dad was satisfied and John didn't become any sicker than he was already.

Mum regretted the timing of her trip with John being ill, and she missed everyone very much. Each letter contained instructions about where to write to her next and expressions of gratitude for the mail she received. She often wrote that she hoped we would be able to travel together after I left school at the end of the following year in December 1971. After some of the difficulties in my early teenage years, it seemed a new and positive note was creeping into our relationship.

34
A Love of Freedom

Journeys to and from school at the beginning and end of each term were hugely exciting. That magnetic pull of the home on the hill high above the meandering Murray River with the magnificent view of the Alps lasted right through my school career and well beyond into my later life.

There were a number of us from Toorak College and other schools who travelled by train on the Albury line from Melbourne. After the school taxi had delivered us and our cases to Spencer Street railway station (now Southern Cross station), we were free as birds until our parents met us at our destination – unless Dad happened to be on the same train. On one occasion, after being denied scrambled eggs on the *Spirit of Progress*, he acquired some eccentric fame by bringing the incident to the attention of Parliament, as if the existence or otherwise of scrambled eggs were an issue of major importance. Famous or infamous, he was a good sport and wisely sat working on parliamentary correspondence in another carriage well away from the noise and mischief of us teenagers. We hitched up our skirts, and anyone lucky enough to have some make-up might have put some on. There were reunions with old friends, romances blossomed and I didn't see much of Dad until we arrived at Wangaratta or Wodonga where he left his car.

The times when I flew from Corryong or Albury I thought I was missing out on the fun on the train. Years later in Europe, friends were amazed when I told them I had flown part of the way to school on a DC-3; I didn't know how lucky I was. Fortunately, James and Annabel Mackinnon from Tintaldra, and later Harry and then Penny Chisholm from Khancoban Station, joined Harry, me and John, travelling on the same trains or planes, so I was seldom alone. On one plane trip James's luggage containing his mother's cake tins went to Albany in Western Australia rather than Albury. This incompetence by the airline surprised and amused us. Wasn't it supposed to be run by grown-ups? James and I chortled to each other. Was Mrs Mackinnon going to have to find some new tins for next term's cakes, I wondered?

Albury railway station was my favourite. Its very long platform and the tower over the station entrance made it seem like the kingpin of all country railway stations and so much grander than the one at Spencer Street. If he wasn't travelling on the same train, Dad usually met us at either Wangaratta or Wodonga – both towns were in his electorate and he could combine collecting us with political business. Meeting us in Albury meant crossing the river and adding time to his journey. Granny was the only one of the family who managed to get out at the wrong station but, even then, someone recognised her and the stationmaster offered to phone Mum and get a message to Dad.

Dad enjoyed driving, particularly when he knew the roads well. 'If I am alone,' he told me, 'I like to sing. Driving has the same effect on me as a bath does on others! Sometimes I sing "Wild Colonial Boy" if I'm thinking about my old Uncle Jack rattling in his buggy – a speedy model it was too, with solid rubber tyres – over to the council meetings at Tumbarumba. If I think the bush

I'm driving through is looking particularly beautiful, I sing "The Road to Gundagai".'

'You must have sung almost every song you know a thousand times over or more when you're driving to party meetings and to see people in different places in the electorate,' I remarked.

'I've sung them all and I wish I knew many more Australian songs than I do. I tried to learn a few more while I was in Changi. Some of the AIF boys had a pretty good repertoire.'

We were lucky that Dad didn't sing when he had passengers. Instead, he told yarns about incidents that had taken place in years gone by on the route between Wodonga and Towong Hill. When we arrived at Shelley, for instance, he delighted in telling us about Granny M's first journey to the Upper Murray, before she and Granddaddy M were married. She was chaperoned by her brother-in-law, Dr Willie Chisholm. She remembered this first trip best and perhaps she had enjoyed telling Dad and Aunt Hon about it as much as Dad liked to tell us. Dad described the road along which Granny M would have travelled as a 'jazzed-up goat track'. They stopped at the pub at Shelley where the publican's wife, who 'was a real piece of old Ireland', served the only dish available, rabbit and rice. Dad seemed tickled by the idea that the variation of rabbit and rice was rice and rabbit, and often repeated the story with all the drama possible in his voice as he drove. I could imagine Dad on stage – politics was probably the next best thing for him! Mum tells the story slightly differently in *Towong Hill: Fifty Years on an Upper Murray Cattle Station*, but it was Dad's originally. He, too, was a great storyteller and Mum was a wonderful scribe.

From the day Granny M arrived at the Mitchell family homestead at Bringenbrong it rained for six weeks. The roof of the old house leaked, the Murray flooded its banks and the roads, such as they were at that time, were cut. Unless a stockman managed to ford the floodwaters and collect the mail from Corryong there was no communication with the world outside the station. For many years a post on the riverbank a few hundred metres downstream from where the Bringenbrong Bridge is now marked the ford. When the river was flooding it was not a crossing to be taken lightly. The Bringenbrong homestead smelled of damp and of wet clothing and saddles. When eventually Granny M was able to go across to Towong Hill, she was taken in the poison cart sitting next to an open can of rabbit poison. On her last evening at Bringenbrong before setting off on her return journey to Sydney, Granny M was utterly fed up and retired to her bedroom only to find that a wet sheepdog had beaten her to it and was curled up sound asleep on her bed. It could have ended the romance, but Granny M was made of stern stuff.

Not surprisingly, she yearned for a more comfortable form of transport and in 1911 insisted that the family should have a car. 'Them Mitchellses is gettin' one of them moti-cars,' Dad used to narrate in a broad country accent of the times to me and anyone else whether we wanted to hear it or not. 'The local people reckoned it would be the death of them all,' he went on. 'They said that their horses would bolt at the very sound of it!' Lady Urquhart at Cudgewa Station already had a car and another in the district might have seemed too much.

'Then Uncle Jack got a motor car – a Talbot, I think. This would have been about 1912,' Dad went on, warming to his story. 'Uncle Jack told Granddaddy M he thought that because they were both skilled in the forge and should be able to fix a car when it broke down they would be good drivers. Granddaddy M should be particularly good because he had a good ear for music and would hear when the car was going to break down. Uncle Jack might have been all right in the forge, shoeing horses, making carriage wheels and that sort of thing, but he didn't have the right touch with those new-fangled machines, as they sometimes called cars in the old days.

'The first time Uncle Jack and Aunt Fanny drove over to see Granddaddy and Granny M he ran into the garden fence before he remembered how to stop the thing. Then, when they left, they had to crank up the car. He climbed into his seat, found reverse and went slap bang into the rose which Mother was trying to grow. Uncle Jack swore terribly and Auntie Fanny sat there looking shocked and saying, "Jock dear, Jock dear, please …" Meanwhile, Uncle would be well into his next tirade. No sooner was Uncle back in the seat than he crashed into the other fence. He'd forgotten how to stop the thing again.'

I thought Dad was one of the most eccentric characters I knew but his stories had characters who were sometimes more eccentric. If we were giving others a lift I tried to discourage him from telling stories so he wouldn't embarrass me. It was a mistake to think I could do so: my negative vibes seemed to encourage him to make the stories more colourful. Maybe it was only me who was embarrassed – quite possibly people enjoyed his stories, even though they knew he exaggerated a bit. Some people called him the Hon Tom but others called him Mr History, and the sobriquet was appropriate.

Mum welcomed us home from school with freshly made sponge cakes. Occasionally she made them in billies so they were very tall, rather like a cake version of Dr Seuss's Cat-in-the-Hat hat, but without the red and white stripes. She greased the inside of the billy before scattering it with caster sugar, thus giving a delicious crunch to the cake's texture. After Mum took a cake out of the oven she put it on a rack under a wire cover to cool and keep it safe from marauding flies. A wonderful aroma of baking would fill the kitchen.

On the first night back at home I would lie in bed, listening to the sounds of cattle on the river flats. Through the windows I could see the familiar silhouette of the trees in the garden and beyond them the outline of the hills surrounding the Murray Valley.

In my early years at school I looked forward to school holidays as if my life depended on them. Later I felt some ambivalence. In my diary for the summer of 1970 I described how, before the holidays started, Sally, a friend from western Victoria, had remarked that she hoped her dad would let her do some work with a tractor when she got home, while Penny, who came from Gippsland, would also be working outside on the property with her dad. I wouldn't have minded if someone could teach me how to drive a tractor or to be useful on the property. I might have been able to plough the firebreaks that lay in huge ribbons across the paddocks on the north side of the house at Towong Hill.

In my last couple of years at school, James Mackinnon (who was at Geelong Grammar) and I were often in touch, finding partners for each other for school dances and making arrangements for the holidays. Once James came to a school dance at Toorak College to be a partner for one of my friends. He took one look at our headmistress, Miss Cerrutty, with her ample bosom and skinny, pin-like legs, then turned to me and asked, 'Honor, where is her broomstick?' I never knew if Miss Cerrutty heard or not, but surely she must at least have sensed mischief from the ripple of laughter following James's remark.

If I ever imagined that by going to boarding school I would be distanced from family friction, I was wrong. It cropped up at unexpected moments. Before my final speech day in 1971, Miss Cerrutty asked Dad to sit with the distinguished guests on the stage. Mum was not invited to sit with him. Luckily Indi and Harry had come down for the occasion and were able to sit with her, but Mum saw the lack of invitation as a slight and she was furious. Harry and Indi were cross about something Miss Cerrutty said, or should have said and didn't say, with regard to me, though I can't remember the details.

Cerri and I had not got on very well in my last few terms. Mum didn't like her and I had had enough of school and Cerri, and

Mum's antipathy towards her. Despite the tension, it was good to have so many members of my family there. Indi, in particular, had been a kind help on a number of occasions during my time at school. Harry had also done exams for some extra school subjects he needed that term and it was good of him to come to my speech day. He had been living at 49 Murphy Street and Granny had expected him to talk to her in the evenings so it had been hard for him to study. He'd had a frustrating year.

In the same way that the age gap between Indi and I meant we were never at school at the same time, so John arrived at Geelong Grammar as Harry left. The physical barrier of Port Phillip Bay, which lay between Toorak College and Geelong Grammar, further divided brother and sister. We were all very different characters from birth and in many ways our paths diverged still further while we were at boarding school. Mum and Dad wouldn't have wanted that to happen and before Christmas 1971 Mum was writing to Uncle Ian suggesting that Harry and I were at 'cross purposes'. Harry said he thought I was lucky because in some ways I'd had a better time at school than he had and enjoyed sport more. I reckoned he was lucky because he was going to inherit our home, just as Dad had done. It upsets me now to think of this knowing that it wasn't going to work out like that.

On leaving school there wasn't to be the skiing trip to Europe that Mum had hoped we might do together. I think I realised at the time it was little more than a dream so it didn't really matter. James Mackinnon and I had already been talking about meeting up to play tennis and the possibility of a woolshed dance at Lankeys Creek near Holbrook. Along with other friends I also had an invitation from John Darling, whom I had met while skiing at Thredbo and later at a dance at Geelong Grammar, to a party his parents were giving in Sydney and I was looking forward to catching the train along with James and other friends from Melbourne – it left in the evening after speech day. Mum had bought me a beautiful dress and I was excited about wearing it to the party. The fact that I would have very few other suitable clothes to wear while I was staying with Aunt Margaret in Sydney no longer seemed to matter on my last day at school.

Whatever it was that Cerri had done or said on speech day was not going to take away my happiness and, strangely, I didn't feel the slights that my family had been conscious of. More importantly, freedom was only hours away. What I was going to do when I returned from Sydney was tomorrow's problem. Never before, or since, have I been so carefree as I was that evening when Mum dropped me at Spencer Street station to catch the Sydney train.

One of the greatest gifts that Toorak College had given me was a love of freedom and some friends with whom to enjoy it. I could feel myself expanding into every inch of it. During various enjoyable occasions with the Swaneys and other friends I began to see possibilities and careers beyond school and the way of life I knew. At last I was moving on, breaking out of the golden cage that had been childhood.

35

The Time Warp

If I thought my bid for freedom and frivolity in Sydney just after leaving school would herald a problem-free spreading of my wings into adulthood, I was wrong. While I was never an angel, I returned to Towong Hill a tarnished creature. With a cigarette burn in my beautiful dress my halo was more non-existent than ever – not that I had smoked, but I had a feeling Mum didn't believe me when I told her about the chap who had waved his arm backwards in a sweeping gesture and caught my dress with his cigarette. Mum said I had behaved badly and there would be consequences. But if there were, I already had other things on my mind and didn't notice.

Back at Towong Hill after the party in Sydney, my apparent lack of gratitude to my family on speech day had caused some upset. Had I forgotten to thank them for coming down, I wondered? Mum said something to me, but I can't remember her exact words, just the feeling I hadn't endeared myself to anyone. I might have been on the cusp of adulthood but, humiliatingly, within the family circle various members seemed to still consider me a rather gauche child. If that were so, they were right, not that I wanted to admit it; it was synonymous with feeling like a

The Time Warp

nuisance, and I certainly had awkward memories about that. Was I so socially inept that every foray I made into the adult world was going to bring criticism, I wondered? The more gauche I felt, the more gauche I became. If this was what leaving school and growing up was all about, then it was an anticlimax. But there would be other opportunities for freedom and I tucked that comforting thought away in my mind.

Next issue: what was I to do back at Towong Hill? Mum enjoyed tennis so I knew we would play a lot and she would organise tennis parties. But with the rest of my life ahead of me, that seemed directionless. I dreaded the exam results as I didn't expect to do well enough to be accepted into courses that I would be interested in and that my parents would consider worthwhile. There had never been much for me to do at home, and increasingly it felt like a cage. Having finally left school after many years away boarding, I felt as if I was stepping back into a time warp.

One day Mum said, 'If you can roast a joint of meat, stew apples, make a good white sauce and a light sponge cake, you can cook just about anything.' She had asked me to stir the white sauce to stop it going lumpy and there was a huge roast in the oven beneath. I nodded, knowing better than to say that I had seen my schoolfriend Penny's mother making delicious desserts like lemon meringue pie with methods and ingredients that looked very different from those needed for a sponge cake or stewing apples.

Domestic life at Towong Hill had a character of its own. Menus didn't seem to have changed much since my early childhood. Mum admitted that she had been married for six years before she cooked a meal on the 'range' at Towong Hill.[1] Except for grilled chops, steaks, roasts, and her delicious sponge cakes, Mum still didn't cook much, and neither did she like it. She hated onions, garlic, cream and chocolate, saying they all made her ill. The roast legs or shoulders of lamb and sirloins of beef she routinely prepared were huge. After the evening meal Mum would put the left-overs in the safe, an open cupboard covered in flywire mesh. The left-overs were then used as cold meat for lunch for a few days and a lot was fed to the dog.

For Mum, time spent in the kitchen was time wasted, and she didn't encourage me to cook much either. She liked me to help her because it was an opportunity to talk, but she didn't want to completely hand over any aspect of meal preparation. She liked to keep control and she didn't like new ideas or different foods. Mum thought I was criticising her if I took any initiative, and responded with frosty silence. Apart from the *Presbyterian Women's Cookbook*, the only other recipe book in the house was one by Constance Spry. Both editions had been published before the war and were very rarely referred to. Mum knew by heart the few recipes she wanted to use.

Mum talked about the stories that 'Aunt' Emily Scammell told her when she worked as a cook at Towong Hill during the war and how they prepared food together to donate to the Red Cross, but I never heard about the meals Emily cooked. I have no idea whether her cooking was experimental or simple, but I suspect the latter. It wouldn't have mattered to Mum so long as it was edible and contained plenty of healthy fruit and vegetables from the garden.

In the postwar years, it became harder and harder to find anyone to employ as a cook. We had one lady who braided her hair, wrapping the shiny plaits around her head, and arrived with a galah in a large cage. She didn't drive and Towong Hill must have been very lonely for her. On her days off she sat in her sitting room and talked to her bird. I can't recall whether the bird replied or not, but they both seemed too introspective for much dialogue.

Another cook was better at chopping down trees than she was at preparing food. She was too butch for Mum, and her husband, if indeed he was her husband, was too effeminate. He increasingly

The Time Warp

needed his wife to help him with the heavy jobs in the garden, which meant she did less and less cooking. Mum became frustrated with them while I became fascinated by their behaviour and near role reversal. While Mum could be devastatingly direct when talking to her own children, she agonised for ages before she finally sacked them.

Another, Mrs G, was allegedly married to Tom, a former First World War digger. They too had a parrot they had reared themselves. It used to screech about wanting a 'bloody drink' and knew a few other choice swear words about old Tom and his plans to go to the pub. Mum was horrified when she discovered that Annabel Mackinnon and I had found out Mrs G and Tom were not married. We were all sorry when we heard that they had made plans to marry, but unfortunately Tom died before they could do so.

Finally there was Mrs M from Corryong, whom we all loved dearly and who was still coming to us on special occasions when I left school. In the kitchen we'd all offer to top up her drink, not realising that other members of the family might already have done so; the evenings when she cooked were cheerful and highly amusing. Mum was beginning to make more friends locally and sometimes for special occasions or after a tennis party she invited people to stay on for a meal. Mrs M cooked Mum's 'short-cut' casseroles, sticking firmly to the requirement that the ingredients should not include onions or garlic. If she was ever aware that the casseroles were known as Mrs Mitchell's F...ing Fricassee in certain circles, she never let on. She held the Towong Hill record for high-speed washing-up and she could almost throw plates and glasses into the sink and seldom, if ever, chip, crack or break anything. She was a marvel with a great character and a heart of pure gold.

Cooks might come and go but little really changed in a kitchen dating from the thirties and forties. It was like cooking in a museum and I felt the need to treat the prewar utensils with a special reverence. A school friend called in once at lunchtime; I suspect she wished she hadn't as afterwards she told me she reckoned that the camembert Mum had offered her was at least six months old. The dried herbs and spices at the back of the store cupboards may even have been prewar and I don't think they were ever used. Mum preferred to use fresh herbs, if she remembered she even had them. Although she had planted quite an extensive herb garden, often it became overgrown with weeds. Its cultivation depended on Mum's varying levels of enthusiasm but, except in drought, it usually flourished, despite spells of being forgotten.

Mum had never installed a dishwasher. She bought one – or at least someone did – but Mum changed her mind about it. Later she explained with remarkable logic that it wouldn't save her work, reasoning that she would be left to fill and empty it by herself. Without one, at least the menfolk of the family dried and put away the dishes. By that stage the amount of domestic effort Mum was prepared to expend was very carefully calculated!

Once there was no longer a cook, Mum worked and read at the kitchen table. The Aga kept her warm and she wrote while she waited for meals to cook. This method was not always successful: a baking tray full of roast vegetables was once left in the 'top right', the hottest oven, for two weeks, and it was only discovered when we couldn't find the roasting dish. After some thought, Mum remembered that she had done a roast when she'd had a visitor a fortnight earlier. Presumably the conversation was so good that they hadn't realised or were too polite to mention the lack of vegetables. When the dish was found she described the charred remains as charcoal apostles and rocked with laughter at her own irreverence.

Mum didn't like cooking but she hated ironing. Her scorch rate was high, perhaps simply because she didn't iron very often.

Upstairs above the kitchen in the linen room was a wardrobe containing her evening and cocktail dresses, suits, skirts and blouses. Many of the garments dated from the Queen's visits in 1954 and 1963, but each garment was associated with at least one special occasion – and also a wonderful repertoire of stories. Whatever her attitude to ironing and other domestic tasks, Mum usually rose to special occasions and dressed immaculately for them, but one could never be certain – it depended on whether she wanted to attend the event or not. Mostly, but certainly not always, someone else did any necessary mending, alteration and ironing.

For me, the saddest aspect of the linen room was the cupboard filled with unused wedding presents. Was everything Mum needed already at Towong Hill, I wondered? Why didn't she want to use her and Dad's own things rather than those of Winifred and Walter Edward? In many instances the presents still had cards in the boxes, and I don't think Mum even knew what the deeper recesses of the cupboard held. If she opened the cupboard and saw a box she recognised she would tell me about the person who had given whatever was inside to them. If she didn't recognise a box she might open it to find the card before beginning her stories. It was a cupboard that could have belonged to Miss Havisham from Charles Dickens' *Great Expectations*. If an early disappointment prevented Mum from making Towong Hill into her own home in a more conventional way, she never said so. Or was it that she found convention mostly an inconvenience to her as a writer? It was a strange domestic world to come home to. I had grown up in some ways at boarding school and now saw things from a slightly more worldly perspective.

Towong Hill was certainly an entirely different world compared to friends' homes I had visited while at school. It was difficult to offer a spur-of-the-moment invitation for a meal or to spend a night as Mum would say she hadn't been given sufficient notice. It was hard to know what 'sufficient notice' meant – it varied according to Mum's plans and whether anyone was going into Corryong and could collect groceries. It was different if Mum liked someone and wanted them to stay, but it was difficult to predict how she might react. That, too, depended on her writing workload.

If Mum possessed the kitchen, she also oversaw and directed everything that was done in the garden; I couldn't even deadhead the roses in case I cut the stem off at the wrong place. The bars of the golden cage were drawn in tightly. One afternoon I sat sullenly in the mottled shade of the deodar in the garden wondering what to do next while watching a couple of magpies circling overhead. Some kookaburras were on the chimney pots scanning the garden below for prey, and I felt sure they had a greater sense of purpose than I did. It seemed like I was sliding backwards, losing everything I had learned or gained at school, back down that dreaded long snake on a board of snakes and ladders. If, as people told me, I had so many more opportunities than other kids, why couldn't I find any escape routes from the golden cage? In the distance dogs were barking and a stockwhip cracked – the men were bringing some cattle in around the bottom of the hill towards the aerodrome paddock and the stockyards. It was time to get off my backside.

I asked Bill Gowing, who had recently taken over from Father Knight as manager, if there was something I could do to help. 'Well, Honor, I don't know,' he said. His brows were knitted with thought, and he understood that the situation, through no fault of his, was unchanged from Father Knight's reign: beyond mustering cattle (which Mum enjoyed immensely and always took part in if she could) it was difficult for Bill to include me in work on the property as even Dad was not involved. Bill's wife, Annie, became a good friend and we spent many happy hours eating peanuts and sipping wine together on the verandah at

The Time Warp

their house. This was some consolation, and Annie's conversation provided a new and often entertaining perspective on life beyond Towong Hill and Toorak College.

At the homestead, both Mum and Dad in their separate interests needed help; they were determined to keep going, but they were not young any more. Mum, though, had never been keen to delegate any writing-related tasks and she wasn't about to start now. Dad responded to my offers by giving me inconsequential tasks. When I complained he said it was 'character building', but I was certain I didn't want my character built in that way.

By the time I left school, Dad had moved into what had been the cook's upstairs accommodation of two rooms and a bathroom at the back of the house. A staircase led down into the back corridor beside the Weasel Hole and a door linked Dad's quarters with the upstairs corridor leading to the other bedrooms. In his new rooms he had more space for his growing assemblages of Dibbs and Mitchell family memorabilia and books. He was still the local member of parliament, but I could feel an increasing sense of nostalgia for the past creeping into his life.

Dad's museum was a noisy corner. He had a brass bell at the top of his staircase and every time he passed the bell on the hour, he rang it the appropriate number of times as is done on naval vessels. Mostly he rang it late in the afternoon when he went upstairs for a bath and to read before dinner. It was strangely out of place in the Upper Murray, miles from the sea, yet for Dad the routine reminded him of a happy part of his childhood and of the stories of the sea that his mother told, or of aspects of their holidays spent at Graythwaite in North Sydney or in the subsequent Dibbs home in Point Piper. Behind the bell was a sepia photograph of the graceful steam yacht *Ena*, on which the Dibbs took family and friends out on the harbour on Saturday afternoons, before the First World War cruelly tore their family, and so many others, asunder.

The memory of starvation in Changi still haunted Dad – perhaps it haunted him even more with passing years. He bought tins, biscuits and packets of rice and threw them into a room already filled with junk, books and papers. Sometimes mice nibbled holes in the packets. Mostly the food was not used unless he woke in the night and didn't have the energy to go downstairs to the kitchen, though usually he'd hobble down, throw the kettle on the Aga stove and cut a huge hunk off a loaf of bread from the Corryong bakery. From upstairs in my bedroom I'd hear the kettle hitting the hob and the rattle of the bread bin. When I asked Dad why he kept food in the storeroom upstairs he reminded me that I didn't know what it was like to starve and how lucky I was. He told me how, in his early days as a POW, 'with our eight dollars of pay Uncle Ken and I managed to order twelve tins of fish at sixty-five cents and four coconuts at five cents. This would allow us two tins a week for the month with a tin not eaten and tucked away in the squirrel store against a rainy day.' The storeroom upstairs had become his new squirrel store.

Mum tried to take no notice of these and other eccentricities, but she didn't like them. She shook her head in silent resignation when she heard him strike the hour on the bell. That was one thing, but playing Scottish music at full volume half a world away from Scotland with the bath running was quite another. Ever more frequently Dad would fall asleep and the bath would overflow and flood the kitchen. Once I found our manager, Bill, mopping up the floor to the strains of the bagpipes above blaring 'Scotland Forever', 'Flower of Scotland' and Dad's other favourites. Bill had already been upstairs to turn off the taps and to attempt to rouse Dad. Meanwhile, Bill's face carried a somewhat amazed look of resignation. Nothing was said then, but later the story was a source of some amusement.

Dad had been old for as long as I could remember, but I didn't realise that he was suddenly ageing more rapidly. Nor was he going to admit it. He was still very active in public life, and like most seasoned politicians he was a great self-publicist – he loved being in the public eye and his family was part of his publicity machine, whether any of us liked it or not. Dad couldn't resist phoning through to the editor of the local newspaper any news he received of my doings. If I hadn't been a shy young adult who wanted nothing more than to blend in with the crowd I might have threatened to write a story about a politician sleeping in an overflowing bath. But he didn't have to call my bluff – I wouldn't have dared.

'People are interested in you,' Dad told me, but I couldn't understand it. Why should anyone be interested in me? It wasn't as if I was brilliant or beautiful. I was gauche and grumpy and becoming even grumpier with the unwanted and sometimes inaccurate publicity. Dad wanted to be seen out and about with his family supporting him, but he was also a terrible old snob. If I talked to people in Corryong or around the electorate he was pleased, but it didn't mean he would let me ask them to the house.

When I went through a stage of telling Dad as little as possible about my comings and goings, he responded by finding out my news from others, so it was often put in the papers anyway. Either way I lost. It embarrassed Mum, as well, that Dad 'blew his own trumpet', but she, too, courted publicity on her own terms, mostly separately from Dad. Sometimes she spoke about one or two of us by name when being interviewed, but mostly she referred to us simply as 'the children', almost as if we were props in her show. Sometimes Indi's artistic talent was mentioned, or that Harry was good with his hands and enjoyed hiking when he was at Timbertop, or that John liked building.

Of my parents, it was Dad who was the most vocal. If there were a few moments' silence during a meal, Dad would fill them with an unsolicited lecture on a remote point of history about which he had been reading. He took scant notice if someone wanted to talk about something else or simply preferred a little peace and quiet and time with their own thoughts. Dad had his captive audience around what he called 'the pre-birth-control dining room table' that could seat about eighteen when all the leaves were in use.

In his book *The Piddingtons*, Russell Braddon describes Dad in Changi: 'His grasp of other men's subjects was phenomenal and was his hobby as a prisoner of war. He was a good talker, a good teacher, an interesting man.'[2] Even then, some thirteen years before he died, to help cope with the difficulties of old age he was probably reverting to the strategy that helped him survive Changi. It was this grasp of 'other men's subjects' and his apparent determination to know more about them than anyone else that annoyed his family to the extent that, on occasion, I thought he was the most irritating man I had ever met. Frequently he held forth quite loudly without thinking of putting in his hearing aids or even noting whether others wanted to talk about the same subject. With Harry away overseas and Indi working in Melbourne during the summer after I left school, Mum, John and I made a sparse and not altogether appreciative audience at mealtimes at the grand table in the dining room.

Recently, after reading some of Dad's medical notes, my husband, Mark, asked perceptively, 'Don't you think your father was scared that he would lose his memory again as he had done as a result of his car accident just before the fall of Singapore?' I am sure Mark is right. As a result of that accident Dad had a suspected fractured skull and bad concussion. In May 1942, about three months later, Uncle Ken Burnside suggested that he could try recovering his memory by writing his autobiography. Throughout his remaining years as a POW, Dad wrote 'Midway Peak'. He seemed to have such a good memory that I simply hadn't realised just how hard he must have worked to retain it.

That summer Mum reluctantly agreed that I could read her two adult novels, *Flow River, Blow Wind* (1953) and *Black*

Cockatoos Mean Snow (1956). If the Brumby books had helped me understand Mum in an inspiring way, these novels I found interesting but distressing.

Flow River, Blow Wind throws light on the concerns and difficulties experienced by two local families when their sons return from the war. Joseph and Sara's marriage almost falls apart in the months after he is sent home early because he was injured in North Africa where he had been serving with the 9th Division. In the depth of his despair, Joseph finds himself thinking, 'Something has broken, and I have fallen out of the picture.'[3] On the other hand, Sara realises that Joseph may have felt they were all taking their work on the land far too seriously. Like Mum and Dad, each of Mum's fictional characters fails to appreciate the wartime experiences of the other. Ultimately Sara and Joseph come together again, thus highlighting something that Mum and Dad apparently didn't achieve, even though they both said on different occasions that they deeply wanted to rediscover their prewar happiness. It always seemed to me that their discord far outweighed their enjoyment in each other's company. Perhaps things were better between them when I was away, but if this were so, I never knew.

Mum's second adult novel, *Black Cockatoos Mean Snow*, is a picture of family life – it could almost have been our family – on a fictional property, Willie Ploma, in the Upper Murray in the early 1950s. Just like the Mum of old, Leonie 'was built to ride horses – and jodhpurs showed off her long slender legs'.[4] The novel emphasises the frustrations that Mum herself had felt: 'Now everything seemed to conspire to hold them more and more – not just the children, but the labour position that was worse than ever.'[5] I realised that Mum could easily have written something of her own frustrations into the character of Leonie, who is desperate to get away from her responsibilities and have fun. Even more unsettling was the fact that Mum had foretold the heavy snowfalls in 1956, the year that the book was published. Leonie perished in the snow, trying to escape her responsibilities and cross the mountains to join her brother. Had Mum wanted to escape that much in the years after she'd published *Flow River, Blow Wind* in 1953, the year I was born? Had she been unable to imagine a future with us all at Towong Hill? Mum always said that the screech of black cockatoos foretold bad weather coming, but even the title seemed a bad omen to me.

The more I thought about the book, the sadder and more unsettling I found it. It confirmed to me that while Mum undoubtedly loved her children, she found them and running the house a terrible tie. In *Black Cockatoos Mean Snow* Leonie says, 'I will not live here without both a cook and a nurse,' – much the same thing Mum had told us over the years.[6]

Mum also expressed some of her feelings through Michael, Leonie's husband: 'He would love to be in the mountains himself now: love to be unmarried: love to be without the responsibility of children.'[7] Just as Michael thinks that the only way he can 'redeem himself and the situation' is through his painting, similarly Mum saw the only way to redeem herself was by writing and selling her books.

I was even more disconcerted when I realised that I had been rather like Leonie's youngest son, Roddy, who is fearful that his parents will not come home. Just as in Leonie and Michael's household, there was a feeling of uncertainty at Towong Hill. Was Mum foretelling the fortunes of her own family in another way, I wondered? But, as ever, I didn't dare ask her about her possible fears – or indeed mine. On one hand I regretted reading the book, yet in a strange way I was grateful that it confirmed some of my instincts about Mum.

I was becoming increasingly uneasy about my future. I knew Mum and Dad didn't expect me to get brilliant results in my exams but I was likely to get something more than straight passes.

The Time Warp

One afternoon when we were in the kitchen putting a roast in the oven for dinner, Mum said, 'You will have to do something. You can't stay here.' On another occasion, she remarked, 'But you shouldn't go too far away so that you can come and help us if we need you.' Again I felt the bars of the golden cage closing in. Dad was less prescriptive. He told me, 'You will just have to make up your mind. I will help as much as I can, but with the cattle market in the state it is, I can't do much.' I knew the sort of help I could expect, if I was lucky, from Indi's experience in trying to win over Dad's support to take up a place at Monash University to do an Arts degree. If it wasn't cattle prices, there would be some other reason, I was sure of that. I would have to work things out for myself.

'I am so delighted. You have done so well,' Mum said as I told her my results. But her patent relief undercut her enthusiastic words: I read the subtext of her response to mean that I hadn't done as badly as she feared I might; she knew I got nervous before exams. I couldn't find Dad out at the workshop so Mum and I drove down to the lagoon in the Land Rover. Some time later Dad appeared in his station wagon and parked immediately behind us. He didn't say much when I told him my results. They were okay, but not good enough to impress a Jesus College, Cambridge, alumnus.

Dad spread his towel in front of the Land Rover and dozed off in the sunshine, then refused to move when it was time for Mum and me to return to the house to make lunch. As the Land Rover didn't have very effective brakes, my concern was not to roll forward in case I him; instead I backed too suddenly and fast and went straight into one of the headlights on his car. I was almost beyond caring; it seemed as if things couldn't get much worse. Dad must have sensed my feelings. He looked annoyed but didn't say anything, in the same way he had remained silent all those years before when we reported that the Land Rover had skidded off the road and turned upside down in a creek on the Alpine Way.

It seemed my results were good enough to qualify for some university courses, and for some extraordinary reason I received a scholarship to study at Swinburne College of Technology (now Swinburne University). Mum and Dad invited Annie and Bill to the homestead for a drink to celebrate.

Later Mum said, 'I don't think you will be able to cope with university.' I should have stood firm but the carpet shot from under my feet: Mum was encouraging me with one hand and holding me back with the other. I ended up not accepting the place at Swinburne.

On another occasion Mum said that Aunt Hon and Uncle Moreton educated my cousin Suzanne, only to find that she hardly ever went home again. She didn't want me to have a similar escape ticket. Aunt Eve once said that during the war she had heard Grandfather and Mum arguing about who needed her most – Granny and Grandfather in Melbourne or Mum at Towong Hill. Eve said, 'I then asked myself what Eve wanted to do.' Eve was the second daughter, just as I was, and the family had expected her to always be around to help them. But after the war, Eve began to travel.

Finally Dad agreed to support me at university, provided I did any 'reasonable' job he requested of me at home. The vision of Dad asking me to do masses of inconsequential tasks came rushing to mind – I couldn't bear the thought of all that 'character building'. As it turned out, it wasn't as bad as I thought. If I were lucky he would simply ask for a cup of 'strong, black and hairy tea' made in his Changi mug, a pannekin upon which a dentist had engraved his name while in Changi, and a yarn. Somewhat surprisingly, I thoroughly enjoyed his reminiscences about the Upper Murray, family history and of his travels both before he met Mum and then after they were married, even if they were not helping me much in deciding on my future.

One afternoon Barbie Waters, who lived further down the river towards Jingellic, telephoned, asking if I had any idea what courses her son Bill, who'd been at Geelong Grammar, might be able to apply for. He was away at the time and Barbie was trying to make sense out of the careers literature. When I suggested that with his results he could do theology, Barbie responded with a wonderfully mischievous giggle at the thought of Bill being associated with such a serious subject and perhaps ultimately wearing a dog collar. I started laughing too – this light-hearted Barbie had taken me by surprise. I don't think my parents would have viewed any flippant discussion of my future favourably.

A few weeks later in February when we stopped at Dead Horse Gap for a quick picnic lunch on our way to take a look at the Australian National University in Canberra, where I'd also been offered a place as an Arts student, Mum said, 'You could always write.' The implication was that she didn't think I would need to go to university to do it.

'What a joke,' I replied sullenly. 'I haven't gone anywhere yet. There's nothing for me to write about that either you or Dad hasn't already written about. Or are about to write about.'

Where was the space for my generation among the gods of the previous generation, I wondered? I had read about the '68 student demonstrations in Paris and of the mock crucifixion one Easter at Monash University. The demonstrators had a point: our parents' generation seemed to have all the heroes from the war and all the answers to the extent that there was little or no room for anyone else. Though to me some students had gone overboard in proving their case: those who staged the mock crucifixion seemed to have forgotten that millions of people sacrifice aspects of their lives for others, even if it is just helping someone else in the smallest way.

Rather than listening to what Mum was saying, I walked over to the area where there had once been a yard for stockmen to keep their horses. I thought of how in *The Silver Brumby* Thowra managed to jump into those very yards where I stood and persuade the beautiful mare Golden to take that incredible leap into the unknown and gallop off with him through the snow to the Secret Valley. If the Secret Valley had provided a safe haven and home for the Silver Brumby and his herd, it had provided a metaphorical haven for Mum too. I searched for something similar in my own imagination, but nothing would come. Golden returned once to her master when her first foal, Kunama, was born before once again cutting her ties and choosing freedom and running with Thowra. My home and upbringing held a far greater sway over me than Golden's master had over her. I knew I could not turn my back on my childhood home forever without looking back.

Perhaps if I had given Mum the chance to warm to her theme I would have heard how she had taught herself to write, and I might have responded more positively. But I hadn't given her a chance to talk about her chosen career as a writer – the thing she loved perhaps most of all and really knew how to do. Many years later I understood what she had been trying to tell me when I finally found the keys to unlock the drawers of the davenport desk she bequeathed me. It was stuffed to overflowing with cuttings, correspondence and her early attempts at writing stories – if I had ever thought her path to success had been a smooth one, I was entirely wrong. She always said she hadn't liked school and didn't perform well, so she had done better in her life than she ever expected, or indeed admitted. I'd lost my chance to say that I understood and to thank her for her advice, example and, above all, for sowing seeds of inspiration.

I accepted the place at ANU and began the term wondering whether I had made the right choice. If I'd ever thought I was breaking free from my family, my choice of majors in political science and Australian history with a sub-major in English was a dip into the individual and collective interests of both my parents. Looking back, I am glad now I made the choices I did. During the decades I lived overseas, my understanding of Australian history and literature helped me appreciate the country and the era in which I had grown up.

On my first evening in the queue for dinner in the Ursula College dining room, I met the tall, bubbly Jude McGrath and we had dinner together. Later in the courtyard we met Jan Kronborg, whose father, Eric, later stood against Al Grassby in the seat of Riverina in the 1972 elections. Gradually, as I began to relax and enjoy the company of others, I discovered some of them had very similar concerns to me about whether they were coping. My Australian history tutor, Mrs Penny, gave me a pass for my very first university essay and for the first time it seemed as if there was a glimmer of hope.

36
'A Man Who Would Have Sons'

Once during the summer after I left school, Dad was yarning about his and Mum's wedding day. 'Numerous telegrams were read,' he recalled, 'but one was unsigned, bearing the Corryong postmark. It said, "May all your worries be little ones," and was not read at the reception.' Almost thirty-seven years later, at the end of May 1972, it was as if a bad fairy's wish had become a reality.

On 29 May 1972 our manager, Bill, and his wife, Annie, kindly drove me back to the ANU in time for me to begin the second term of my first year. They had not been to Canberra before so after they dropped me off they were going to visit the Australian War Memorial. I was feeling as unsettled as I had at the beginning of the first term, again questioning whether I should be there and, indeed, whether I should have returned. Something didn't seem right and I hadn't felt so lonely since my first days at boarding school.

After starting to unpack, I went in search of the friends I had made in the first term to hear news of their vacation. I had had an exciting holiday, beginning with a week of intervarsity tennis in Hobart. In Launceston Jude McGrath had invited me to stay and meet some of her schoolfriends before I flew back to Melbourne and returned to Towong Hill for the last couple of weeks of the break, which included a combined celebration for Harry's twenty-second birthday on 26 May and my nineteenth, which would be a couple of weeks later.

It was maybe two evenings after the party that Harry, Mum and Dad had an argument. Beforehand, Harry came to my room to say goodbye and give me a birthday present as I would be returning to Canberra the next morning. He told me he was intending to visit friends near Orange he had met on his overseas trip earlier in the year, and perhaps stay with them a while. Indi heard some of the angry exchange between Harry and Mum and Dad, but I was upstairs packing and tidying up in preparation for my departure with Annie and Bill early the next morning.

When I arrived very few people had returned to Ursula College and the campus seemed bleak and empty. By late afternoon the sunshine had vanished and the sky was overcast and threatening rain. I wanted a friend to talk to, but with nobody around I knew, I returned to my college room to finish unpacking, find my books and plan my timetable for the week ahead. I remember the events of that afternoon and early evening down to the finest detail. Having said that, I don't know precisely what the time was except that it was after dinner when I heard a knock at my door. Rather than a friend coming for a yarn, as I had hoped, it was Monsignor Burke, the college chaplain, asking if he could come in to talk to me. I felt myself tense. Something wasn't right.

I can't remember what words he used to tell me that Harry had been killed in a car accident near Lithgow, and I don't know if I even replied. I do remember thinking that dying in a car accident was so shockingly violent and must have hurt terribly.

Later, others told me the details of what had happened but I couldn't remember what they said either, only that Harry was dead. I don't remember any more about that night except that

I kept waking, seeing Harry's face flickering, like frames of a black-and-white film flashing before my eyes.

I sat up in bed thinking I hardly knew him and, if it was true that he had died, I no longer had a chance to. I lay down again, feeling ill. I had lost the brother who had broken the ice on the trough and then wiped the cow poo off by backside by scraping me against a wire fence. I had lost the brother who, like a mischievous leopard, had leapt in and out of bed in his short blue pyjamas with brown spots all those years ago in St Andrew's Hospital. I had lost the brother who laughingly pointed out that Dad had probably swallowed the crucifix from the Christmas pudding. Surely what Monsignor Burke had told me was a nightmare and hadn't really happened? I wanted to go home and find Harry there. I wished Bill and Annie hadn't left already.

In another moment of horrible understanding I realised that I didn't really *know* anyone in my family. I suppose I knew Indi best from when she had helped me buy clothes and had me to stay in her Melbourne flat for some weekends away from school. But Indi was almost seven years older than me and although we had skied together quite a bit in the year after she left school and before I went to boarding school, I didn't feel as if we had shared enough for me to know her well.

Next morning one of the nuns who lived at and helped run Ursula College must have told me that Bruce Chisholm, Dad's relative and good family friend, was coming over from Khancoban Station to collect me. If Bruce was coming it must be true that something terrible had happened to Harry, but I still didn't really believe it. I can't even remember if I packed any luggage or if someone else came to help me, or what I did while I waited for Bruce. Nor do I remember much about the trip, except that we drove over the Alpine Way and the chill of the late autumnal mountain air nipped me as it always did. At Leather Barrel Creek

Bruce offered me a nip of brandy or whisky from his hipflask. It turned out the flask was empty, but he suggested the smell of something strong might help anyway. I dreaded arriving home and finding that the nightmare was true.

All I recall of arriving at Towong Hill is that Barbie Waters had given Mum a liquidambar tree that could be planted in Harry's memory. Apart from being quite sure that Harry would walk in the homestead's back door at any moment, I can't recall anything else. My next memory would have been a few days later standing numb at the graveside, bleak clouds squashing us down into the earth, burying us with Harry in the Corryong Cemetery. Only I still didn't believe that he was in the coffin.

Friends told me who was at the funeral a few days later; all I can remember is the congregation singing the first lines of Psalm 121: 'I will lift up mine eyes unto the hills, from whence cometh my help.' From the Anglican Church in Corryong we could see the bush-covered hills surrounding the Corryong Valley, but the mountains were invisible beneath shrouds of cloud. I hadn't wanted Psalm 121 in the service as I knew that not even the mountains could help a family who had only ever wanted the best for their eldest son and brother. It was too late to correct misunderstandings and misplaced ambitions; nothing could reverse this tragedy.

Mum and Dad told me what had happened and Indi did too, yet still I couldn't consciously comprehend what they said or wrote to me. I started to dream about a hill, a grey Mini Minor and a truck. I saw Harry lying on the ground with his head on a kind, middle-aged woman's lap as she talked and comforted him. That woman was Enid O'Dowd, and she wrote to Mum and phoned her each Christmas and on the anniversary of Harry's death for the rest of her life. Once I answered the phone when she called, and when I heard her warm and gracious words about Harry my voice seized up.

One year, around the time of our birthdays, Harry and I had speculated about what we would be like in the year 2000, when he would be fifty and I would be forty-seven. It had never occurred to either of us that one of us might no longer be alive then.

The sun never shone properly at Towong Hill again after Harry died. It was always glary and hazy. The purity had gone out of the light, just as innocence had been ripped from our lives.

Just as I had read *Flow River, Blow Wind* and *Black Cockatoos Mean Snow* to learn more about Mum, I tried to remember Harry and understand his relationship with Mum through re-reading *Winged Skis* many years later. Mum began writing the ski thriller in 1960 especially for him. I tried to recall and find out as much as I could about events surrounding the writing of the book as, while I knew Harry had not enjoyed the Brumby books if indeed he had read them at all, he, like me, had probably always wanted Mum to dedicate a book to him.

Following the publication of *The Silver Brumby* and *Silver Brumby's Daughter*, Mum was enjoying the fruits of her success as a children's writer and, as by then we were all able to ski, could for the first time since having a family ski throughout the winter and for as long as the snow lasted. As she explained in a letter to Dorothy Tomlinson in reference to the new book she was working on, 'Skiing is booming in this country and I hoped we would catch the boom.'

Mum imbued Barry, the hero of *Winged Skis*, with a love of skiing and the mountains that she hoped Harry either already had or would develop. I don't know whether in fact he had discovered 'the treasures of the snow'[1] to the degree Mum would have liked. Perhaps, like me, he discovered some of them, but possibly at the time not as many as Mum might have wished. I think he enjoyed skiing because it was something he could do with his mother and family. Where Harry and his fictional counterpart were most alike was in their wonderful ability for making friends and winning the respect of other skiers. Particularly in the early sixties, Harry was renowned for his good cheer both on and off the slopes, and those days were probably among the happiest of his life. Sometimes Mum used to refer to him affectionately as 'Happy'.

In *Winged Skis* Mum painted an idealistic world where Barry the hero satisfactorily balanced becoming a good skier and touring the mountains accompanied by his parents with his correspondence schooling. His relationship with his parents is almost too close, well-mannered and problem-free for a truly convincing story, but Mum would not have wanted to create a young role model with wild or undesirable characteristics and be held responsible for encouraging such traits in her own or anyone else's family. She might also have wished that her own family was better mannered and less argumentative. Ironically, the Miltons didn't seem to have the same high expectations of their Barry as Mum and Dad had about their offspring, and Barry didn't disappoint his parents.

The story is set in country that Mum had explored extensively in 1941, the winter immediately after Dad embarked with the 8th Division AIF to Malaya. In *Australia's Alps* she had already written about her various expeditions on the Main Range, to the Ramsheads and to the Cascades in the winter of 1941, and *Winged Skis* was another opportunity for her to explore this beloved country, this time with the added challenge of writing for young teenagers. She could dream that once again she was skiing and exploring the peaks and valleys she adored, but this time with her beloved son. In reality, at the time Mum was writing *Winged Skis* Harry had not had a chance to venture much beyond Thredbo, the Ramsheads, Dead Horse Gap, the summit of Mt Kosciusko and perhaps the Main Range in winter. The book was a promise of great adventures to come and suggested that there was so much to which Harry could look forward.

The idea that Barry might ski as much as he wished, provided he did his correspondence lessons, was a little too close to home. It had been Mum's original aim that so long as we did our schoolwork we could ski as much as possible each winter. Again, the reality in our family was different. In the early sixties Harry would have been at the Corryong primary school and about to start at Geelong Grammar. I don't recall Mum ever taking him out of school so that we could all ski; perhaps he was dropped at the school bus before we set off for Thredbo and someone else picked him up in the afternoon while Mum returned from Thredbo with John and me. By this time I was already aware from some of Dad's remarks that he thought Mum was taking us to Thredbo too often and this was a source of friction between them.

Re-reading *Winged Skis* I felt uncomfortable with the idea that Barry was so obviously Harry; there was only one letter differentiating their names! Correspondence with Mr Gaywood at Hutchinson in Melbourne mentions that Dorothy Tomlinson at the publisher's London office objected to the book being dedicated to Harry because it made it more obvious that Harry was the model for Barry in the story. Mum argued that Harry had even asked that the hero be named after him. While he might have done at one point, I wonder if he would have felt comfortable with it as he grew up?

Mum pressed ahead with a surprising indifference to the warnings. She usually took her publisher's advice, but she and Dorothy Tomlinson didn't always see eye to eye, and in this instance Mum brushed aside her counsel. The hero's name was not the only source of my discomfort. There was also the fine line between fiction and the reality of our lives, which would embarrass me later when I went to school. I never knew what Harry really felt about *Winged Skis* and perhaps he didn't really know himself. Sometimes these sorts of thoughts take years to germinate, possibly because when one is very young one feels bad harbouring critical thoughts of a parent.

Dorothy Tomlinson expressed other reservations about the manuscript in a letter to Mum dated 10 September (probably 1962).

> *Incident takes the place of sustained action, and the descriptions of skiing, well done as they are, become monotonous. In my opinion, too, the mixture of fine writing and a children's adventure story does not really work and I think boys would probably react against this monotonously happy and successful atmosphere, as Barry develops into the perfect skier, scrupulously obeys the mountain rules and enjoys so many rapturous days of skiing; they might also feel a tinge of embarrassment at the passages where Barry and Michael discuss poetry.*

Given these misgivings, it is surprising that *Winged Skis* was ever published. Much to Mum's delight, however, a review by Noel Streatfeild in the British press paid tribute to her 'superb gift for creating atmosphere: the excitement of skiing; the feeling of being able to fly over untrodden snow; the exquisite beauty of snow-covered mountains; the feeling of achievement at the end of a long day in terrible weather when, by willpower only, the end of the journey is reached'.[2] In an August 1964 review in *Ski Australia*, Dorothy Ryman also paid tribute to Mum's writing about the mountains, but she was not blind to the 'slender plot'.[3]

Winged Skis never enjoyed the financial success of the Brumby books, yet it was highly commended in the Children's Book of the Year Awards in 1965. Annette Macarthur-Onslow's evocative sketches might have been part of its success. It was the first teenage story to be set in the Australian snowfields and, despite criticism, it does have a certain appeal for those who enjoy skiing.

Mum took great care in her research. In an undated letter to Dorothy Tomlinson, she mentions that she had given a copy of the manuscript to the head ski instructor at Thredbo, asking him to check that the opinions expressed by the ski instructors in the story were credible. Mum explained: 'I had intended having Barry hurt, but the children begged me not to.' It is possible that Mum found our feedback less than helpful on some occasions, but here she heeded it. Even when I re-read *Winged Skis* as an adult I was glad that Barry had not been injured.

Having a book written just for him didn't really help Harry to read fluently or independently. It must have been a sad disappointment not just for Mum, but probably even more so for Harry. I never knew if when he first went to boarding school he too found that Mum's books could be a source of some embarrassment among his peers. It was not until I read a letter dated 14 December 1960 from Mum to her friend and fellow writer Henrietta Drake-Brockman that I realised Mum understood Harry had reading difficulties. She explained that she was working on a story for Harry, 'but he battles reading so much that it is a rather thankless task. He does not even like being read to. It is most extraordinary.' Having dedicated her first two children's books to Indi, Mum had to persist. If Harry had not had a book dedicated to him he would have felt left out.

It was seldom if ever heard of then, but my own subsequent research indicates that Harry may have suffered from dyslexia. The tragedy was that Mum and Dad most likely didn't realise that Harry's problems could not be cured with just a little more time and effort from Harry himself. He probably needed professional help, but at that time such difficulties were not sufficiently understood, and appropriate help was not readily available. I don't think it helped Harry's confidence that most of the time he had to wear thick glasses; a family friend Mrs Hay told me that not long after he started boarding school at Geelong Grammar he tried to get rid of them by burying them beside the school playing fields.

But Harry was particularly fortunate in the care and understanding he received from many of the masters at Geelong Grammar, and the friendships he developed with those who knew him at the school. His obituary in the school magazine, *The Corian*, remarked, 'In all parts of the school [Harry's] cheerfulness, his courage and perseverance earned him respect from all members of the community.'[4] To visit the school and share memories with some of his old masters and friends has always brought me great pleasure.

However, nothing could compensate for the discrepancy between Dad's ambition for Harry to follow him to Jesus College, Cambridge, and the reality that Harry was struggling academically. I remember that Harry frequently seemed to be in trouble for poor school reports. In 1967, Harry's final year at Geelong Grammar, his future career became a battleground not only between him and Dad, but also between Dad and Mum. Arguing that it would give him the time and opportunity to develop, Dad was insistent, against Harry's wishes, that he should go jackarooing near Warren in New South Wales. Their correspondence reveals a sad breakdown in communication. While Dad clearly thought he was making himself available for discussions and was irritated that Harry didn't jump at the opportunities being offered to him to talk about his future, Dad made little effort to initiate conversations with Harry, nor indeed to assist him with his enquiries about possible alternative careers. Unfortunately there was little constructive response from Dad to Harry's clearly thought out and well-written letters explaining his wishes. Obviously he had gone to great trouble and I suspect that a kind master at Geelong Grammar may well have helped him. Harry really wanted to do a diploma in electronics; he would have thrived in the computer age. In many ways he was born before his time.

There had been earlier problems in their relationship. Sometime during the summer of 1963 Mum remarked in a letter to Granny that 'Tom went camping on his own after all his theories of a man taking his son out alone, Harry said he was too nasty to him and he wouldn't go. I feel sorry for Tom, but wondered if it might not bring him to his oats a bit.' Harry found Mum easier to talk to so it was understandable that, perhaps even without realising he was doing so, he attempted to have Mum not only support him but also argue his case for his future for him. Spotting injustice in the way Dad was treating Harry, Mum went into the fray to battle for her son and his attempt to pursue a career for which he would be suited. In doing so she may have made Harry's situation and his relationship with Dad even more difficult; as I had discovered at school, she could be too fierce an ally.

Harry suggested that he might be able to train in electronics in the army if he were called up as part of the National Service scheme that was introduced in 1964. Judging by a letter from Dad to Harry, it seems that Harry did not make the necessary enquiries about whether it would be possible to do his vocational training in the army and it was Mum who wrote letters asking about courses available at technical colleges. Dad responded by insisting again that Harry go jackarooing: he didn't see that Harry was suffering as a result of his dictatorial stance; probably he was too busy to notice. Even by the standards of the day Dad's attitudes could be old-fashioned.

Mum's efforts on Harry's behalf did not help her relationship with Dad and tensions escalated. Both could be malicious to each other. Mum, miserable and unable to influence Dad's decisions, begged Harry to write politely to his father, pointing out to him during long discussions that 'if you really quarrel with Dad it is going to make life most frightfully difficult for me, and for the others too'.

'A Man Who Would Have Sons'

Dad didn't budge. After Harry stayed with him in Sydney on his way up north to start his jackarooing job, Uncle Edward wrote to Mum saying that he understood she had 'a serious problem' in attempting to settle Harry's future. Uncle Edward tried to be helpful and supportive, but there was little he could do for either Harry or Mum. There was only one player in this drama who needed to back down and that was not going to happen. Mum was convinced she was right, and mostly she probably was. Dad thought he was right too, but almost anyone who knew our family probably realised that in this instance he was not entirely justified. If Dad was strong-willed when he came home from Changi, he seemed all the more so now.

My suspicion is that Dad ultimately acquired a special type of stubborn determination from his experience of human nature while in captivity and that he felt that those who had not endured similar experiences were comparatively naive and spoilt. Perhaps it was this perception that made him feel that he alone had the background necessary to make the important decisions in the family. Dad and some of his fellow POWs may have thought that their experience gave them something more to offer their communities, and by extension their own families, on their return home. In captivity Dad would have seen the best and the worst of people, and he probably came to his own conclusions about what brought out the best in a person. Perhaps Dad thought the psychology he learned in Changi would work on his own family, but I don't know. Dad didn't talk much about his experiences in Changi beyond studying geology, history, Banjo Paterson's poetry and reading everything he could lay his hands on. He didn't mind talking about the Changi Ski Club, a group of keen skiers who discussed where they had skied and where they might venture after the war. He also mentioned helping Uncle Ken with his malarial research, writing a prize-winning essay – and starvation. Hunger was always at the forefront of anything he said about Changi.

In the summer of 1967–68, Harry was turning eighteen. There were three years until he reached twenty-one, the golden age of majority. It would have been interesting to see what might have happened if he had stood his ground and refused to take up the jackarooing position. When at the time I heard that Dad had threatened to disinherit him if he didn't go, it reminded me that Dad claimed Granddaddy M had said Dad could play 'ducks and drakes' with the property if he wished. Dad could do as he liked but Harry didn't even have a say in his choice of career without fear of retribution.

If Harry had left home, Dad might have reported his son missing to the police and Harry and Dad would have had to cope with the publicity his actions would undoubtedly have attracted. But I can't help feeling that if he had chosen this course, Dad's friends and colleagues would have understood Harry's plight and tried to talk Dad around to reason. Perhaps Dad was challenging Harry to stand up to him more. I really don't know if Dad would have changed his will, as he threatened, but I think it unlikely that he intended to torment Harry as he did. I don't think Dad could see what he was doing. It was hard for us all to witness what Harry endured.

As children we had been brought up to obey our parents and this Harry continued to do. But it left huge rifts between father and son and between Dad and Mum. There were moments when Mum felt that Harry was turning against her too, simply because she couldn't help him find a way of dealing with his father. All in all, 1971 was a particularly tough year for both Harry and Mum. Thankfully, Harry had a trip to Europe in early 1972 to look forward to.

Dad used to tell me how much he missed his father after his death in 1917. It seems strange that a man who had made such an admission should then alienate his own son, but possibly Dad was unaware of the impact his decisions were having on Harry and indeed his entire family. It will never be known to what extent the explanation for this behaviour lay in wartime events. Uncle Jack used to roar the hell out of Dad when he was helping in the stockyards at Khancoban, and perhaps Dad felt that what worked for one generation was good enough for the next. Probably he thought it was 'character building'. With the possible exception of his own father, Dad's role models in the family had been volatile. Either he couldn't see or refused to admit that such behaviour can have damaging consequences.

As the time came for each of us to leave school, our careers became a battlefield between Mum and Dad. Being the eldest, Indi blazed the way, but the main focus was on the boys' careers. I was fortunate not to be within the radar of expectations. Dad argued that spending money on tertiary education for women was 'the expensive way to the kitchen sink', and believed Indi and I would marry and give up thoughts of careers. Initially he hadn't been keen to support Indi to go to Monash University to do an Arts degree.

Mum fought for each of us to be able to pursue a field of our choice, even if we didn't really know what we wanted to do. While her support was reassuring, the increasing discord between her and Dad was deeply upsetting. When his time came, John encountered similar problems to Harry's with Dad and family life reached a new low. It was about that time that Mum stopped singing and playing her piano accordion. From the late 1960s there was hardly ever any music in the house. It seemed that an ill wind was blowing in our lives.

Some years ago Mum gave me one of Harry's children's books about a little red engine that had to climb difficult hills. It puffed away saying, 'I think I can, I think I can' as it climbed. The spine of the little book was broken and its pages were bent, as if it had been read over and over again, perhaps more by Mum than by Harry. The most fitting epitaph for Harry was that he died trying, probably trying harder than any of us were aware.

His death brought an end to his impossible quest to discover a niche for himself, or to even be permitted to look for one. It had been an awful situation for the long-awaited and much-desired son. At the time of his death Mum wrote, 'The boy for whom we had dreamt nearly 40 years before – the boy who would become a man riding over the Towong Hill paddocks – another Mitchell for the Murray – a man who would have sons … & he was no longer living. Love, laughter and light … had gone.'

37
Wings to Find My Life

Just prior to beginning university in 1873, at the age of eighteen, Thomas William Mitchell, Dad's uncle and Grandaddy M's eldest brother, died of meningitis in West Melbourne. As a result Great-Grandfather Thomas Mitchell wouldn't allow any of his other sons to follow their elder brother's footsteps into tertiary education, or so Dad said. Dad's elder brother, Thomas Hugh Mitchell (known as Uncle Hughie), was born on 21 February 1905 and died unexpectedly of unknown causes just three weeks later on 15 March, having lived only twenty-one days. Malcolm Chisholm, Dad's cousin and eldest son of Pinkie (née Emma Isabella Mitchell) and Willie Chisholm, was killed in August 1914 in the First World War. Was it, I wonder, a coincidence that Harry, another eldest son, should also die so young? Was the family caught in an intergenerational pattern, or was it just a series of tragic accidents?

The coronial inquest into Harry's death said: 'Contusion of the brain and lacerations to both lungs accidentally received when the motor vehicle he was driving collided with another motor vehicle travelling in the opposite direction.'[1] If discord between Mum and Dad had often unsettled me, Harry might have felt dogged by it to the point of distraction. Was Harry feeling so desperate about his future that he was not concentrating adequately on driving his grey Mini nor on the other traffic on the road? I haven't seen the stretch of road on which he died and I don't want to, because the road alone cannot provide any answers. It was a place where our lives changed forever. Afterwards my childhood was severed, as if divided by an impenetrable wall from the rest of my life.

Mum often remarked, 'Changi touched you all, even though it happened before you were born.' I have two questions I never asked in my parents' lifetimes in response to Mum's comment. First, what happened in Changi that 'touched' us all? And secondly, was Changi to blame for everything that went wrong after Dad returned at the end of the war? I didn't ask Mum before she died as I didn't want to cause further hurt when there was enough already. Later, I decided to do my own research.

In the wake of Victory over Japan Day on 15 August 1945 and prior to Dad's arrival in Sydney on 10 October, Mum wrote a series of long, loving letters to him, describing her life during the war and filled with excitement about his imminent return. These letters should have prophesied a happy postwar life. In an undated cable to 'VX43577 Capt T W Mitchell 8th Divn HQ Care 2 Aust POW Reception Group Singapore', Mum wrote: 'Thrilled see your name in list longing your return try to inform me ships name and where meet you love Elyne.' Dad said he thought about the 'hell' they would create together when he returned – meaning the sort of adventures and happy days of exploration they'd enjoyed in the mountains before the war.

While undoubtedly there were some happy family occasions, the seeds of controversies had been sown well before Mum and Dad argued about my name, and reached a zenith in the desperate arguments over Harry's future. Mum had a keen sixth sense, perhaps greater than she ever realised. As early as 1943 she wrote about feeling a growing sense of doom after the fall of Singapore.

Apparently there were three urgent telegrams among the correspondence addressed to Dad on the hospital ship HMS *Largs Bay* in early October 1945. One informed him that his account had been credited with fifty-two pounds and a chequebook was being held for him by his trustees. He told me that he'd thought that fifty-two pounds (of his own) was a fortune after what he'd been living on. The second telegram came from Mum and was received by Dad when the ship called at Brisbane. It concerned her arrangements for meeting him in Sydney and advised him to consider 'FEDERAL', probably meaning federal politics. On another fragment, presumably relating to the same telegram as there is no signature on it, Mum goes on to say, 'Situation very changed stop glad your strength improving stop so looking forward to seeing you all love … Elyne Mitchell.'

The third telegram was from Granny Chauvel, welcoming Dad and informing him that he would be met on the ship when it arrived in Brisbane by General Stanke.[2] Also coming to meet him on the ship would be Brigadier Ronald Hopkins, who had been Grandfather's aide-de-camp after the First World War and was a Chauvel family friend, and who would deliver a letter from Mum. (There would have been insufficient fuel available for Mum to travel to Brisbane.) Granny had activated her contacts to ensure that Dad would receive a good welcome.

Dad described the atmosphere on board ship after their departure from Singapore as quiet and thoughtful. He recalled that at one point soon after sailing they were served roast beef. Even though while in captivity he had dreamed of roast dinners, when the real thing was in front of him, his stomach had shrunk so much as a result of starvation he could hardly touch it, yet he hated seeing so much wonderful food going to waste. He also recalled 'feeling flat' and that it was difficult to be excited, as he worried that 'he wouldn't measure up in Mum's eyes to the man he had been before the accident' that landed him in hospital on

10 February 1942, just five days before the surrender of Singapore. I can only guess how the uncertainty, privations, hardship, rough treatment and suffering Dad experienced over the three and a half years he spent as a prisoner of war might have affected his attitudes as a man, a husband and a father. He didn't discuss his wartime experience with me much except to tell each of us from time to time how lucky we were not to know hunger. Dad's determined, dictatorial streak may have been exacerbated by his experiences as a POW. As a result of her wartime experience, Mum, equally, had become more independent and determined. Such strong wills were destined to clash.

It was a sobering thought, also, to realise that I owed my life to two atomic bombs – Little Boy dropped on 6 August on Hiroshima and Fat Man dropped on 9 August 1945 on Nagasaki. Had they not been deployed, Dad may never have returned from Changi. Yet the very event that indirectly made my conception possible killed over two hundred thousand people and brought immeasurable suffering for decades to many more. It didn't seem to me that the hope expressed by General Douglas MacArthur in his address before the Japanese were invited to sign the Instrument of Surrender on 2 September 1945 that 'a better world shall emerge out of the blood and carnage of the past' had come to pass.

In 1996 John Wyett, a senior staff officer in the 8th Division, wrote: 'A whole generation of our people has grown up strangers to their own heritage, uninformed about crucial aspects of their history and deprived of the pride they should rightly have' because of the veterans' of the 8th Division's 'reluctance to discuss it'. He goes on to explain: 'The enormous number of casualties, the hurt, the suffering, the infinite exhaustion and the final disappointment were all too much to talk about.'[3] Dad's reluctance to talk about his experience could have contributed to a number of sad misunderstandings in our family. But it may simply have been too dreadful and painful for Dad to speak about. It is not my place to pass judgement on a man whose sufferings were beyond my imagination.

Separation, uncertainty and profound loneliness would also have wrought changes in Mum. Changi – shorthand in our family for Dad's prisoner-of-war experiences – could not be answerable for everything. In November 1944 Mum had written candidly to Aunt Hon:

> *I hope to hell Thos still thinks he made a good choice when he comes home! I don't really know why, but for quite a while now the fact that in many ways I am changing and changing has got me by the short hairs. I expect I would feel even more disturbed if I thought I had not changed ... gone forward ... at all in these years but still ... Of course I have mainly gone along the highways opening up from the tracks that Tom and I had already mapped out together and he wanted me to go on and on ... confidently ... on my own.*

Those final words – 'to go on and on ... confidently ... on my own' – are pretty well what she did. Dad had shown her a road ahead and she took it, almost entirely without him, but never leaving him either.

After Dad's homecoming in October 1945, Mum was more determined than ever to pursue her career as a writer. The house and property with its meandering river and lagoons and the mountains beyond had become an essential backdrop for her writing and she was doing well. Rather than modifying her ambitions, the arrival of babies seemed only to reinforce them, and it seems there was increasingly little room in her life for marriage and family as we children grew up and needed more of her time in many different ways.

In the weeks following Harry's death I felt as if I had not only lost a brother but a part of both parents and of each sibling too.

It was as if something from all of us went with Harry and we increasingly forged separate paths. John returned to school and I think Indi returned to studying for her law degree. I know I strived to recapture some sort of normality at university, but when I tried to laugh it felt false and wrong – nothing was the same. The bottom had fallen out of my world.

Mum poured her grief into her poetry and diaries. Just as she used to record our weights for the first year of our lives, she counted the number of words she wrote each day, as if she needed a progress chart of her efforts to 'get cracking' again. Harry had always been her blue-eyed boy; in death his stature soared and his memory filled every nook and cranny of Towong Hill. His room was left as he had left it when he set off on his fateful journey. In comparison, I had always found myself to be lacking a mysterious yet vital ingredient. Mum wanted to feel needed by her family but, it seemed to me, only on her terms. After Harry's death she was often miserable and bad-tempered to the extent that Indi once told her not to forget that she still had three children – to no apparent affect.

Dad became more silent and devoted himself to political work in his electorate and at Parliament House where, among other involvements, he was a member of the library committee, which, thankfully, he enjoyed. While in Changi he had kept a bamboo stick on which he cut a notch for every week he spent as a POW. 'When I think things are getting tough,' he told me, 'I rub my hands up and down the stick to remind myself of the weeks when things were *really* tough.' I don't know how often he sat with his stick in his hands; he probably would have never told me. One afternoon he handed it to me so that I too could rub my hands along it, but for me there were no ghastly memories associated with the notches and I had no idea of his benchmark of pain. Instead I thought of the little girl with bandaged eyes in St Andrew's Hospital when Harry and I were having our tonsils taken out, but my memory of her misery didn't seem to be relevant to the pain I felt over Harry. For her there was hope of recovery and there was no such hope for Harry.

Silver Brumby Whirlwind was published in 1973, the year after Harry's death. It was dedicated 'To Harry, to all those marvellous mountain days'. The book was a great tribute to a much-loved son. Significantly, in her author's note, Mum acknowledges that the book was inspired not only by the suggestion of Carol Clark, one of her American readers, but also Indi's idea for the ending – Thowra's disappearance in a whirlwind of snow somewhere among the Ramsheads, near his birthplace. It was Indi who had persuaded Mum in the late sixties, and again after Harry died, to explore the northern end of the High Country, thus introducing new landscapes into her wanderings and new direction into her writing.

Slowly but surely Mum began to write more, in memory of Harry and to thank God for his life and all his love and laughter. She dedicated *Chauvel Country* to Harry as well as her parents and her brother Edward, all of whom had by then died. For Mum these tributes were never sufficient; it was almost as if her beloved parents, brother and son became an inspiration, the stars to which she could attach her chariot.

If early in my childhood I felt there was little space or role for me, after Harry died the feeling was even more acute. Strangely, I reckoned Harry was the lucky one. I couldn't compete with either his memory or Mum's creative ambitions and I didn't have the maturity to help Mum in the way Indi did, despite the fact that she must have found it very difficult to cope with her own grief. John tried very hard to help Mum in his own way too. Being now the only son and the youngest, perhaps Harry's death was hardest of all for him. In his anxiety to make arrangements for his succession, Dad made John the new focus of his attention. It was a tough burden for such young shoulders to bear. It was not only sad for father and son, but for the whole family. I felt I had moved right out onto the edge of the family circle and, at any moment, I might tumble off the family map completely. Yet my parents had brought me into this world in which I had to live and I had to find a way of doing so.

In *Silver Brumbies of the South*, the hero, Baringa, grandson of Thowra, the Silver Brumby, knew he had to venture out and explore the world in order to find his own mares and his own Secret Valley or safe haven. Perhaps Mum had been trying to tell me that I would need to find a secret valley of my own and make my own life.

A few days after Harry's funeral, kind friends Charlie and Remy came over from Canberra to take me back to university. I was tempted to withdraw for the year as I didn't feel ready to return, but in the absence of an acceptable alternative plan, the wisest course of action seemed to be to continue as best I could. In retrospect I don't think I would have forgiven myself if I hadn't and I am glad I found the steel to do so.

I skied in the intervarsity championships that August and again the following year. Somebody clapped a pair of waxed skis on my feet and pushed me between the starting flags for the cross-country ski race about which I can remember nothing except that I never looked back and have enjoyed cross-country skiing ever since. My childhood was over by then and much of those early adult years after Harry died are blurred. Soon after, Indi was married and moved to Townsville. John became ill and was sometimes in hospital. I'd had stomach surgery but it didn't provide the relief I'd hoped for and I didn't feel I was making a good recovery. I knew I had to take control of my own life and I needed to get away to do so. Friendships were defined and redefined and some patient, loyal friends stayed with me. I am immensely grateful to them.

In June 1974 I celebrated my twenty-first birthday and coming of age twice: once with friends in Canberra and again with the family at Towong Hill. It felt like I had acquired few attributes of adulthood. With Mum and Dad preoccupied, the gilded cage against which I had plotted and fought for so long disintegrated, but at first I scarcely knew what to do with the freedom. Like the Silver Brumby's grandson Baringa, in 1976 I chose to venture out and explore the world. For thirty-four years half a world distanced me from the trouble spots at home that the Second World War had left smouldering between Mum and Dad. For thirty-two of those years I have been married to Mark Auchinleck, who served for thirty-seven years in the British army before retiring in 2005.

Together we moved nineteen times, living in five different countries on three continents. We lived in Germany for the last decade of the Cold War and witnessed the country's reunification. Apart from Mark's operational tours in Northern Ireland, the First Gulf War, Bosnia and Sierra Leone, I have accompanied him on every posting, with Sarah and James joining us on holidays from boarding school and, later, university. They were with me during the 1999 earthquake when we were living in Izmir, Turkey, and a few years later when Mark was defence attaché in Ankara we all lived through the 2003 bombing of the British Consulate-General in Istanbul and the early years of the war in Iraq. Unsurprisingly, both our children have worked in defence. We've now returned to live in Australia. We've called our part of the original Towong Hill holding 'Baringa', in gratitude for the inspiration of Elyne's equine hero. Sometimes we all meet in the mountains to go bushwalking or to explore the snowy peaks on snowshoes.

Close to five decades separate me from my childhood now. In *Towong Hill: Fifty Years on an Upper Murray Cattle Station* Mum wrote: 'Always remembering how important my own childhood memories have seemed to me, I hoped to give each child its own memories – something to build on, something to treasure for life.'[4]

Mum certainly gave me memories on which I could build and truly 'something to treasure for life'. Although as a child I found

Mum and Dad's stories daunting, they ultimately gave me wings to find my life, which, in the words of Constantine Cavafy, has been a 'long road full of adventure, full of knowledge'. It was not the sort of life Mum and Dad intended and nor did it have to be. That way I haven't lived in their shadows and I have had a life apart – my life. And that is all part of another story.

Notes

Prologue
1. *Digest of World Readers*, Melbourne, December.
2. 'Horse stars in her 7th book', *The Sun*, 3 October 1958, p. 40 and 'Authoress writes about Horses and mountains', *Weekly Times*, 15 October 1958, p. 63.
3. Elyne Mitchell, *The Silver Brumby*, pp. 172–3.

2 A Name Like Honor
1. *The Herald*, 9 June 1953, p. 12.
2. First page of a letter from Elyne Mitchell to Mr White dated 18 May 1953. The rest of the letter is missing.

3 Cranky Ghosts
1. *Corryong Courier*, 17 May 1894.
2. *Albury Daily News and Wodonga Chronicle*, 20 September 1917, p. 2.
3. John T. Francis, *Lives of Romance*, p. 65.
4. ibid.

4 Working in a Wild Museum
1. Elyne Mitchell, *Chauvel Country*, p. 249.

6 Each Item Had a Story
1. Elyne Mitchell, *Chauvel Country*, p. 83.

7 Brilliant Times and Places
1. Elyne Mitchell, *Chauvel Country*, p. 3.
2. Philippe Batters, *Prahran's Heritage: No. 9 Murphy Street Resident, Talks Given at Meetings of the Prahran Historical Society*, p. 7.
3. *Chauvel Country*, p. 245.

8 'Like a Wave Lifting Everything'
1. Letter from Elyne Mitchell to Eve Maberly, 6 March 1954.
2. 'Arrangements for the Queen's Visit', *Corryong Courier*, 7 March 1963, p. 10.

11 The Bittersweet Schoolroom
1   Elyne Mitchell, *Black Cockatoos Mean Snow*, p. 6.

12 So Many Stories
1   Dad wrote something similar in his local history, *Corryong and the Man from Snowy River District*, 1981, Wilkinson Printers, Albury, p. 11.
2   Elyne Mitchell, *Flow River, Blow Wind*, p. 147.

13 The Coming of the Brumbies
1   Elyne Mitchell, *The Silver Brumby*, pp. 36–37.
2   ibid, p.16.
3   Elyne Mitchell, *Australia's Alps*, p. 57.
4   ibid, p. 129.
5   Elyne Mitchell, *Black Cockatoos Mean Snow*, pp. 23–24.
6   Elyne Mitchell, *The Silver Brumby*, pp. 17–18.
7   Elyne Mitchell, *Silver Brumby's Daughter*, p. 129.
8   Elyne Mitchell, *Silver Brumbies of the South*, p. 16.
9   ibid, p. 58.
10 Elyne Mitchell, *Silver Brumby Whirlwind*, p.17.
11 ibid, p. 19.
12 Elyne Mitchell, *Towong Hill: Fifty Years on an Upper Murray Cattle Station*, p. 98.
13 Elyne Mitchell, *Chauvel Country*, p. 254.
14 *The Silver Brumby*, p. 161.
15 Letter from Elyne Mitchell to Paul Hodder-Williams, 15 October 1962.

17 Pushing the Boundaries
1   Elyne Mitchell, *Chauvel Country*, p. 93.
2   'His Suggestion Popped Back', *People*, 12 September 1951, p. 37.

20 War Secrets
1   There is a colour photograph of the lily pond at Blowering in the visitor centre in Tumut.
2   'Woman Runs Big Fat Stock Station', 5 February 1944, *Pix*, p. 8.
3   ibid, p. 8.

21 War Friends and Waterskiing
1   Elyne Mitchell, *Chauvel Country*, p. 264.

23 Visitors to Our World
1   Elyne Mitchell, *Images in Water*, p. 32.
2   ibid, p. 32.

24 Typical Upper Murray Fun
1   Elyne Mitchell, 'Living with Distance' (unpublished), p. 5.
2   Letter from Elyne Mitchell to Sibyl Chauvel, 26 January 1952.
3   Letter from Lilian Chauvel to Elyne and Tom Mitchell, 13 January 1937.

25 Early Skiing
1   Elva Breen, 'Roundabout for Women', *The Herald*, 11 October 1958, p. 33.
2   *People*, 12 September 1951, p. 38.

26 Skiing is Serious
1   Elyne Mitchell, *A Vision of the Snowy Mountains*, p. 25.
2   Jill Craig, 'Elyne and Her Mountains', *Border Mail*, 17 July 1985, p. 4.

27 The Magic of Summer Skiing
1   Elyne Mitchell, *Silver Brumby's Daughter*, p. 14.
2   ibid, p. 17.
3   ibid, p. 194.
4   ibid, p. 198.
5   Elyne Mitchell, 'Once Forgotten Corner', *Riverlander*, April 1964, p. 8.

28 Adventures on the Alpine Way
1   Elyne Mitchell, 'Through Adversity – to the Snow', *The Age Literary Supplement*, 3 September 1966, p. 21.
2   Elyne Mitchell, *Towong Hill: Fifty Years on an Upper Murray Cattle Station*, p. 177.
3   Elyne Mitchell, 'Through the Australian Alps in a Jeep', *Australian Geographical Magazine Walkabout*, 1 April 1949, p. 29.
4   Elyne Mitchell, *The Colt from Snowy River*, Acknowledgements.
5   ibid.

29 Skiing the World
1. Elyne Mitchell, Travel Journal, 1938.
2. ibid.
3. Elyne Mitchell, *Chauvel Country*, p. 210.
4. ibid, p. 215.
5. Letter from Tom Mitchell to Winifred Mitchell, 27 August 1938, p. 11.
6. Thomas Mitchell, 'Midway Peak', p. 303.

30 Accident and Intrigue
1. Karl Roesen survived the war; Dad visited him when he was in Europe in 1965. Hannes died in 1955 having never returned to St Anton. I have not been able to discover the fate of Frau Roesen.
2. Tom Mitchell, 'Skiing the World', p. 263.

31 Moths in the Lamplight
1. Dad also described this in his unpublished ski memoir, 'Skiing the World', p. 13.
2. Elyne Mitchell, *Chauvel Country*, p. 200.
3. *Chauvel Country*, p. 200, quoting 'Skiing the World', pp. 137–38.
4. ibid.

35 The Time Warp
1. Elyne Mitchell, *Speak to the Earth*, p. 27.
2. Russell Braddon, *The Piddingtons*, pp. 104–5.
3. Elyne Mitchell, *Flow River, Blow Wind*, p. 76.
4. Elyne Mitchell, *Black Cockatoos Mean Snow*, p. 19.
5. ibid, p. 67.
6. ibid, p. 67.
7. ibid, p. 117.

36 'A Man Who Would Have Sons'
1. The Book of Job, Chapter 38, Verse 22, quoted in Elyne Mitchell, *Winged Skis*, p. 88.
2. Noel Streatfeild, 'Book Page', *Elizabethan*, April 1964.
3. Dorothy Ryman, 'Winged Skis by Elyne Mitchell', *Ski Australia* (August 1964), p. 39.
4. *The Corian: The Journal of the Geelong Church of England Grammar School and the Old Geelong Grammarians*, April 1973, p. 121.

37 Wings to Find My Life

1. Inquest held on 14 September 1972 by J.H. Power, Coroner for the District of Lithgow.
2. Lieutenant General Victor Paul Hildebrand Stanke was General Officer Commanding Queensland Lines of Communication, 1943–46.
3. John Wyett, *Staff Wallah*, p. xvi.
4. Elyne Mitchell, *Towong Hill: Fifty Years on an Upper Murray Cattle Station*, p. 80.

Bibliography

Monographs
Andrews, Dr Arthur, *First Settlement of the Upper Murray 1835-1845 with a Short Account of over Two Hundred Runs 1835 – 1880*, D. S. Ford Printers, 729 George St Sydney, 1920

Braddon, Russell, *The Piddingtons*, Werner Laurie, London, 1950

Francis, John T., *Lives of Romance*, Mitchell & Co, 45 Clerkwell Close, 1914

Hill, A.J. *Chauvel of the Light Horse*, Melbourne University Press, Melbourne, 1978

Mitchell, Elyne, *Australia's Alps*, Angus and Robertson, Sydney, 1942

Mitchell, Elyne, *Speak to the Earth*, Angus and Robertson, Sydney, 1945

Mitchell, Elyne, *Soil and Civilization*, Angus and Robertson, Sydney, 1946

Mitchell, Elyne, *Images in Water*, Angus and Robertson, Sydney, 1947

Mitchell, Elyne, *Flow River, Blow Wind*, George G. Harrap & Co. Ltd, London, 1953

Mitchell, Elyne, *Black Cockatoos Mean Snow*, Hodder and Stoughton, London, 1956

Mitchell, Elyne, *The Silver Brumby*, Hutchinson, London, 1958

Mitchell, Elyne, *Silver Brumby's Daughter*, Hutchinson, London, 1960

Mitchell, Elyne, *Kingfisher Feather*, Hutchinson & Co, London, 1962

Mitchell, Elyne, *Winged Skis*, Hutchinson & Co, London, 1964

Mitchell, Elyne, *Silver Brumbies of the South*, Hutchinson, London, 1965

Mitchell, Elyne, *Jinki: Dingo of the Snows*, Hutchinson Group *(Australia)* Pty Ltd, Melbourne, 1970

Mitchell, Elyne, *Light Horse to Damascus*, Hutchinson of Australia, Melbourne, 1971

Mitchell, Elyne, *Silver Brumby Whirlwind*, Hutchinson Australia, Melbourne 1973

Mitchell, Elyne, *Light Horse: The Story of Australia's Mounted Troops*, Macmillan Australia, 1978

Mitchell, Elyne, *The Colt from Snowy River*, Hutchinson, London, 1980

Mitchell, Elyne, *Chauvel Country*, Macmillan Australia, Melbourne, 1983

Mitchell, Elyne, *A Vision of the Snowy Mountains*, Macmillan, Melbourne, 1988

Mitchell, Elyne, *Towong Hill: Fifty Years on an Upper Murray Cattle Station*, Macmillan, Melbourne, 1989

Mitchell, T.W., *Ski Heil*, The Sydney and Melbourne Publishing Company, 1937

Mitchell, Mitchell, the Hon. T. W, C.M.G, *Corryong and the "Man from Snowy River District*, printed and published by Wilkinson Printers, Albury, NSW, 1981

Peck, Harry, *Memoirs of a Stockman*, Stock and Land Publishing Company Pty Ltd, Melbourne, 1972

Wyett, John, *Staff Wallah*, Allen & Unwin, Sydney, 1996

Newspaper Articles

Albury Daily News and *Wodonga Chronicle*, Thursday, 20 September 1917

'Arrangements for the Queen's Visit', *Corryong Courier*, 7 March 1963, p. 10

'Authoress writes about Horses and Mountains', *Weekly Times*, 15 October 1958, p. 63

Breen, Elva, 'Roundabout for Women', *The Herald*, 11 October 1958, p. 33

Corryong Courier, 17 May 1894

Craig, Jill, 'Elyne and her Mountains', *Border Mail*, 17 July 1985, p. 4

The Herald, 9 June 1953, p. 12

'His Suggestion Popped Back', *People*, 12 September 1951, p. 36–39

'Horse Stars in her 7th Book', *The Sun*, 3 Octctober 1958, p. 40

Mitchell, Elyne, 'Through Adversity – to the Snow', *The Age Literary Supplement*, 3 September 1966

'Noel Streatfeild's Book Page', *Elizabethan*, April 1964

Journal Articles

Mitchell, Elyne, 'Through the Australian Alps in a Jeep', *Australian Geographical Magazine Walkabout*, 1 April 1949

Mitchell, Elyne, 'Once Forgotten Corner', *Riverlander*, April 1964

Journals

Batters, Phillipe, *Prahran's Heritage No. 9 Murphy Street Resident Talks Given at Meetings of the Prahran Historical Society* (Prahran Historical Society Inc. 1992)

Ski Australia, August 1964

Snowy Review (House Magazine for the Snowy Mountains Authority)

The Corian: *The Journal of the Geelong Church of England Grammar School and the Old Geelong Grammarians*, April 1973

'Woman Runs Big Fat Stock Station', *Pix*, 5 February 1944, p. 8

Bibliography

Correspondence
A.C. to Tom and Elyne Mitchell, 28 August 1939
Lilian Chauvel to Elyne and Tom Mitchell, 13 January 1937
Elyne Mitchell to Eve Maberly, 6 March 1954
Elyne Mitchell to Dr Euan Littlejohn, 9 April 1945
Elyne Mitchell to Dr Euan Littlejohn, 5 May 1945
Elyne Mitchell to Dr Euan Littlejohn, 2 June 1945
Elyne Mitchell to Dr Euan Littlejohn, 25 June 1945
Elyne Mitchell to Harry Mitchell (copied to author), March 1968
Elyne Mitchell to Honnor Lodge, 10 November [1944]
Elyne Mitchell to Tom Mitchell, 26 December 1941
Elyne Mitchell to Tom Mitchell, 19 August 1945
Elyne Mitchell to Tom Mitchell, 21 August 1945
Elyne Mitchell to Tom Mitchell, 20 September 1945
Elyne Mitchell to Sibyl Chauvel, 26 January 1952
Elyne Mitchell to Sibyl Chauvel, 2 February 1952
Elyne Mitchell to Sibyl Chauvel, dated 26 January 1952
Elyne Mitchell to Sibyl Chauvel, dated 26 January 1952
Elyne Mitchell to Mr White, 18 May 1953 (the first page only – the rest of the letter is missing)
Lilian Chauvel to Elyne and Tom Mitchell, 13 January 1937
Sibyl Chauvel to Elyne Mitchell, 9 November 1938
Winifred Mitchell to Honnor Mitchell, 8 June 1953

Correspondence with Publishers and Literary Agents
Elyne Mitchell to Dorothy Tomlinson, Editor Children's Books, Hutchinson and Co London, 11 November 1963
Elyne Mitchell to Paul Hodder-Williams, 15 October 1962
Dorothy Tomlinson, Hutchinson, to Elyne Mitchell, 10 September [no year]
Mr Voss Smith, Australasian Manager of Hutchinson, to Elyne Mitchell, 6 August 1957
Mr Voss Smith, Australasian Manager of Hutchinson, to Elyne Mitchell, 28 September, 1957

Telegrams
Undated cable to 'VX43577 Capt T W Mitchell 8th Divn HQ Care 2 Aust POW Reception Group Singapore'

Unpublished Manuscripts
Mitchell, Elyne, 'Living with Distance' (1952)
Mitchell T. W., 'Midway Peak' (1942-44)
Mitchell, T.W., 'Skiing the World' (1938–40) Elyne also contributed to this and typed the manuscript

Travel Journals and Diary Fragment
Elyne Mitchell's diary fragment, Sunday, 9 August 1942
Mitchell, Elyne, Travel Journal 1938, unpublished
Mitchell, Elyne, 'Austrian Diary' (17 December 1938 – 22 March 1939)

Death Certificates
1873 Deaths in the District of West Melbourne in the Colony of Victoria, Schedule B 712
Walter Edward Mitchell (New South Wales Death Certificate 1917/009462)
John F. H. Mitchell (New South Wales Death Certificate 13149/1921)

Inquests
Inquest held on 14 September 1972 by J. H. Power, Coroner for the District of Lithgow

Acknowledgements

My thanks go firstly to my family for their support and patience throughout the six years I have taken to research and write this book. I am especially grateful to my husband, Mark, and daughter, Sarah, for their assistance with proof reading. Lucy Hemsley played a significant inspirational role in the many hours we spent together in her house in Somerset in England discussing our Australian childhoods in the 1950s. Christina Hughes-Onslow (née Hay) in London contributed similarly, reminding me of some of our shared childhood experiences.

I thank too Fiona Inglis and her staff at Curtis Brown for their guidance and support. Shona Martyn and Fiona Henderson, my publishers at HarperCollins, have been most helpful; indeed it was Fiona's challenge many years ago which inspired me to write the memoir. Still with HarperCollins, I am very grateful for Amanda O'Connell's professional editing and advice and also to Deonie Fiford, Simone Ford and Rowena Lennox: together they have made a marvellous team with which to work. I also thank Natalie Winter for her beautiful cover design.

Professor Richard Freadman and Professor Sue Thomas at La Trobe University have so ably and enthusiastically picked up where Elyne left off, rekindling my interest in Australian autobiography and providing inspiring guidance. *Elyne Mitchell: A Daughter Remembers* is the creative element in a Ph.D at La Trobe University. My gratitude also goes to Dr Evelyn Kerslake at the Open University in England for early guidance about Family History Research.

Marie-Louise Ayers and Emma Jolley at the National Library of Australia have helped with my research. The staffs of the State Libraries of Victoria and New South Wales, the Boroondara Library in Hawthorn and the Elyne Mitchell Library in Corryong have also played an important role, as have the Registries of

Births, Deaths and Marriages in Victoria and New South Wales that provided all the certificates I needed for family history research. The Australian War Memorial in Canberra answered many questions relating to military history. I am grateful to the Victorian Writers Centre and the Fellowship of Australian Writers (Queensland) for practical advice and encouragement. The Man from Snowy River Museum with its assemblages of Mitchell family memorabilia has been a useful source of reference.

Prue Webb, the archivist at St Catherine's School, provided access to the school archives and information about Elyne's education, while Janet Howse, the archivist at Cranbrook School in Sydney, assisted with similar information about my father Tom's formative years.

Michael Collins Persse, a distinguished and long-standing member of staff at Geelong Grammar, has been a family friend and shared reminiscences over many decades. My relative Tim Honnor, who shares my interest in our mutual family histories, has also provided background information.

I wish to thank Euan Littlejohn and Dr Rowan Swaney for their assistance with my manuscript. I am very grateful to Prue Grieve for many interesting hours talking about our extended family histories. Over the years Mary Greenshields has been a wonderful support and has helped immensely in so many different ways.

It has been a great pleasure for me to include family photographs in *Elyne Mitchell: A Daughter Remembers* taken by my parents and Upper Murray photographers Albert Mildren, Jim Nicholas and Glenn Wilson.

I thank too my extended family and friends, particularly those from the Upper Murray, my teachers and the nuns and staff of Ursula College and Bruce Hall at ANU, all of whom have contributed in some way to my early years and indeed to my memoir. Last, but certainly not least, is my special gratitude to my parents for all they have given me – individually and together.

ON THE TRAIL
OF THE
SILVER BRUMBY

Generations of Australians have fallen in love with the silver brumbies of Elyne Mitchell's classic children's stories. Now, for the centenary of Elyne's birth, comes this celebration in words and pictures of the brumby heartland: the glorious Australian Alps that were Elyne's inspiration and great passion.

Featuring the best of Elyne Mitchell's non-fiction writing about her beloved high country, *On the Trail of the Silver Brumby* is lavishly illustrated with archival images and new photography of the Alps by her grandson James Auchinleck. From thrilling accounts of exploring these untamed places on foot, skis and horseback to tales of wild brumby chases and evenings spent yarning round the campfire, Elyne's words bring the mountains vividly to life.

On the Trail of the Silver Brumby allows readers to follow Elyne and her brumby heroes through their kingdom and discover for themselves a world of snowy alps, secret valleys, sparkling cascades and summer fields of wildflowers.

THE SILVER BRUMBY
CENTENARY EDITION

To many people the name Elyne Mitchell is synonymous with *The Silver Brumby*, the timeless classic that has captivated the hearts and imaginations of young readers since it was first published in 1958.

This special edition commemorates the centenary of Elyne Mitchell's birth and contains *The Silver Brumby* and three other favourites: *Silver Brumby's Daughter*, *Silver Brumbies of the South* and *Silver Brumby Kingdom*. These much-loved classics tell the story of Thowra, the magnificent silver stallion, king of the brumbies. Whether you are enjoying the Silver Brumby series for the first time or rediscovering it after many years, this is a book to be treasured.

Also included in this beautiful edition is a specially commissioned biographical note of Elyne Mitchell, who was born in 1913 and went on to become one of Australia's most successful and popular authors. The biographical note also contains photographs that depict Elyne in many other areas of her long and distinguished life, including that of daughter, wife, mother, sportswoman, horsewoman, farmer and environmentalist.